Frontispiece. *A Visit to the Bazaar, Cairo,* by William Prinsep, 1870. An amateur artist and member of a large trading family of Calcutta, Prinsep returned to England in 1842 via the so-called Overland Route. This lively water-colour, in which the mid-Victorian fashions of the European tourists contrast with the oriental dress of the local population, is one of many made by the artist as a pictorial record of his journey through Egypt.
Photograph: Martyn Gregory Gallery.

Title Page. Title page of *The Route of The Overland Mail to India,* watercolour attributed to Henry Fitzcook, 1850-52. Fitzcook seems to have made scaled-down versions of the images in Telbin and Grieve's popular diorama of the same name for more widespread publication as lithographs. The title page illustrates some of the people and costume to be encountered along the so-called Overland Route – men and women from Cairo, an Ottoman Turk and a Bedouin Arab.
The Peninsular and Oriental Steam Navigation Company.

Notes of a Journey

from

CORNHILL TO GRAND CAIRO

by

WILLIAM MAKEPEACE THACKERAY

New Introduction by Sarah Searight. Illustrations compiled by Briony Llewellyn

Cockbird Press

HEATHFIELD

New edition first published 1991

Cockbird Press Ltd

P.O. Box 356, Heathfield, East Sussex TN21 9QF.

British Library Cataloguing in Publication Data

Thackeray, W.M. (William Makepeace) *1811 - 1863*
[Notes of a Journey from Cornhill to Grand Cairo...]
Cornhill to Grand Cairo. - 3rd. ed.
1. Middle East. Description & travel, 640 - 1990
I. [Notes of a Journey from Cornhill to Grand Cairo...]
II. Title
916.2043

ISBN 1-873054-01-7

Designed by Peter Guy

Production by Rupert Wheeler

Map by Denys Baker

Typeset by The Setting Studio, Newcastle

Produced by Mandarin Offset
Printed and bound in Hong Kong

CONTENTS

ILLUSTRATIONS

PUBLISHER'S NOTE

The publisher acknowledges gratefully those
institutions, both private and public, who have
lent illustrations for this book. Many people
have been generous with their time and expertise
and of great assistance to Briony Llewellyn in the
compilation of these illustrations. Thanks are
owed particularly to Charles Newton of the Victoria and Albert Museum, Tony Carroll of The
Fine Arts Society, Stephen Rabson and Lyn
Palmer of the P&O Company, and Karen Taylor
of Sotheby's. Thanks also to Helen Guiterman,
Krystyna Matyjaszkiewicz and Pieter van der
Merwe. Many of the illustrations lent by the
Victoria & Albert Museum are drawn from their
Searight Collection, an extensive visual record of
North Africa and the Middle East. This magnifi-
cent collection, containing 2000 items, was
originally formed by Rodney Searight to whom a
special debt of gratitude is owed.

Thanks are particularly due to Martin Marix
Evans and John Taylor for their patient advice
on numerous matters, to Michael Barnsley for
helping with classical references and to Sue
Mertens for undertaking the Index.

The transliteration of Arabic words is not an
exact science, and is often made less so by the
idiosyncracies of writers and painters from earlier periods whose English spellings were
conditioned by their own native languages. We
have retained the original spelling in Thackeray's
text and in the titles to all illustrations. A standard modern form has been adopted in the
Introduction, Notes to the text and in the cap-
tions, as well as for a few words in Thackeray's
text where their victorian form is particularly
obscure.

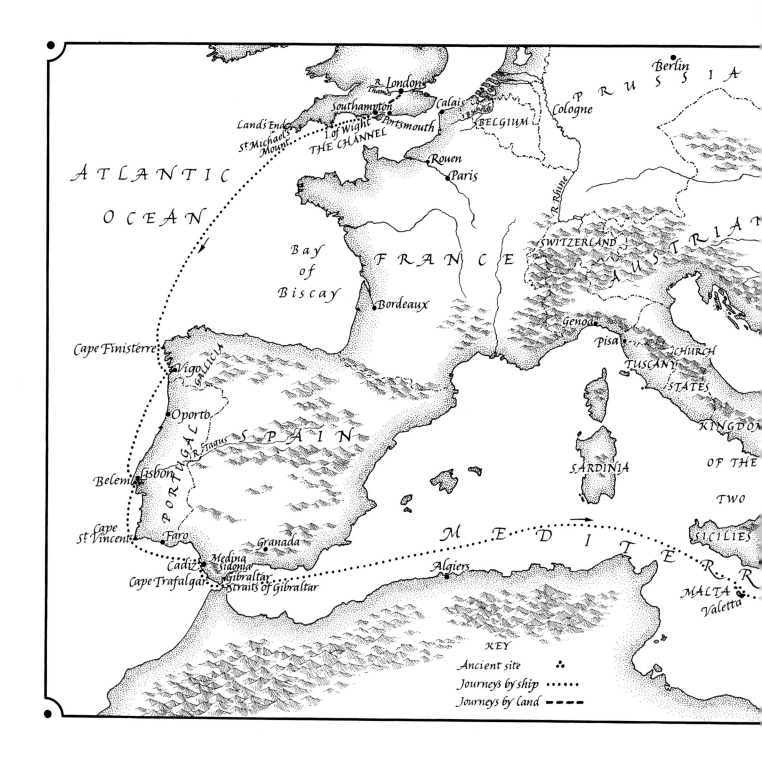

ATLANTIC

OCEAN

Berlin

R. London
Thames

Southampton
Land's End
St Michael's
Mount
I. of Wight
THE CHANNEL
Portsmouth
Calais

PRUSSIA

Cologne

BELGIUM

R. Scheldt

Rouen
Paris

R. Rhine

SWITZERLAND

AUSTRIA

Bay
of
Biscay

FRANCE

Bordeaux

Genoa

Pisa

TUSCANY
STATES

CHURCH

Cape Finisterre
Vigo

GALICIA

SPAIN

CORSICA

SARDINIA

KINGDOM

OF THE

Oporto

PORTUGAL

R. Tagus

Belem *Lisbon*

MEDITE

Cape
St Vincent
Faro
Granada

TWO

Algiers

SICILIES

R R

Cadiz
Medina
Sidonia
Gibraltar
Cape Trafalgar
Straits of Gibraltar

MALTA
Valetta

KEY

Ancient site   ⸫

Journeys by ship   ······

Journeys by land   ─ ─ ─

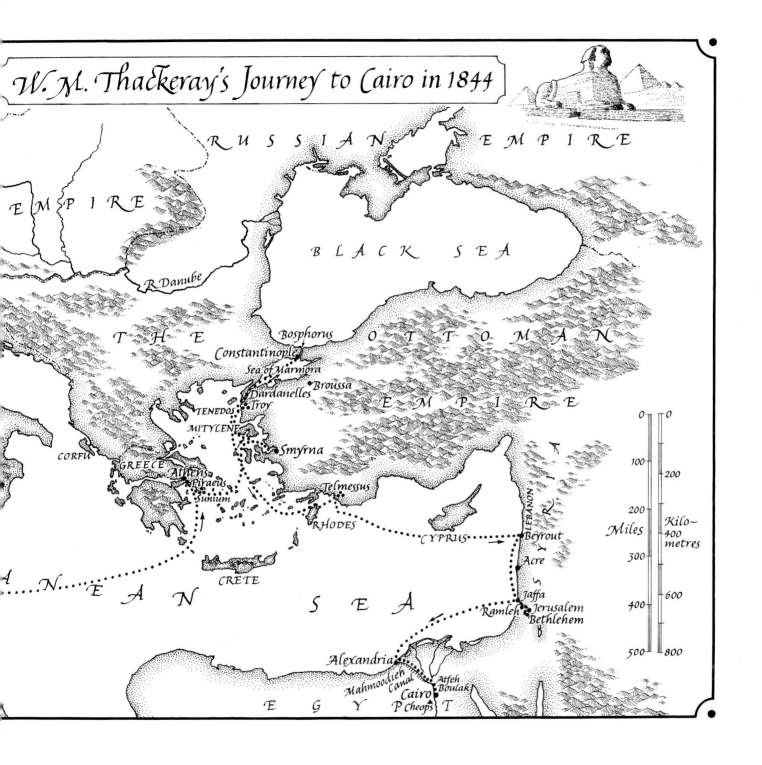

W. M. Thackeray's Journey to Cairo in 1844

RUSSIAN EMPIRE

EMPIRE

BLACK SEA

R. Danube

THE

OTTOMAN

Bosphorus

Constantinople

Sea of Marmora

Broussa

EMPIRE

Dardanelles

Troy

TENEDOS

MITYLENE

Smyrna

CORFU

GREECE

Athens

Piraeus

Sunium

Telmessus

RHODES

CYPRUS

CRETE

SEA

LEBANON

Beyrout

Acre

SYRIA

Jaffa

Ramleh

Jerusalem

Bethlehem

Alexandria

Mahmoodieh Canal

Atfeh

Boulak

Cairo

P Cheops

EGYPT

0

100

200

300

400

500

Miles

0

200

400

600

800

Kilo~
metres

Portrait of William Thackeray, by Daniel Maclise, c.1840. A pencil drawing of Thackeray at the time when he was establishing his reputation as a writer, and shortly before he embarked on his journey from 'Cornhill to Grand Cairo.'
National Portrait Gallery.

INTRODUCTION

WILLIAM MAKEPEACE THACKERAY leapt at an invitation in July 1844 to join a friend on a voyage by steamship to the eastern Mediterranean. He was thirty three, a poorly paid though moderately successful journalist, his wife was in a lunatic asylum outside Paris and he had been obliged to leave their two small daughters in the care of his mother and stepfather, also in Paris. He was, as usual, out of money. 'Come...,' said his friend James Emerson Tennent, 'in all your life you will never probably have a chance again to see so much in so short a time'.

By the 1840s the Levant and Egypt were all the rage with the general public. Illustrated albums of the Bosphorus and the Holy Land by such artists as Thomas Allom and W.H. Bartlett, dioramas of the so-called Overland Route to India via Egypt and displays of antiquities from the banks of the Nile fed a public imagination already whetted by gothic tales of Arabian nights.

A voyage offered Thackeray scope to break out of the mould of critical and satirical journalism by which he earned an inadequate living. As London emptied for the summer and he attended a last dinner in the Reform Club for Tennent given by another friend, William Bevan, Thackeray offered only a token demur to Tennent's suggestion. 'With every glass of claret the enthusiasm somehow rose, and the difficulties vanished.' When Tennent suggested that the shipping company Peninsular & Oriental might give him a berth, in return for some favourable publicity, Thackeray could no longer resist. Peninsular & Oriental obliged, and two days later, so did Thackeray. *Notes of a Journey from Cornhill to Grand Cairo*, first published in 1846, was the result.

He certainly capitalized on the opportunity the trip offered. It gave him time to finish the final parts of his first full-length work of fiction, *The Luck of Barry Lyndon*, serialised in *Fraser's Magazine*, a literary periodical of con-

servative outlook which gave Thackeray his steadiest source of income. On several occasions in his diary of the trip Thackeray mentions the problems of keeping ahead of the printer, the serial parts presumably sent back to London on the little steam packet boats that were now operating all over the Mediterranean. He also wrote articles about his trip for *Punch*, founded four years earlier and firmly established by 1842 when Thackeray began writing for it.

He made his reputation as a contributor with these travel articles, written under the pseudonym 'Fat Contributor' (he was reckoned to weigh between 210 and 252 lb.) and later published as a collection, *Punch in the East. Cornhill to Cairo* is an expansion of these articles. *Punch* paid well, 'more than double of that I get anywhere else', he told his mother. This improved income no doubt gave him relative peace of mind, on his return from the east, to settle down to his great masterpiece, *Vanity Fair*.

It was the improving means of communication with India that were the stimulus for P&O's services to the East and Thackeray's own boyhood experience illustrates the immediate social need they served. Born in Calcutta in 1811, the only member of a third generation of Thackerays to live in India, he was sent home in 1816 after his father's death, at the age of five, already older than many children who were to face the dismal parting. After a four month voyage via the Cape of Good Hope to England, he was raised by Anglo-Indian relatives (kinder to him, however, than Kipling's foster parents were to be) and he did not see his mother again for another four years.

The need to speed up communications with the East had been recognised as a strategic priority since the Napoleonic Wars. Napoleon's expedition to Egypt in 1798 had been aimed at interrupting British links with India and ultimately at ousting the British from India. While a military disaster, the expedition instigated, with its accompanying

Front Cover of an early edition of the satirical periodical *Punch,* founded in 1840 and firmly established by 1842 when Thackeray began contributing to it.

party of savants, that great interest in Egypt's ancient glories which is reflected in many of Thackeray's comments. Commercial interest in India had been expanding since the East India Company's monopoly of trade had ended in 1813.

Life was never easy for Thackeray, least of all in the early years before he was recognised for the literary brilliance of *Vanity Fair*. He was educated at Charterhouse (Slaughter House in *Vanity Fair*), where he made friends with John Leech, later as celebrated a contributor to *Punch* as Thackeray himself. At Cambridge in 1829 he befriended Edward Fitzgerald (Fitz Omar as he was known after the publication in 1859 of his translation of Omar Khayyam's verses). But Thackeray's law studies paled before the attractions of travel and, a year later, Cambridge had yielded to Weimar in Germany. He tried law again at London's Middle Temple in 1831, though without any great enthusiasm.

Taking himself to Paris a year later, shortage of cash had Thackeray trying his hand at journalism. He also thought of being an artist and studied Old Masters in the Louvre; he frequently mentions sketching during his travels to the East and the little caricatures which illustrate *Cornhill to Cairo* are evidence of his competence, although a friend and more successful caricaturist, George Cruikshank, suggested that 'he had not the patience to be an artist with pencil or brush.' In the same year, recognising the political and cultural significance of the capital of an Ottoman Empire already exciting avaricious European glances, he applied unsuccessfully to be *The Morning Chronicle's* Constantinople correspondent. Instead he found a job as a Paris contributor to *Galignani's Messenger*, a less distinguished publication.

Thackeray married Isabella Shawe in 1836 in Paris. The marriage began happily enough but after giving birth to three daughters in quick succession (the middle one dying at the age of only eight months), Isabella succumbed to severe, often suicidal depression and at the end of 1840 Thackeray was compelled to place her in an asylum near Paris. He was then working as a freelance journalist, in particular for *Fraser's Magazine*, *The Morning Chronicle* and the newly founded *Punch* and was making a small reputation for his no-nonsense style of literary criticism, this being in contrast to the popular pseudo-romanticism that fol-

lowed inelegantly in the footsteps of Byron and Scott. 'That man *never* wrote from the heart', comments Thackeray in Athens apropos Byron's attitude to Nature, 'Our native bard! *Mon Dieu!*'

Thackeray now developed the nom de plume of Michael Angelo Titmarsh, by which he referred to himself in *Cornhill to Cairo*, perhaps relishing the fact that Micaelangelo, like himself, had a broken nose. Both first and second editions of *Cornhill to Cairo* acknowledged Titmarsh as author, Thackeray only emerging as author in the third edition, re-published here. The name Titmarsh is said by Thackeray's biographer, Gordon Ray, to have been adopted from a seventeeth century printer of tracts, Samuel Titmarsh, with offices at the King's Head at the Royal Exchange in Cornhill, a commercial district of London.

Thackeray's three-month journey from Cornhill to Cairo in fact took him via Lisbon, Cadiz, Gibraltar and Malta to Constantinople, Beirut and Palestine, as well as Egypt. From Egypt he returned to Malta for quarantine and went thence to Italy where he spent the winter. His account reflects contemporary political as much as cultural interest in the eastern Mediterranean, in particular European concern over the well-being of the Ottoman Empire, seen as threatened by Russian expansion southwards to the shores of the Black Sea.

War between Russia and Turkey in 1828 had led a year later to the Treaty of Adrianople, whose terms effectively turned the Black Sea into a Russian, as opposed to a Turkish, lake. Further disintegration of the empire was threatened with the French invasion of Algeria in 1830 and its campaign against Morocco; Thackeray saw the French fleet in the Straits of Gibraltar returning from its bombardment of Mogador in Morocco. Britain, for the time being, wanted to preserve the Ottoman Empire intact because of growing concern with faster and more secure communications with India. All routes to India, except the long voyage via the Cape of Good Hope, lay through the Ottoman Empire. The Eastern Question, as the fate of the empire became known in the course of the nineteenth century, had thus already begun to dominate relations between Britain, France and Russia when Thackeray set forth in 1844.

On several occasions Thackeray alludes to the Egyptian invasion of Syria. In 1833 Tsar Nicholas I came to the

Southampton Docks. A colourful crowd of men, women and children are gathered on the quay for the departure of one of P&O's steamers for Alexandria, carrying passengers on their way to India. The watercolour, attributed to Henry Fitzcook, is one of 32 published as lithographs in 1850-52 in a portfolio entitled *The Route of The Overland Mail to India.* The Peninsular and Oriental Steam Navigation Company.

rescue of the Ottoman Sultan Mahmud II when the Sultan's Egyptian vassal, the viceroy Muhammad Ali, sent his son Ibrahim to invade Syria. Russian support enabled the Turks to stem the Egyptian invasion at Bursa (famous for the 'Broussa silks' mentioned by Thackeray), but the subsequent Egyptian occupation of Syria caused considerable anxiety to the British government: it put the Egyptians in control of the two possible land routes to India – one via Syria and the Euphrates river and the other through Egypt. The Syrian route had been investigated in 1836 by Colonel Francis Chesney but his schemes were defeated by Egyptian obstruction and Mesopotamian anarchy.

Eventually, joint British, French and Austrian action forced the Egyptians out of Syria in 1840, with Syria becoming the scene of intensified European rivalry, hence Thackeray's acquaintance with the British warship *Trump*, which had been lying off the Syrian coast in case of further trouble. France, Britain and Russia all appointed consuls to preserve their interests, often cloaking their political intentions with claims to be protecting one or other of the Christian communities which had proliferated in this vital crossroads of the Near East.

Thackeray found these consuls conspicuously at work in Jerusalem: the Russians were set up as guardians of the Greek Orthodox community (their convent, built by the Russians, had the Russian double-headed eagle over the doorway), the French of the Catholics (as also of the Maronites in Mount Lebanon) and the British had upset everyone by allowing the London Society for Promoting Christianity among the Jews to set up, with the Prussian government, an evangelising Protestant bishopric. Ten years after Thackeray's visit the overbearing Russian protection of the Orthodox Church was to lead to the Crimean War.

Thackeray himself demonstrates – in his descriptions of Constantinople and Jerusalem – the francophobia and even stronger russophobia which then characterised British attitudes to its rivals in the eastern Mediterranean, the latter in particular fed by such extremists as David Urquhart. Urquhart had been a diplomat at the British Embassy in Constantinople, partly responsible for the curious *Vixen* incident of 1836, when this British vessel was arrested by the Russians in the eastern Black Sea allegedly for supplying weapons to Circassian rebels. On his return to London, Urquhart published a succession of virulent attacks on what he saw as the Russian threat and the supineness of the British government in facing up to it, Palmerston 'drugging the Sultan's champagne for the benefit of Russia', as Thackeray interpreted Urquhart's viewpoint.

Conversion of the Jews to Christianity was symptomatic of the anti-Semitism which prevailed throughout Europe, growing stronger as the century progressed. Although it was less violent and pervasive in Britain than on the continent, Thackeray's own expression of anti-Semitism on several occasions in his account strikes one today as vitriolic and repugnant but is a salutary reminder of how acceptable it was to a large segment of his readers. In Thackeray's day Jews were excluded from national, though no longer from municipal, office. Opponents of Jewish emancipation argued that Jews were cosmopolitan, Britain only a temporary resting place, Palestine their real home. Shylock still dominated the average British view of the Jews and Jewish villains figure in several of Walter Scott's novels.

In 1844, the year of Thackeray's voyage, Disraeli (who was converted to Christianity in 1817 at the age of thirteen) published *Coningsby*, an exaltation of Jews and Jewishness which Thackeray parodied in *Punch* as Codlingsby. British Jews were a closely-knit community, dominating banking and money-lending circles and Thackeray's own extravagance may well have led him both to borrow from them and to resent the humiliation of having to do so. The Polish Jews whom he describes so unkindly were the Sephardic precursors of a major diaspora from persecution in eastern Europe in the latter part of the century, fuelling the overt anti-Semitism that led eventually to the concentration camps of Nazi Germany.

Moving on from Palestine, Thackeray found Egypt in 1844 relatively free of the tensions which marked European relations with other parts of the Ottoman Empire. This was largely due to the determination of its ruler, Muhammad Ali, to modernize the country with the help of the European entrepreneurs and technicians, mainly French, who flocked to the country in the wake of Napoleon's expedition. Foreign engineers would, for instance, have set up the 'steam-engine manufactories' noted by Thackeray on the banks of the Nile. Muhammad Ali's own acquisition of power was complete by 1811 after his slaughter of the Mamluks, his predecessors in the seat of power. Thackeray visiting the citadel of Cairo duly describes the 'famous leap, by which one of the corps (of Mamluks) escaped death, at the time that his Highness the Pasha arranged the general massacre...'.

As a route to India, Egypt's significance had been appreciated at least since the 1770s but most emphatically since the 1820s by an energetic publicist named Thomas Waghorn, brilliantly described by Thackeray. Waghorn appreciated the fact that steam vessels such as Thackeray's *Lady Mary Wood* and *Iberia*, by being independent of the vagaries of Mediterranean, Red Sea and monsoon winds, could dovetail their timetables at the Egyptian terminus ports of Alexandria and Suez and thus vastly improve the speed of communications with India. The 220 mile stretch overland between the two ports through Egypt gave its name to the whole venture. Waghorn's main concern was the mails, the lucrative mail contract being essential to the profitability of the project.

Ten years prior to Thackeray's journey, Waghorn had won approval from Muhammad Ali to develop the route through Egypt, with little or no encouragement from the Post Office in Britain, organising camel caravans from Alexandria direct to Suez to carry mail bags and Welsh coal for steamboats arriving from India, and a system of resting places on the dreary track from Cairo to Suez for passengers. Thackeray himself, staying at the Hôtel d'Orient in Cairo, found it built to accommodate 'a hundred Christian people, or more, [who] come from England and from India every fortnight'. As passenger numbers swelled, Waghorn's somewhat *extempore* arrangements were superseded by more efficient services, especially on the desert stretch, provided by Messrs Hill & Raven. Even then a passenger once complained that the champagne served at the halfway house was warm.

The voyage by sea to Egypt was meanwhile being absorbed by Peninsular & Oriental. This company had been founded, initially as the Peninsular Steam Company, by Brodie Willcox and Arthur Anderson in 1837, from offices off Cornhill in London. The next year saw Isambard Kingdom Brunel launch his magnificent paddle steamer *Great Western*, the largest steam vessel afloat, to be surpassed the year before Thackeray's voyage by his even larger screw-

Portrait of Lieutenant Thomas Waghorn. A passionate advocate of the Overland Route through Egypt as the fastest transit for passengers and mail to and from India, Waghorn's energetic activities are brilliantly encapsulated by Thackeray (see chapter XV). The wood engraving is from the 8th November 1845 issue of *The Illustrated London News.*

propelled *Great Britain*. The marine steam engine had evolved rapidly since the first passenger-carrying prototype, the *Charlotte Dundas*, chugged along the Forth & Clyde Canal in 1801.

The steamboat's potential for easing the distance between India and Britain was recognised as early as 1820 by Calcutta merchants who, together with leading steam

enthusiasts in Britain, financed a voyage from Falmouth to Calcutta in 1825 via the Cape of Good Hope by the tiny steamboat *Enterprize*. *Enterprize's* arrival alongside the Calcutta quay was witnessed by Waghorn, then employed as a pilot on the Hooghly river. A more significant landmark in the development of steam communications was a voyage in 1830 from Bombay to Suez by the *Hugh Lindsay*, a steamboat built in Bombay and financed by the Bombay Government to prove that steam engines could prevail against the seasonal monsoons that effectively closed Bombay to much of the outside world for several months a year.

By 1844 steamships were departing regularly for the Mediterranean and Alexandria. 'The paddle wheel is the great conqueror!' wrote Thackeray. The matching service up the Red Sea was less satisfactory, however, mainly because of East India Company parsimony in using underpowered vessels against its difficult winds. In 1840 Peninsular Steam won the mail contract to Alexandria, adding 'Orient' to the company's name, and subsequently the route from Calcutta to Suez (on which Thackeray's vessel the *Lady Mary Wood* would steam), but not until 1852 did the company win the Bombay-to-Suez run.

The company also in due course set up its own arrangements for the transit of Egypt; in Thackeray's day it was still run by Messrs Hill & Raven. Steamboats also proved invaluable for the transit of Egypt. Muhammad Ali's foreign advisers persuaded him to dig the Mahmudiyyah Canal from just outside Alexandria to the Nile at Atfah, its barges initially pulled by horses but soon by diminutive steam tugs, as were the barges they linked up with on the Nile.

Thackeray's description of his trip was part of a flourishing body of travel literature about the Near East. In his diary he mentions amongst his reading matter Kinglake's *Eothen* (only just published), James Morier's *Adventures of Hajji Baba* and *Antar, a Bedooeen Romance*. He must also have been familiar with a frivolous account of the Overland Route, *Sand and Canvas*, published in 1840 by Samuel Bevan, brother of Thackeray's friend William and with whom Thackeray stayed in Rome after finishing his homeward voyage at Naples. Thackeray's own publication *Our Street* describes the typical Eastern traveller: 'Hang it', says Titmarsh disparagingly of Clarence Bulbul, 'has not everyone written an Eastern book?'.

Carlyle unkindly compared Thackeray's acceptance of P&O's hospitality with 'the practice of a blind fiddler going to and fro on a penny ferry boat in Scotland and playing tunes to the passengers for halfpence'. But the 'passengers' must have approved: a second edition of Thackeray's 'Eastern book' followed the first by a few months, only the second unserialised book which he had attempted (the first was his *Irish Sketchbook*, published in 1842).

Often witty, sometimes flippant, always observant, Thackeray reflects on paper the mounting interest which the general public had developed in the Orient. J. F. Lewis, the artist whom he visited in Cairo and clearly knew well, was achieving a similar success on canvas with his brilliant evocations of Cairo street scenes. When Thackeray chooses, as in describing the landscape of the Holy Land, he can also be reverent. As the anonymous review in Dickens' *Daily News* claimed, *Cornhill to Cairo* established Thackeray as a true humorist, letting 'the public into the secret of their own peculiar characters'.

'Thackeray was a big man, a ripe man, and a complete man' wrote Gordon Ray. In general Thackeray saw the world in the same light as ordinary people; this is the great appeal of his no-nonsense attitude to the 'East', avoiding both the hushed reverence which characterised so much contemporary literature about the area, and the minutiae of guide books which were to weigh down the luggage of those who followed in growing numbers in Thackeray's footsteps. His was a distinctive and unconventional talent, admirably suited to both the exoticism of oriental life and the mundanities by which the outsider survives the exoticism. His success confirmed Thackeray in his literary vocation, leading to the full maturity of his talent in his next full length book, *Vanity Fair*.

SARAH SEARIGHT
London, September 1990

Facing Page. *P&O Steamship 'Iberia' approaching the Rock of Gibraltar*. The *Iberia* was one of the P&O steamships in which Thackeray sailed during his Mediterranean voyage, and he dedicated his book to its Captain, Samuel Lewis. Although this picture was not painted until 1887, the artist, R. H. Neville-Cumming, copied an engraving, published in 1836, of an earlier painting by the marine artist W. J. Huggins. The Peninsular and Oriental Steam Navigation Company.

Chapter I: VIGO

THE sun brought all the sick people out of their berths this morning, and the indescribable moans and noises which had been issuing from behind the fine painted doors on each side of the cabin happily ceased. Long before sunrise, I had the good fortune to discover that it was no longer necessary to maintain the horizontal posture, and, the very instant this truth was apparent, came on deck, at two o'clock in the morning, to see a noble full moon sinking westward, and millions of the most brilliant stars shining overhead. The night was so serenely pure, that you saw them in magnificent airy perspective; the blue sky around and over them, and other more distant orbs sparkling above, till they glittered away faintly into the immeasurable distance. The ship went rolling over a heavy, sweltering, calm sea. The breeze was a warm and soft one; quite different to the rigid air we had left behind us, two days since, off the Isle of Wight.[1] The bell kept tolling its half hours, and the mate explained the mystery of watch and dog-watch.

The sight of that noble scene cured all the woes and discomfitures of sea-sickness at once, and if there were any need to communicate such secrets to the public, one might tell of much more good that the pleasant morning-watch affected; but there are a set of emotions about which a man had best be shy of talking lightly, – and the feelings excited by contemplating this vast, magnificent, harmonious Nature are among these. The view of it inspires a delight and ecstasy which is not only hard to describe, but which has something secret in it that a man should not utter loudly. Hope, memory, humility, tender yearnings towards dear friends, and inexpressible love and reverence towards the Power which created the infinite universe blazing above eternally, and the vast ocean shining and rolling around – fill the heart with a solemn, humble happiness, that a person dwelling in a city has rarely occasion to enjoy. They are coming away from London parties at this time: the dear lit-tle eyes are closed in sleep under mother's wing. How far off city cares and pleasures appear to be! How small and mean they seem, dwindling out of sight before this magnificent brightness of Nature! But the best thoughts only grow and strengthen under it. Heaven shines above, and the humbled spirit looks up reverently towards that boundless aspect of wisdom and beauty. You are at home, and with all at rest there, however far away they may be; and through the distance the heart broods over them, bright and wakeful like yonder peaceful stars overhead.

The day was as fine and calm as the night; at seven bells, suddenly a bell began to toll very much like that of a country church, and on going on deck we found an awning raised, a desk with a flag flung over it close to the compass, and the ship's company and passengers assembled there to hear the captain read the Service in a manly respectful voice. This, too, was a novel and touching sight to me. Peaked ridges of purple mountains rose to the left of the ship, – Finisterre and the coast of Gallicia. The sky above was cloudless and shining; the vast dark ocean smiled peacefully round about, and the ship went rolling over it, as the people within were praising the Maker of all.

In honour of the day, it was announced that the passengers would be regaled with champagne at dinner;[2] and accordingly that exhilarating liquor was served out in decent profusion, the company drinking the captain's health with the customary orations of compliment and acknowledgment. This feast was scarcely ended, when we found ourselves rounding the headland into Vigo Bay, passing a grim and tall island of rocky mountains which lies in the centre of the bay.

Whether it is that the sight of land is always welcome to weary mariners, after the perils and annoyances of a voyage of three days, or whether the place is in itself extraordinarily beautiful, need not be argued; but I have seldom seen

On the Way to India – Sunday at Sea, engraving from *The Graphic*, 10 April 1875. Although later in date than Thackeray's voyage, this scene – apart from the costumes of the congregation – tallies well with Thackeray's account of the Sunday Service on board the *Lady Mary Wood* more than 30 years earlier.
The Peninsular and Oriental Steam Navigation Company.

anything more charming than the amphitheatre of noble hills into which the ship now came – all the features of the landscape being lighted up with a wonderful clearness of air, which rarely adorns a view in our country. The sun had not yet set, but over the town and lofty rocky castle of Vigo a great ghost of a moon was faintly visible, which blazed out brighter and brighter as the superior luminary retired behind the purple mountains of the headland to rest. Before the general background of waving heights which encompassed the bay, rose a second semicircle of undulating hills, as cheerful and green as the mountains behind them were grey and solemn. Farms and gardens, convent towers, white villages and churches, and buildings that no doubt were hermitages once, upon the sharp peaks of the hills, shone brightly in the sun. The sight was delightfully cheerful, animated, and pleasing.

Presently the captain roared out the magic words, 'Stop her!', and the obedient vessel came to a stand-still at some three hundred yards from the little town, with its white houses clambering up a rock, defended by the superior mountain whereon the castle stands. Numbers of people, arrayed in various brilliant colours of red, were standing on the sand close by the tumbling, shining, purple waves: and there we beheld, for the first time, the royal red and yellow standard of Spain floating on its own ground, under the guardianship of a light blue sentinel, whose musket glittered in the sun. Numerous boats were seen, incontinently, to put off from the little shore.

And now our attention was withdrawn from the land to a sight of great splendour on board. This was Lieutenant Bundy, the guardian of her Majesty's mails,[3] who issued from his cabin in his long swallow-tailed coat, with anchor

In the Bay of Vigo, in Galicia, after George Vivian, from his volume of lithographs, *Scenery of Portugal & Spain,* 1839. Vivian was one of several British artists to visit Spain in the 1830s.
Victoria and Albert Museum.

Lieutenant Bundy and the Royal Mail going ashore at Vigo, wood engraving by William Thackeray.

buttons; his sabre clattering between his legs; a magnificent shirt-collar, of several inches in height, rising round his good-humoured sallow face; and above it a cocked hat, that shone so, I thought it was made of polished tin (it may have been that or oilskin), handsomely laced with black worsted, and ornamented with a shining gold cord. A little squat boat, rowed by three ragged *gallegos,* came bouncing up to the ship. Into this Mr Bundy and her Majesty's royal mail embarked with much majesty; and in the twinkling of an eye, the royal standard of England, about the size of a pocket-handkerchief, – and at the bows of the boat, the man-of-war's pennant, being a strip of bunting considerably under the value of a farthing, – streamed out.

'They know that flag, sir,' said the good-natured old tar, quite solemnly, in the evening afterwards: 'they respect it, sir.' The authority of her Majesty's lieutenant on board the steamer is stated to be so tremendous, that he may order it to stop, to move, to go larboard, starboard, or what you will; and the captain dare only disobey him, *suo periculo.*

It was agreed that a party of us should land for half an hour, and taste real Spanish chocolate on Spanish ground. We followed Lieutenant Bundy, but humbly in the

[22]

P&O Steamship 'Lady Mary Wood' passing the Rock of Gibraltar. Thackeray sailed in the *Lady Mary Wood* from Southampton to Gibraltar. The lithograph by William Delamotte is from the series *Views of the Overland Journey to India*, published in 1847.
The Peninsular and Oriental Steam Navigation Company.

providor's boat; that officer going on shore to purchase fresh eggs, milk for tea (in place of the slimy substitute of whipped yolk of egg, which we had been using for our morning and evening meals), and, if possible, oysters, for which it is said the rocks of Vigo are famous.

It was low tide, and the boat could not get up to the dry shore. Hence it was necessary to take advantage of the offers of sundry *gallegos*, who rushed barelegged into the water, to land on their shoulders. The approved method seems to be, to sit upon one shoulder only, holding on by the porter's whiskers; and though some of our party were of the tallest and fattest men whereof our race is composed,[4] and their living sedans exceedingly meagre and small, yet all were landed without accident upon the juicy sand, and forthwith surrounded by a host of mendicants, screaming, 'I say, sir! penny, sir! I say, English! tam your ays! penny!', in all voices from extreme youth to the most lousy and venerable old age. When it is said that these beggars were as ragged as those of Ireland, and still more voluble, the Irish traveller will be able to form an opinion of their capabilities.

Through this crowd we passed up some steep rocky steps, through a little low gate, where, in a little guard-house and barrack, a few dirty little sentinels were keeping a dirty little guard; and by low-roofed, whitewashed houses, with balconies, and women in them, – the very same women, with the very same head clothes, and yellow fans and eyes, at once sly and solemn, which Murillo painted, – by a neat church into which we took a peep, and, finally, into the Plaza del Constitucion, or Grand Place of the town, which may be about as big as that pleasing square, Pump Court, Temple.[5] We were taken to an inn, of which I forget the name, and were shown from one chamber and storey to another, till we arrived at that apartment where the real Spanish chocolate was finally to be served out. All these rooms were as clean as scrubbing and whitewash could make them; with simple French prints (with Spanish titles) on the walls; a few rickety half-finished articles of furniture; and, finally, an air of extremely respectable poverty. A jolly, black-eyed, yellow-shawled Dulcinea conducted us through the apartment, and provided us with the desired refreshment.

Sounds of clarions drew our eyes to the Place of the Constitution; and, indeed, I had forgotten to say, that that majestic square was filled with military, with exceedingly small firelocks, the men ludicrously young and diminutive for the most part, in a uniform at once cheap and tawdry, – like those supplied to the warriors at Astley's,[6] or from still humbler theatrical wardrobes: indeed, the whole scene was just like that of a little theatre; the houses curiously small, with arcades and balconies, out of which looked women apparently a great deal too big for the chambers they inhabited; the warriors were in ginghams, cottons, and tinsel; the officers had huge epaulets of sham silver lace drooping over their bosoms, and looked as if they were attired at a very small expense. Only the general – the captain-general (Pooch, they told us, was his name: I know not how 'tis written in Spanish)–was well got up, with a smart hat, a real feather, huge stars glittering on his portly chest, and tights and boots of the first order. Presently, after a good deal of trumpeting, the little men marched out of the place, Pooch and his staff coming into the very inn in which we were awaiting our chocolate.

Then we had an opportunity of seeing some of the civilians of the town. Three or four ladies passed, with fan and mantle; to them came three or four dandies, dressed smartly in the French fashion, with strong Jewish physiognomies. There was one, a solemn lean fellow in black, with his collars extremely turned over, and holding before him a long ivory-tipped ebony cane, who tripped along the little place with a solemn smirk, which gave one an indescribable feeling of the truth of *Gil Blas*,[7] and of those delightful bachelors and licentiates who have appeared to us all in our dreams.

In fact we were but half an hour in this little queer Spanish town; and it appears like a dream, too, or a little show got up to amuse us. Boom! the gun fired at the end of the funny

Balcony Scene, Spain. Elegant Spanish ladies leaning over decorative balconies was an image often used by Victorian artists to evoke the exoticism of Mediterranean Spain. The example here is an engraving from a special feature on Spain in *The Illustrated London News,* 4 October 1845.

little entertainment. The women and the balconies, the beggars and the walking Murillos, Pooch and the little soldiers in tinsel, disappeared, and were shut up in their box again. Once more we were carried on the beggars' shoulders out of the shore, and we found ourselves again in the great stalwart roast-beef world; the stout British steamer bearing out of the bay, whose purple waters had grown more purple. The sun had set by this time, and the moon above was twice as big and bright as our degenerate moons are.

The providor had already returned with his fresh stores, and Bundy's tin hat was popped into its case, and he walking the deck of the packet denuded of tails. As we went out of the bay, occurred a little incident with which the great incidents of the day may be said to wind up. We saw before us a little vessel, tumbling and plunging about in the dark waters of the bay, with a bright light beaming from the mast. It made for us at about a couple of miles from the town, and came close up, flouncing and bobbing in the very jaws of the paddle, which looked as if it would have seized and twirled round that little boat and its light, and destroyed them for ever and ever. All the passengers, of course, came crowding to the ship's side to look at the bold little boat.

'I SAY!' howled a man; 'I say! – a word! – I say! *Passagero! Passagero! Passage-e-ero!'*. We were two hundred yards ahead by this time.

'Go on', says the captain.

'You may stop if you like', says Lieutenant Bundy, exerting his tremendous responsibility. It is evident that the lieutenant has a soft heart, and felt for the poor devil in the boat who was howling so piteously *'Passagero!'*

But the captain was resolute. His duty was *not* to take the man up. He was evidently an irregular customer – someone trying to escape, possibly.

The lieutenant turned away, but did not make any further hints. The captain was right; but we all felt somehow disappointed, and looked back wistfully at the little boat, jumping up and down far astern now; the poor little light shining in vain, and the poor wretch within screaming out in the most heart-rending accents a last faint, desperate – 'I say! *Passagero-o!'*

We all went down to tea rather melancholy; but the new milk, in the place of that abominable whipped egg, revived us again; and so ended the great events on board the *Lady Mary Wood*[8] steamer, on the 25th August 1844.

Chapter II: L I S B O N – C A D I Z

A GREAT misfortune which befalls a man who has but a single day to stay in a town, is that fatal duty which superstition entails upon him of visiting the chief lions of the city in which he may happen to be. You must go through the ceremony, however much you may sigh to avoid it; and however much you know that the lions in one capital roar very much like the lions in another; that the churches are more or less large and splendid; the palaces pretty spacious, all the world over; and that there is scarcely a capital city in this Europe but has its pompous bronze statue or two of some periwigged, hook-nosed emperor, in a Roman habit, waving his bronze baton on his broad-flanked brazen charger. We only saw these state old lions in Lisbon, whose roar has long since ceased to frighten one. First we went to the church of St Roch,[1] to see a famous piece of mosaic work there. It is a famous work of art, and was bought by I don't know what king, for I don't know how much money. All this information may be perfectly relied on, though the fact is we did not see the mosaic work; the sacristan, who guards it, was yet in bed; and it was veiled from our eyes in a side chapel by great dirty damask curtains, which could not be removed, except when the sacristan's toilette was done, and at the price of a dollar. So we were spared this mosaic exhibition; and I think I always feel relieved when such an event occurs. I feel I have done my duty in coming to see the enormous animal – if he is not at home, *Virtute mea me*, etc. – we have done our best, and mortal can do no more.

In order to reach that church of the forbidden mosaic, we had sweated up several most steep and dusty streets – hot and dusty, although it was but nine o'clock in the morning. Thence the guide conducted us into some little dusty-powdered gardens, in which the people make believe to enjoy the verdure, and whence you look over a great part of the arid, dreary, stony city. There was no smoke, as in honest London, only dust – dust over the gaunt houses and

The Tagus, from *The Route of The Overland Mail to India,* 1850-52, watercolour attributed to Henry Fitzcook. Several ships, under different flags, and numerous small fishing boats, are seen at the mouth of this great river.
The Peninsular and Oriental Steam Navigation Company.

Lisbon from Caxias on the North Bank of the Tagus, oil painting by Charles Henry Seaforth, 1840. The busy harbour is depicted, with fishing boats on the shore and large ships sailing at the mouth of the river.
Photograph: The Fine Art Society.

the dismal yellow strips of gardens. Many churches were there, and tall, half-baked looking public edifices, that had a dry, uncomfortable, earthquaky look, to my idea.[2] The ground-floors of the spacious houses by which we passed, seemed the coolest and pleasantest portions of the mansion. They were cellars or warehouses, for the most part, in which white-jacketed clerks sat smoking easy cigars. The streets were plastered with placards of a bull-fight, to take place the next evening (there was no opera at that season); but it was not a real Spanish tauromachy – only a theatrical combat, as you could see by the picture, in which the horseman was cantering off at three miles an hour, the bull tripping after him with tips to his gentle horns. Mules interminable, and almost all excellently sleek and handsome, were pacing down every street: here and there, but later in the day, came clattering along a smart rider, on a prancing

Spanish horse; and in the afternoon a few families might be seen in the queerest, old-fashioned little carriages, drawn by their jolly mules, and swinging between, or rather before, enormous wheels.

The churches I saw were of the florid periwig architecture – I mean of that pompous, cauliflower-kind-of ornament, which was the fashion in Louis the Fifteenth's time,[3] at which unlucky period a building mania seems to have seized upon many of the monarchs of Europe, and innumerable public edifices were erected. It seems to me to have been the period in all history when society was the least natural, and perhaps the most dissolute; and I have always fancied that the bloated artificial forms of the architecture partake of the social disorganization of the time. Who can respect a simpering ninny, grinning in a Roman dress and a full-bottomed wig, who is made to pass off for a hero; or a

fat woman in a hoop, and of a most doubtful virtue, who leers at you as a goddess? In the palaces which we saw, several court allegories were represented, which, atrocious as they were in point of art, might yet serve to attract the regard of the moraliser. There were Faith, Hope, and Charity restoring Don John to the arms of his happy Portugal: there were Virtue, Valor and Victory saluting Don Emanuel: Reading, Writing and Arithmetic (for what I know, or some mythologic nymphs) dancing before Don Miguel – the picture is there still, at the Ajuda; and, ah, me! where is poor Mig? Well, it is these state lies and ceremonies that we persist in going to see; whereas a man would have a much better insight into Portuguese manners, by planting himself at a corner, like yonder beggar, and watching the real transactions of the day.

A drive to Belem is the regular route practised by the traveller who has to make only a short stay, and accordingly a couple of carriages were provided for our party, and we were driven through the long merry street of Belem, peopled by endless strings of mules, – by thousands of *gallegos*, with water-barrels on their shoulders, or lounging by the fountains to hire, – by the Lisbon and Belem omnibuses, with four mules, jingling along at a good pace; and it seemed to me to present a far more lively and cheerful, though not so regular, an appearance as the stately quarters of the city we had left behind us. The little shops were at full work – the men brown, well-dressed, manly, and handsome: so much cannot, I am sorry to say, be said for the ladies, of whom, with every anxiety to do so, our party could not perceive a single good-looking specimen all day. The noble blue Tagus accompanies you all along these three miles of busy, pleasant street, whereof the chief

The North Bank of the Tagus, Buenos Ayres, Lisbon, oil painting by Charles Henry Seaforth, 1840. The view is from the terrace of the British Mission, and looks across the Tagus to the Cacilhas on the far side.
Photograph: The Fine Art Society.

Left. *Lisbon: The Fort of Belem near the mouth of the Tagus*, lithograph after George Vivian, from *Scenery of Spain & Portugal*, 1839.
Victoria and Albert Museum.

Right. *Lisbon: The Aqueduct from the Garden of the Mai d'Aqua*, after George Vivian. The aqueduct that Thackeray endured 'a dismal excursion of three hours' to visit, terminated within the walls of Lisbon. The lithograph is from Vivian's volume of views, *Scenery of Portugal & Spain*, 1839.
Victoria and Albert Museum.

charm, as I thought, was its look of genuine business – that appearance of comfort which the cleverest court architect never knows how to give.

The carriages (the canvas one with four seats and the chaise in which I drove) were brought suddenly up to a gate with the Royal Arms over it; and here we were introduced to as queer an exhibition as the eye has often looked on. This was the state-carriage house, where there is a museum of huge, old, tumble-down, gilded coaches of the last century, lying here, mouldy and dark, in a sort of limbo. The gold has vanished from the great, lumbering, old wheels and panels; the velvets are woefully tarnished. When one thinks of the patches and powder that have simpered out of those plate-glass windows – the mitred bishops, the big-wigged marshals, the shovel-hatted *abbé* which they have borne in their time – the human mind becomes affected in no ordinary degree. Some human minds heave a sigh for the glories of bygone days; while others, considering rather the lies and humbug, the vice and servility, which went framed and glazed and enshrined, creaking along in those old juggernaut cars, with fools worshipping under the wheels, console themselves for the decay of institutions that may have been splendid and costly, but were ponderous, clumsy, slow, and unfit for daily wear. The guardian of these defunct old carriages tells some prodigious fibs concerning them: he pointed out one carriage that was six hundred years old in his calendar; but any connoisseur in bricabrac can see it was built at Paris in the Regent Orleans' time.

Hence it is but a step to an institution in full life and vigour, – a noble orphan school for one thousand boys and girls, founded by Don Pedro, who gave up to its use the superb convent of Belem, with its splendid cloisters, vast airy dormitories, and magnificent church.[4] Some Oxford gentlemen would have wept to see the desecrated edifice, – to think that the shaven polls and white gowns were banished from it to give place to a thousand children, who have not even the clergy to instruct them. 'Every lad here may choose his trade', our little informant said, who addressed us in better French than any of our party spoke, whose manners were perfectly gentlemanlike and respectful, and whose clothes, though of a common cotton stuff, were cut and worn with a military neatness and precision. All the children whom we remarked were dressed with similar neatness, and it was a pleasure to go through their various rooms for study, where some were busy at mathematics, some at drawing, some attending a lecture on tailoring, while others were sitting at the feet of a professor of the science of shoemaking. All the garments of the establishment were made by the pupils; even the deaf and dumb were drawing and reading, and the blind were, for the most part, set to perform on musical instruments, and got up a concert for the visitors. It was then we wished ourselves of the numbers of the deaf and dumb, for the poor fellows made noises so horrible, that even as blind beggars they could hardly get a livelihood in the musical way.

Hence we were driven to the huge palace of Necessidades,[5] which is but a wing of a building that no King of Portugal ought ever to be rich enough to complete, and which, if perfect, might outvie the Tower of Babel. The mines of Brazil must have been productive of gold and silver, indeed, when the founder imagined this enormous edifice. From the elevation on which it stands it commands the noblest views, – the city is spread before it, with its many churches and towers, and for many miles you see the magnificent Tagus, rolling by banks crowned with trees and towers. But, to arrive at this enormous building you have to climb a steep suburb of wretched huts, many of them with dismal gardens of dry, cracked earth, where a few reedy sprouts of Indian corn seemed to be the chief cultivation, and which were guarded by huge plants of spiky aloes, on which the rags of the proprietors of the huts were sunning themselves. The terrace before the palace was similarly encroached upon by these wretched habitations. A few millions, judiciously expended, might make of this arid hill one of the most magnificent gardens in the world; and the palace seems to me to excel for situation any royal edifice I have ever seen. But the huts of these swarming poor have crawled up close to its gates, – the superb walls of hewn stone stop all of a sudden with a lath-and-plaster hitch; and capitals, and hewn stones for columns, still lying about on the deserted terrace, may lie there for ages to come, probably, and never take their places by the side of their brethren in yonder tall bankrupt galleries. The air of this pure sky has little effect upon the edifices, – the edges of the stone look as sharp as if the builders had just left their work; and close to the grand entrance stands an outbuilding, part of which may have been burnt fifty years ago, but is in such cheerful preservation, that you might fancy the fire had occurred yesterday. It must have been an awful sight from this hill to have looked at the city spread before it, and seen it reeling and swaying in the time of the earthquake. I thought it looked so hot and shaky, that one might fancy a return of the fit. In several places still remain gaps and chasms, and ruins lie here and there as they cracked and fell.

Although the palace has not attained anything like its full growth, yet what exists is quite big enough for the monarch of such a little country; and Versailles or Windsor has not apartments more nobly proportioned. The Queen resides in the Ajuda, a building of much less pretensions, of which the yellow walls and beautiful gardens are seen between Belem and the city. The Necessidades are only used for grand galas, receptions of ambassadors, and ceremonies of state. In the throne-room is a huge throne, surmounted by an enormous gilt crown, than which I have never seen anything larger in the finest pantomime at Drury Lane; but the effect of this splendid piece is lessened by a shabby old Brussels carpet, almost the only other article of furniture in the apartment, and not quite large enough to cover its spacious floor. The looms of Kidderminster have supplied the web which ornaments the 'Ambassadors' Waiting-room', and the ceilings are painted with huge allegories in distemper, which pretty well correspond with the other furniture. Of all the undignified objects in the world, a palace out at elbows is surely the meanest. Such places ought not to be seen in adversity, – splendour is their decency, – and when no longer able to maintain it, they should sink to the level of their means, calmly subside into manufactories, or go shabby in seclusion.

There is a picture-gallery belonging to the palace that is quite of a piece with the furniture, where are the mythological pieces relative to the kings before alluded to, and where the English visitor will see some astonishing pictures of the Duke of Wellington, done in a very characteristic style of Portuguese art. There is also a chapel, which has been decorated with much care and sumptuousness of ornament,- the altar surmounted by a ghastly and horrible carved figure in the taste of the time, when faith was strengthened by the shrieks of Jews on the rack, and enlivened by the roasting of

closed, and we were entertained with a legend of some respectable character who had made a good livelihood there for some time past lately, having a private key to this very aqueduct, and lying in wait there for unwary travellers, like ourselves, whom he pitched down the arches into the ravines below, and there robbed them at leisure. So that all we saw was the door and the tall arches of the aqueduct, and by the time we returned to town it was time to go on board

Cadiz: The Landing Place, oil painting by F. Williams, 1827. A similar scene to that which Thackeray would have encountered when he went ashore at Cadiz in 1844.
Government Art Collection.

heretics. Other such frightful images may be seen in the churches of the city; those which we saw were still rich, tawdry, and splendid to outward show, although the French, as usual, had robbed their shrines of their gold and silver, and the statues of their jewels and crowns. But brass and tinsel look to the visitor full as well at a little distance, – as doubtless Soult and Junot thought, when they despoiled these places of worship,[6] like French philosophers as they were.

A friend, with a classical turn of mind, was bent upon seeing the aqueduct, whither we went on a dismal excursion of three hours, in the worst carriages, over the most diabolical clattering roads, up and down dreary parched hills, on which grew a few grey olive trees and many aloes. When we arrived, the gate leading to the aqueduct was

the ship again. If the inn at which we had sojourned was not of the best quality, the bill, at least, would have done honour to the first establishment in London. We all left the house of entertainment joyfully, glad to get out of the sunburnt city, and go *home*. Yonder in the steamer was home, with its black funnel and gilt portraiture of Lady Mary Wood at the bows; and every soul on board felt glad to return to the friendly little vessel. But the authorities, however, of Lisbon are very suspicious of the departing stranger, and we were made to lie an hour in the river before the Sanita boat, where a passport is necessary to be procured before the traveller can quit the country. Boat after boat, laden with priests and peasantry, with handsome red-sashed *gallegos* clad in brown, and ill-favoured women,

The Alameda at Cadiz and Convent of the Virgin del Carmen, 1836, from the second of four *Jennings' Landscape Annuals,* illustrated with engravings after David Roberts, following his visit to Spain and Morocco in 1832-33. In a review of the *Annuals* Thackeray praised Roberts's 'admirable designs'. Victoria and Albert Museum.

came and got their permits, and were off, as we lay bumping up against the old hull of the Sanita boat; but the officers seemed to take a delight in keeping us there bumping, looked at us quite calmly over the ship's sides, and smoked their cigars without the least attention to the prayers which we shrieked out for release.

If we were glad to get away from Lisbon, we were quite as sorry to be obliged to quit Cadiz, which we reached the next night, and where we were allowed a couple of hours' leave to land and look about. It seemed as handsome within as it is stately without; the long narrow streets of an admirable cleanliness, many of the tall houses of rich and noble decorations, and all looking as if the city were in full prosperity. I have seen no more cheerful and animated sight than the long street leading from the quay where we were landed, and the market blazing in sunshine, piled with fruit, fish, and poultry, under many-coloured awnings; the tall white houses with their balconies and galleries shining round about, and the sky above so blue that the best cobalt in all the paint-box looks muddy and dim in comparison to it. There were pictures for a year in that market-place – from the copper-coloured old hags and beggars who roared to you for the love of heaven to give money, to the swaggering dandies of the market, with red sashes and tight clothes, looking on superbly, with a hand on the hip and a cigar in the mouth. These must be the chief critics at the great bull-fight house yonder, by the Alameda, with its scanty trees and cool breezes facing the water. Nor are there any corks

[31]

Spanish Peasant Girl,
watercolour by John
Frederick Lewis, 1832-34.
Photograph: Sotheby's.

to the bulls' horns here as at Lisbon.[7] A small old English guide who seized upon me the moment my foot was on shore, had a store of agreeable legends regarding the bulls, men, and horses that had been killed with unbounded profusion in the late entertainments which have taken place.

It was so early an hour in the morning that the shops were scarcely opened as yet; the churches, however, stood open for the faithful, and we met scores of women tripping towards them with pretty feet, and smart black mantillas, from which looked out fine dark eyes and handsome pale faces, very different from the coarse brown countenances we had seen at Lisbon. A very handsome modern cathedral, built by the present bishop at his own charges, was the finest of the public edifices we saw; it was not, however, nearly so much frequented as another little church, crowded with altars and fantastic ornaments, and lights and gilding, where we were told to look behind a huge iron grille, and beheld a bevy of black nuns kneeling. Most of the good ladies in the front ranks stopped their devotions, and looked at the strangers with as much curiosity as we directed at them through the gloomy bars of their chapel. The men's convents are closed; that which contains the famous Murillos has been turned into an academy of the fine arts; but the English guide did not think the pictures were of sufficient interest to detain strangers, and so hurried us back to the shore, and grumbled at only getting three shillings at parting for his trouble and his information.

And so our residence in Andalusia began and ended before breakfast, and we went on board and steamed for Gibraltar, looking, as we passed, at Joinville's black squadron,[8] and the white houses of St Mary's across the bay, with the hills of Medina Sidonia and Granada lying purple beyond them. There's something even in those names which is pleasant to write down; to have passed only two hours in Cadiz is something – to have seen real donnas with comb and mantle – real caballeros with cloak and cigar – real Spanish barbers lathering out of brass basins, – and to have heard guitars under the balconies; there was one that an old beggar was jangling in the market, whilst a huge leering fellow in bushy whiskers and a faded velvet dress came singing and jumping after our party, – not singing to a guitar, it is true, but imitating one capitally with his voice, and cracking his fingers by way of castanets, and performing a dance

such as Figaro or Lablache might envy.[9] How clear that fellow's voice thrums on the ear even now; and how bright and pleasant remains the recollection of the fine city and the blue sea, and the Spanish flags floating on the boats that danced over it, and Joinville's band beginning to play stirring marches as we puffed out of the bay.

The next stage was Gibraltar, where we were to change horses. Before sunset we skirted along the dark savage mountains of the African coast, and came to the Rock just before gun-fire. It is the very image of an enormous lion, crouched between the Atlantic and the Mediterranean, and set there to guard the passage for its British mistress. The next British lion is Malta, four days further on in the midland sea, and ready to spring upon Egypt or pounce upon Syria, or roar so as to be heard at Marseilles in case of need.

To the eyes of the civilian, the first-named of these famous fortifications is by far the most imposing. The Rock looks so tremendous, that to ascend it, even without the compliment of shells or shot, seems a dreadful task – what would it be when all those mysterious lines of batteries were vomiting fire and brimstone; when all those dark guns that you see poking their grim heads out of every imaginable cleft and zigzag should salute you with shot, both hot and cold; and when, after tugging up the hideous perpendicular place, you were to find regiments of British grenadiers ready to plunge bayonets into your poor panting stomach, and let out artificially the little breath left there?[10] It is a marvel to think that soldiers will mount such places for a shilling – ensigns for five and ninepence – a day: a cabman would ask double the money to go half way! One meekly reflects upon the above strange truths, leaning over the ship's side, and looking up the huge mountain, from the tower nestled at the foot of it to the thin flagstaff at the summit, up to which have been piled the most ingenious edifices for murder Christian Science ever adopted. My hobby-horse is a quiet beast, suited for Park riding, or a gentle trot to Putney and back to a snug stable, and plenty of feeds of corn: – it can't abide climbing hills, and is not at all used to gunpowder. Some men's animals are so spirited that the very appearance of a stone wall sets them jumping at it; regular chargers of hobbies, which snort and say – 'Ha, ha!' at the mere notion of a battle.

Chapter III: THE *LADY MARY WOOD*

Our week's voyage is now drawing to a close. We have just been to look at Cape Trafalgar, shining white over the finest blue sea. (We, who were looking at Trafalgar Square only the other day!). The sight of that cape must have disgusted Joinville and his fleet of steamers, as they passed yesterday into Cadiz bay, and tomorrow will give them a sight of St Vincent.

One of their steam-vessels has been lost off the coast of Africa; they were obliged to burn her, lest the Moors should take possession of her. She was a virgin vessel, just out of Brest. Poor innocent! to die in the very first month of her union with the noble whiskered god of war!

We Britons on board the English boat received the news of the *Groenenland's* abrupt demise with grins of satisfaction. It was a sort of national compliment, and cause of agreeable congratulation. 'The lubbers!' we said; 'the clumsy humbugs! there's none but Britons to rule the waves!', and we gave ourselves piratical airs, and went down presently and were sick in our little buggy berths. It was pleasant, certainly, to laugh at Joinville's admiral's flag floating at his foremast, in yonder black ship, with its two thundering great guns at the bows and stern, its busy crew swarming on the deck, and a crowd of obsequious shore-boats bustling round the vessel – and to sneer at the Mogador warrior, and vow that we English, had we been inclined to do the business, would have performed it a great deal better.

Now yesterday at Lisbon we saw HMS *Caledonia*. This, on the contrary, inspired us with feelings of respect and awful pleasure. There she lay – the huge sea-castle – bearing the unconquerable flag of our country. She had but to open her jaws, as it were, and she might bring a second earthquake in the city – batter it into kingdom-come – with the Ajuda Palace and the Necessidades, the churches, and the lean, dry, empty streets, and Don John, tremendous on horseback, in the midst of Black Horse Square. Wherever we looked we could see that enormous *Caledonia*, with her flashing three lines of guns. We looked at the little boats which ever and anon came out of this monster, with humble wonder. There was the lieutenant who boarded us at midnight before we dropped anchor in the river; ten white-jacketed men pulling as one, swept along with the barge, gig, boat, curricle, or coach-and-six, with which he came up to us. We examined him – his red whiskers – his collars turned down – his duck trousers, his bullion epaulets – with awe. With the same reverential feeling we examined the seamen – the young gentleman in the bows of the boat – the handsome young officers of marines we met sauntering in the town next day – the Scotch surgeon who boarded us as we weighed anchor – every man, down to the broken-nosed mariner who was drunk in a wine-house, and had *Caledonia* written in his hat. Whereas at the Frenchmen we looked with undisguised contempt. We were ready to burst with laughter as we passed the Prince's vessel – there was a little French boy in a French boat alongside cleaning it, and twirling about a little French mop – we thought it the most comical, contemptible French boy, mop, boat, steamer, prince – Psha! it is of this wretched vapouring stuff that false patriotism is made. I write this as a sort of homely apropos of the day, and Cape Trafalgar, off which we lie. What business have I to strut the deck, and clap my wings, and cry 'Cock-a-doodle-doo' over it? Some compatriots are at that work even now.

We have lost one by one all our jovial company. There were the five Oporto wine merchants – all hearty English gentlemen – gone to their wine-butts, and their red-legged partridges, and their duels at Oporto. It appears that these gallant Britons fight every morning among themselves, and give the benighted people among whom they live an opportunity to admire the spirit national. There is the brave,

Deck of the P&O steam vessel, Madras, watercolour by William Carpenter, 1854. The *Madras,* built in 1852, was used for the journey between England and India, and was similar to the vessels in which Thackeray sailed in the previous decade.

The Peninsular and Oriental Steam Navigation Company.

honest major, with his wooden leg – the kindest and simplest of Irishmen: he has embraced his children, and reviewed his little invalid garrison of fifteen men, in the fort which he commands at Belem, by this time, and, I have no doubt, played to every soul of them the twelve tunes of his musical-box. It was pleasant to see him with that musical-box – how pleased he wound it up after dinner – how happily he listened to the little clinking tunes as they galloped, ding-dong, after each other. A man who carries a musical-box is always a good-natured man.

Then there was his grace, or his grandeur, the Archbishop of Beyrout (in the parts of the infidels), His Holiness's Nuncio to the court of her most faithful Majesty, and who mingled among us like any simple mortal, – except that he had an extra smiling courtesy, which simple mortals do not always possess; and when you passed him as such, and puffed your cigar in his face, took off his hat with a grin of such prodigious rapture, as to lead you to suppose that the most delicious privilege of his whole life, was that permission to look at the tip of your nose or of your cigar. With this most reverend prelate was his grace's brother and chaplain – a very greasy and good-natured ecclesiastic, whom, from his physiognomy, I would have imagined to be a dignitary of the Israelite rather than the Romish church – as profuse in smiling courtesy as his lordship of Beyrout. These two had a meek little secretary between them, and a tall French cook and valet, who, at meal times, might be seen busy about the cabin where their reverences lay. They were on their backs for the greater part of the voyage; their yellow countenances were not only unshaven, but, to judge from appearances, unwashed. They ate in private; and it was only of evenings, as the sun was jetting over the western wave, and, comforted by the dinner, the cabin passengers assembled on the quarter-deck, that we saw the dark faces of the reverend gentlemen among us for a while. They sunk darkly into their berths when the steward's bell tolled for tea.

At Lisbon, where we came to anchor at midnight, a special boat came off, whereof the crew exhibited every token of reverence for the ambassador of the ambassador of Heaven, and carried him off from our company. This abrupt departure in the darkness disappointed some of us, who had promised ourselves the pleasure of seeing His

Cape Trafalgar, watercolour attributed to Henry Fitzcook for *The Route of The Overland Mail to India*, 1850-52. A note in the prospectus accompanying the portfolio of lithographs began: 'The sight of this celebrated spot, the scene of Nelson's greatest victory and glorious death, necessarily awakens strong emotions in the bosoms of Englishmen'. The Peninsular and Oriental Steam Navigation Company.

Grandeur depart in state in the morning, shaved, clean, and in full pontificals, the tripping little secretary swinging an incense-pot before him, and the greasy chaplain bearing his crosier.

Next day we had another bishop, who occupied the very same berth his grace of Beyrout had quitted – was sick in the very same way – so much so that this cabin of the *Lady Mary Wood* is to be christened 'the bishop's berth' henceforth; and a handsome mitre is to be painted on the basin.

Bishop No. 2 was a very stout, soft, kind-looking old gentleman, in a square cap, with a handsome tassel of green and gold round his portly breast and back. He was dressed in black robes, and tight purple stockings: and we carried him from Lisbon to the little flat coast of Faro, of which the meek old gentleman was the chief pastor.

We had not been half an hour from our anchorage in the Tagus, when his lordship dived down into the episcopal berth. All that night there was a good smart breeze; it blew fresh all the next day, as we went jumping over the blue bright sea; and there was no sign of his lordship the bishop until we were opposite the purple hills of Algarve, which lay at some ten miles distant, – a yellow sunny shore stretching flat before them, whose long sandy flats and villages we could see with our telescope from the steamer.

Presently a little vessel, with a huge shining lateen sail, and bearing the blue and white Portuguese flag, was seen playing a sort of leap frog on the jolly waves, jumping over them, and ducking down as merry as could be.[1] This little boat came towards the steamer as quick as ever she could jump; and Captain Cooper roaring out, 'Stop her!' to *Lady Mary Wood*, her ladyship's paddles suddenly ceased twirling, and news was carried to the good bishop that his boat was almost alongside, and that his hour was come.

It was rather an affecting sight to see the poor old fat gentleman, looking wistfully over the water as the boat now came up, and her eight seamen, with great noise, energy, and gesticulation laid her by the steamer. The steamer steps were let down; his lordship's servant in blue and yellow livery, like the *(Edinburgh) Review*, cast over the episcopal luggage into the boat, along with his own bundle and the jack-boots with which he rides postillion on one of the bishop's fat mules at Faro. The blue and yellow domestic went down the steps into the boat. Then came the bishop's turn;

but he couldn't do it for a long while. He went from one passenger to another, sadly shaking them by the hand, often taking leave and seeming loath to depart, until Captain Cooper, in a stern but respectful tone, touched him on the shoulder, and said, I know not with what correctness, being ignorant of the Spanish language, 'Señor Bispo! Señor Bispo!', on which summons the poor old man, looking ruefully round him once more, put his square cap under his arm, tucked up his long black petticoats, so as to show his purple stockings and jolly fat calves, and went trembling down the steps towards the boat. The good old man! I wish I had had a shake of that trembling, podgy hand somehow before he went upon his sea martyrdom. I felt a love for that soft-hearted old Christian. Ah! let us hope his *governante* tucked him comfortably in bed when he got to Faro that night, and made him a warm gruel and put his feet in warm water. The men clung around him, and almost kissed him as they popped him into the boat, but he did not heed their caresses. Away went the boat scudding madly before the winds. Bang! another lateen-sailed boat in the distance fired a gun in his honour; but the wind was blowing away from the shore, and who knows when that meek bishop got home to his gruel.

I think these were the notables of our party. I will not mention the laughing, ogling lady of Cadiz, whose manners I very much regret to say, were a great deal too lively for my sense of propriety; nor those fair sufferers, her companions, who lay on the deck with sickly, smiling, female resignation; nor the heroic children, who no sooner ate biscuit than they were ill, and no sooner were ill than they began eating biscuit again: but just allude to one other martyr, the kind lieutenant in charge of the mails, and who bore his cross with what I can't but think a very touching and noble resignation.

There's a certain sort of man whose doom in the world is disappointment, – who excels in it, – and whose luckless triumphs in his meek career of life, I have often thought, must be regarded by the kind eyes above with as much favour as the splendid successes and achievements of coarser and more prosperous men. As I sat with the lieutenant upon deck, his telescope laid over his lean legs, and he looking at the sunset with a pleased, withered old face, he gave me a little account of his history. I take it he is in nowise disinclined to talk about it, simple as it is: he has been seven-and-thirty years in the Navy, being somewhat more mature in the service than Lieutenant Peel, Rear-Admiral Prince de Joinville, and other commanders, who need not be mentioned. He is a very well-educated man, and reads prodigiously, – travels, histories, lives of eminent worthies and heroes, in his simple way. He is not in the least angry at his want of luck in the profession. 'Were I a boy tomorrow,' he said, 'I would begin it again; and when I see my schoolfellows, and how they have got on in life, if some are better off than I am, I find many are worse, and have no call to be discontented.' So he carries her Majesty's mails meekly through this world, waits upon port-admirals and captains in his old glazed hat, and is as proud of the pennon at the bow of his little boat, as if it were flying from the mainmast of a thundering man-of-war. He gets two hundred a year for his services, and has an old mother and a sister, living in England somewhere, who I will wager (though he never, I swear, said a word about it) have a good portion of this princely income.

Is it breaking a confidence to tell Lieutenant Bundy's history? Let the motive excuse the deed. It is a good, kind, wholesome, and noble character. Why should we keep all our admiration for those who win in this world, as we do, sycophants as we are? When we write a novel, our great, stupid imaginations can go no further than to marry the hero to a fortune at the end, and to find out that he is a lord by right. Oh, blundering lick-spittle morality! And yet I would like to fancy some happy retributive Utopia in the peaceful cloudland, where my friend the meek lieutenant should find the yards manned of his ship as he went on board, all the guns firing an enormous salute (only without the least noise or vile smell of powder), and he be saluted on the deck as Admiral Sir James, or Sir Joseph – aye, or Lord Viscount Bundy, Knight of all the orders above the sun.

I think this is a sufficient, if not a complete catalogue, of the worthies on board the *Lady Mary Wood*. In the week we were on board – it seemed a year, by the way – we came to regard the ship quite as a home. We felt for the captain – the most good-humoured, active, careful, ready of captains – a filial, a fraternal regard; for the providore, who provided for us with admirable comfort and generosity, a genial gratitude; and for the brisk steward's lads – brisk in serving the banquet, sympathising in handing the basin – every possible sentiment of regard and good will. What winds blew, and how many knots we ran, are all noted down, no doubt, in the ship's log; and as for what ships we saw – every one of them with their gunnage, tonnage, their nation, their direction whither they were bound, were not these all noted down with surprising ingenuity and precision by the lieutenant, at a family desk at which he sat, every night before a great paper, elegantly and mysteriously ruled off with his large ruler? I have a regard for every man on board that ship, from the captain down to the crew – down even to the cook, with tattooed arms, sweating among the saucepans in the galley, who used (with a touching affection) to send us locks of his hair in the soup. And so, while our feelings and recollections are warm, let us shake hands with this knot of good fellows, comfortably floating about in their little box of wood and iron, across Channel, Biscay Bay, and the Atlantic, from Southampton water to Gibraltar Straits.

Chapter IV: GIBRALTAR

A Jewish Woman of Gibraltar,
in a festa dress (detail),
lithograph by John Frederick
Lewis from his *Sketches of*
Spain & Spanish Character,
1836.
Victoria and Albert Museum.

SUPPOSE all the nations of the earth to send fitting ambassadors to represent them at Wapping or Portsmouth Point, with each, under its own national sign-board and language, its appropriate house of call, and your imagination may figure the main street of Gibraltar; almost the only part of the town, I believe, which boasts of the name of street at all, the remaining houserows being modestly called lanes, such as Bomb Lane, Battery Lane, Fusée Lane, and so on. In Main Street the Jews predominate, the Moors abound; and from the Jolly Sailor, or the brave Horse Marine, where the people of our nation are drinking British beer and gin, you hear choruses of *Garry Owen* or *The Lass I left behind me*; while through the flaring lattices of the Spanish *ventas* come the clatter of castanets and the jingle and moan of Spanish guitars and ditties. It is a curious sight at evening this thronged street, with the people, in a hundred different costumes, bustling to and fro under the coarse flare of the lamps; swarthy Moors, in white or crimson robes; dark Spanish smugglers in tufted hats, with gay silk handkerchiefs round their heads; fuddled seamen from men-of-war, or merchantmen; porters, Gallician or Genoese; and at every few minutes' interval, little squads of soldiers tramping to relieve guard at some one of the innumerable posts in the town.

Some of our party went to a Spanish *venta*, as a more convenient or romantic place of residence than an English house; others made choice of the clubhouse in Commercial Square, of which I formed an agreeable picture in my imagination; rather, perhaps, resembling the Junior United Service Club in Charles Street, by which every Londoner has passed ere this with respectful pleasure, catching glimpses of magnificent blazing candelabras, under which sit neat half pay officers, drinking half-pints of port. The clubhouse of Gibraltar is not, however, of the Charles Street sort; it may have been cheerful once, and there are yet relics of splendour about it. When officers wore pig-tails, and in the time of Governor O'Hara, it may have been a handsome place; but it is mouldy and decrepit now; and though his Excellency Mr Bulwer was living there,[1] and made no complaints that I heard of, other less distinguished persons thought they had reason to grumble. Indeed, what is travelling made of? At least half its pleasures and incidents come out of inns; and of them the tourist can speak with much more truth and vivacity than of historical recollections compiled out of histories, or filched out of handbooks. But to speak of the best inn in a place needs no apology; that, at least, is useful information; as every person intending to visit Gibraltar cannot have seen the flea-bitten countenances of our companions, who fled from their Spanish *venta* to take refuge at the club the morning after our arrival: they may surely be thankful for being directed to the best house of accommodation in one of the most unromantic, uncomfortable, and prosaic of towns.

If one had a right to break the sacred confidence of the mahogany, I could entertain you with many queer stories of Gibraltar life, gathered from the lips of the gentlemen who enjoyed themselves round the dingy table cloth of the clubhouse coffee-room, richly decorated with cold gravy and spilt beer. I heard there the very names of the gentlemen who wrote the famous letters from the *Warspite* regarding the French proceedings at Mogador; and met several refugee Jews from that place, who said that they were much more afraid of the Kabyles without the city, than of the guns of the French squadron, of which they seemed to make rather light. I heard the last odds on the ensuing match between Captain Smith's b. g. Bolter, and Captain Brown's ch. c. Roarer: how the gunroom of Her Majesty's Ship *Purgatory* had 'cobbed' a tradesman of the town, and of the row in consequence: I heard capital stories of the way in which Wilkins had escaped the guard, and Thompson had

Gibraltar, watercolour attributed to Henry Fitzcook, for *The Route of The Overland Mail to India*, 1850-52. Gibraltar was the first coaling station for the outward-bound steamer. The vessel in the right background of the picture is possibly the *Lady Mary Wood*.
The Peninsular and Oriental Steam Navigation Company.

HMS The Victory, with the body of Nelson on board, towed into Gibraltar 28th of October, 1805, seven days after the Battle of Trafalgar,
oil painting by Clarkson Stanfield, 1853. Thackeray visited Gibraltar nearly a decade before this painting was exhibited, but the event it commemorates would have been in the forefront of his mind. The pathos and emotion expressed in Stanfield's painting would still have been keenly felt by most Englishmen. Thackeray was a great admirer of Stanfield's considerable artistic achievements (see chapter VII).
Private Collection. *Photograph:* Sotheby's.

been locked up among the mosquitoes for being out after ten without the lantern. I heard how the governor was an old —— , but to say what, would be breaking a confidence; only this may be divulged, that the epithet was exceedingly com-plimentary to Sir Robert Wilson.[2] All the while these conversations were going on, a strange scene of noise and bustle was passing in the market-place, in front of the window, where Moors, Jews, Spaniards, soldiers were thronging in the sun; and a ragged fat fellow, mounted on a tobacco barrel, with his hat cocked on his ear, was holding an auction, and roaring with an energy and impudence that would have done credit to Covent Garden.

The Moorish castle is the only building about the Rock which has an air at all picturesque or romantic;[3] there is a plain Roman Catholic cathedral, a hideous new Protestant

conversing, or at the open windows of the officers' quarters, Ensign Fipps lying on his sofa and smoking his cigar, or Lieutenant Simson practising the flute to while away the weary hours of garrison dullness. I was surprised not to find more persons in the garrison library, where is a magnificent reading-room, and an admirable collection of books.

In spite of the scanty herbage and the dust on the trees, the Alameda is a beautiful walk; of which the vegetation has been as laboriously cared for as the tremendous fortifications which flank it on either side. The vast rock rises on one side with its interminable works of defence, and Gibraltar Bay is shining on the other, out on which from the terraces immense cannon are perpetually looking, surrounded by plantations of cannon balls and beds of bomb shells, sufficient, one would think, to blow away the whole Peninsula. The horticultural and military mixture is indeed very queer: here and there temples, rustic summer seats, etc., have been erected in the garden, but you are sure to see a great squat mortar look up from among the flower-pots: and amidst the aloes and geraniums sprouts the green petticoat and scarlet coat of a Highlander; fatigue parties are seen winding up the hill, and busy about the endless cannon-ball plantations; awkward squads are drilling in the open spaces: sentries marching everywhere, and (this is a caution to artists) I am told have orders to run any man through who is discovered making a sketch of the place. It is always beautiful, especially at evening, when the people are sauntering along the walks, and the moon is shining on the waters of the bay and the hills and twinkling white houses of the opposite shore. Then the place becomes quite romantic: it is too dark to see the dust on the dried leaves; the cannon balls do not intrude too much, but have subsided into the shade; the awkward squads are in bed; even the loungers are gone, the fan-flirting Spanish ladies, the sallow black-eyed children, and the trim white-jacketed dandies. A fife is heard from some craft at roost on the quiet waters somewhere; or a faint cheer from yonder black steamer at the Mole, which is about to set out on some night expedition. You forget that the town is at all like Wapping, and deliver yourself up entirely to romance; the sentries look noble pacing there, silent in the moonlight, and Sandy's voice is quite musical, as he challenges with a 'Who goes there?'.

church of the cigar-divan architecture, and a Court-house with a portico which is said to be an imitation of the Parthenon: the ancient religious houses of the Spanish town are gone, or turned into military residences, and marked so that you would never know their former pious destination. You walk through narrow white-washed lanes, bearing such martial names as are before-mentioned, and by-streets with barracks on either side; small Newgate-like looking buildings, at the doors of which you may see the serjeants' ladies

'All's well' is very pleasant when sung decently in tune; and inspires noble and poetic ideas of duty, courage, and danger: but when you hear it shouted all the night through, accompanied by a clapping of muskets in a time of profound peace, the sentinel's cry becomes no more romantic to the hearer than it is to the sandy Connaught-man or the bare-legged Highlander who delivers it. It is best to read about wars comfortably in Harry Lorrequer[4] or Scott's[5] novels, in which knights shout their war cries, and jovial Irish bayoneteers hurrah, without depriving you of any blessed rest. Men of a different way of thinking, however, can suit themselves perfectly at Gibraltar; where there is marching and counter-marching, challenging and relieving guard all the night through. And not here in Commercial Square alone, but all over the huge rock in the darkness – all through the mysterious zig-zags, and round the dark cannon-ball pyramids, and along the vast rock-galleries, and up to the topmast flagstaff where the sentry can look out over two seas, poor fellows are marching and clapping muskets, and crying 'All's well,' dressed in cap and feather, in place of honest nightcaps best befitting the decent hours of sleep.

All these martial noises three of us heard to the utmost advantage, lying on iron bedsteads at the time in a cracked old room on the ground floor, the open windows of which looked into the square. No spot could be more favourably selected for watching the humours of a garrison-town by night. About midnight, the door hard by us was visited by a party of young officers, who having had quite as much drink as was good for them, were naturally inclined for more; and when we remonstrated through the windows, one of them in a young tipsy voice asked after our mothers, and finally reeled away. How charming is the conversation of high spirited youth! I don't know whether the guard got hold of them: but certainly if a civilian had been hiccuping through the streets at that hour he would have been carried off to the guard-house, and left to the mercy of the mosquitoes there, and had up before the governor in the morning. The young man in the coffee-room tells me he goes to sleep every night with the keys of Gibraltar under his pillow. It is an awful image, and somehow completes the notion of the slumbering fortress. Fancy Sir Robert Wilson, his nose just visible over the sheets, his night-cap and the huge key (you see the very identical one in Reynold's portrait of Lord

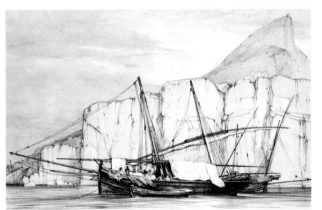

Heathfield)[6] peeping out from under the bolster!

If I entertain you with accounts of inns and nightcaps it is because I am more familiar with these subjects than with history and fortifications: as far as I can understand the former, Gibraltar is the great British depôt for smuggling goods into the Peninsula. You see vessels lying in the harbour, and are told in so many words they are smugglers; all those smart Spaniards with cigar and mantles are smugglers, and run tobaccos and cotton into Catalonia; all the

Spanish Contrabandistas, watercolour by John Frederick Lewis, 1833-36. *Photograph:* Christie's.

Smuggling Feluchos, Gibraltar, lithograph by John Frederick Lewis from his *Sketches of Spain & Spanish Character,* 1836. Lewis visited Spain in 1833-34, at almost the same time as David Roberts, and a decade before Thackeray stopped at Gibraltar. The British garrison town was apparently well-known as a thriving entrepôt for smugglers. Victoria and Albert Museum.

Facing Page. *Gibraltar: View from the Alameda, looking over the Town and Neutral Ground, to the Spanish Territory,* after George Vivian. Vivian seems also to have been struck by the curious 'horticultural and military mixture' on which Thackeray commented. The lithograph is another from Vivian's volume, *Scenery of Spain & Portugal,* 1839. Victoria and Albert Museum.

respected merchants of the place are smugglers. The other day a Spanish revenue vessel was shot to death under the thundering great guns of the fort, for neglecting to bring to, but it so happened that it was in chase of a smuggler; in this little corner of her dominions Britain proclaims war to custom-houses, and protection to free trade. Perhaps ere a very long day, England may be acting that part towards the world, which Gibraltar performs towards Spain now; and the last war in which we shall ever engage may be a custom-house war. For once establish railroads and abolish preventive duties through Europe, and what is there left to fight for? It will matter very little then under what flag people live, and foreign ministers and ambassadors may enjoy a dignified sinecure; the army will rise to the rank of peaceful constables, not having any more use for their bayonets than those worthy people have for their weapons now who accompany the law at assizes under the name of javelin-men. The apparatus of bombs and eighty-four pounders may disappear from the Alameda, and the crops of cannon-balls which now grow there, may give place to other plants more pleasant to the eye; and the great key of Gibraltar may be left in the gate for anybody to turn at will, and Sir Robert Wilson may sleep at quiet.

I am afraid I thought it was rather a release, when, having made up our minds to examine the Rock in detail and view the magnificent excavations and galleries, the admiration of all military men, and the terror of any enemies who may attack the fortress, we received orders to embark forthwith in the *Tagus*, which was to carry us to Malta and Constantinople.[7] So we took leave of this famous rock – this great blunderbuss – which we seized out of the hands of the natural owners a hundred and forty years ago, and which we have kept ever since tremendously loaded and cleaned and ready for use. To seize and have it is doubtless a gallant thing; it is like one of those tests of courage which one reads of in the chivalrous romances, when, for instance, Sir Huon, of Bordeaux, is called upon to prove his knighthood by going to Babylon and pulling out the Sultan's beard and front teeth in the midst of his court there.

But, after all, justice must confess it was rather hard on the poor Sultan. If we had the Spaniards established at Land's End, with impregnable Spanish fortifications on St Michael's Mount, we should perhaps come to the same

conclusion. Meanwhile, let us hope during this long period of deprivation, the Sultan of Spain is reconciled to the loss of his front teeth and bristling whiskers – let us even try to think that he is better without them. At all events, right or wrong, whatever may be our title to the property, there is no Englishman but must think with pride of the manner in which his countryman have kept it, and of the courage, endurance, and sense of duty with which stout old Eliot and his companions resisted Crillion and the Spanish battering ships and his fifty thousand men. There seems to be something more noble in the success of a gallant resistance than of an attack, however brave. After failing in his attack on the fort, the French General visited the English Commander who had foiled him, and parted from him and his garrison in perfect politeness and good humour. The English troops, Drinkwater says, gave him thundering cheers as he went away, and the French in return complimented us on our gallantry, and lauded the humanity of our people. If we are to go on murdering each other in the old-fashioned way, what a pity it is that our battles cannot end in the old-fashioned way too.

One of our fellow travellers, who had written a book, and had suffered considerably from seasickness during our passage along the coasts of France and Spain, consoled us all by saying that the very minute we got into the Mediterranean we might consider ourselves entirely free from illness; and, in fact, that it was unheard of in the inland sea. Even in the Bay of Gibraltar the water looked bluer than anything I have ever seen – except Miss Smith's eyes. I thought, somehow, the delicious faultless azure never could look angry – just like the eyes before alluded to – and under this assurance we passed the Strait, and began coasting the African shore calmly and without the least apprehension, as if we were as much used to the tempest as Mr T.P. Cooke.[8]

But when, in spite of the promise of the man who had written the book, we found ourselves worse than in the worst part of the Bay of Biscay, or off the storm-lashed rocks of Finisterre, we set down the author in question as a gross imposter, and had a mind to quarrel with him for leading us into this cruel error. The most provoking part of the matter too, was, that the sky was deliciously clear and cloudless, the air balmy, the sea so insultingly blue that it seemed as if we had no right to be ill at all, and that the innumerable little waves that frisked round about our keel were enjoying an *anerithmon gelasma* (this is one of my four Greek quotations, depend on it, I will manage to introduce the other three before the tour is done)[9] – seemed to be enjoying, I say, the above-named Greek quotation at our expense. Here is the dismal log of Wednesday, 4th of September: – 'All attempts at dining very fruitless. Basins in requisition. Wind hard ahead. *Que diable allais je faire dans cette galère?*[10] Writing or thinking impossible, so read letters from the Aegean.' These brief words give, I think, a complete idea of wretchedness, despair, remorse, and prostration of soul and body. Two days previously we passed the forts and moles and yellow buildings of Algiers, rising very stately from the sea, and skirted by gloomy purple lines of African shore, with fires smoking in the mountains, and lonely settlements here and there.

Algiers, watercolour attributed to Henry Fitzcook, from *The Route of The Overland Mail to India*, 1850-52. The French occupied Algiers in 1830, and during the 1840s were engaged in the colonisation of the country.
The Peninsular and Oriental Steam Navigation Company.

Malta, watercolour attributed to Henry Fitzcook. Thackeray's vivid description of Valletta's busy harbour is here illustrated in another of the scenes from *The Route of The Overland Mail to India*, published as a portfolio of lithographs in 1850-52.
The Peninsular and Oriental Steam Navigation Company.

On the 5th, to the inexpressible joy of all, we reached Valetta,[11] the entrance to the harbour of which is one of the most stately and agreeable scenes ever admired by seasick traveller. The small basin was busy with a hundred ships, from the huge guard ship, which lies there a city in itself;- merchantmen loading and crews cheering, under all the flags of the world flaunting in the sunshine; a half-score of busy black steamers perpetually coming and going, coaling and painting, and puffing and hissing in and out of harbour; slim men-of-war's barges shooting to and fro, with long shining oars flashing like wings over the water; hundreds of painted town-boats, with high heads and white awnings, – down to the little tubs in which some naked, tawny young beggars came paddling up to the steamer, entreating us to let them dive for halfpence. Round this busy blue water rise rocks, blazing in sunshine, and covered with every imaginable device of fortification: to the right, St Elmo, with flag and lighthouse; and opposite, the Military Hospital, looking like a palace; and all round, the houses of the city, for its size the handsomest and most stately in the world.

Nor does it disappoint you on a closer inspection, as many a foreign town does. The streets are thronged with a lively, comfortable looking population; the poor seem to inhabit handsome stone palaces, with balconies and projecting windows of heavy carved stone. The lights and shadows, the cries and stenches, the fruit shops and fish stalls, the dresses and chatter of all nations; the soldiers in scarlet, and women in black mantillas; the beggars, boatmen, barrels of pickled herrings and maccaroni; the shovel-hatted priests and bearded capuchins; the tobacco, grapes, onions, and sunshine; the sign-boards, bottled-porter stores, the statues of saints and little chapels which jostle the stranger's eyes as he goes up the famous stairs from the water-gate, make a scene of such pleasant confusion and liveliness as I have never witnessed before. And the effects of the groups of multitudinous actors in this busy, cheerful drama, is heightened, as it were, by the decorations of the stage. The sky is delightfully brilliant; all the houses and ornaments are stately; castles and palaces are rising all around; and the flag, towers, and walls of Fort St Elmo look as fresh and magnificent as if they had been erected only yesterday.

The Strada Reale has a much more courtly appearance than that one described. Here are palaces, churches, court-houses and libraries, the genteel London shops, and the latest articles of perfumery. Gay young officers are strolling about in shell jackets much too small for them: midshipmen are clattering by on hired horses; squads of priests, habited after the fashion of Don Basilio in the opera,[12] are demurely pacing to and fro; professional beggars run shrieking after the stranger; and agents for horses, for inns, and for worse places still, follow him and insinuate the excellence of their goods. The houses where they are selling carpet-bags and pomatum were the palaces of the successors of the goodliest company of gallant knights the world ever heard tell of. It seems unromantic; but *these* were not the romantic Knights of St John. The heroic days of the order ended as the last Turkish galley lifted anchor after the memorable siege. The present stately houses were built in times of peace and splendour and decay. I doubt whether the Auberge de Provence, where the Union Club flourishes now, has ever seen anything more romantic than the pleasant balls held in the great room there.

The church of Saint John, not a handsome structure without, is magnificent within: a noble hall covered with a rich embroidery of gilded carving, the chapels of the different nations on either side, but not interfering with the main structure, of which the whole is simple, and the details only splendid; it seemed to me a fitting place for this wealthy body of aristocratic soldiers, who made their devotions as it were on parade, and though on their knees, never forgot their epaulets or their quarters of nobility. This mixture of religion and worldly pride seems incongruous at first; but have we not at church at home similar relics of feudal ceremony? – the verger with the silver mace who precedes the vicar to the desk; the two chaplains of my lord archbishop, who bow over his grace as he enters the communion-table gate; even poor John, who follows my lady with a coroneted prayerbook, and makes his *congé* as he hands it into the pew. What a chivalrous absurdity is the banner of some high and mighty prince, hanging over his stall in Windsor Chapel, when you think of the purpose for which men are supposed to assemble there! The church of the Knights of St John is paved over with sprawling heraldic devices of the dead gentlemen of the dead order; as if, in the next world, they expected to take rank in conformity with their pedigrees, and would be marshalled into Heaven according to the orders of precedence. Cumbrous

handsome paintings adorn the walls and chapels, decorated with pompous monuments of grand masters. Beneath is a crypt, where more of these honourable and reverend warriors lie, in a state that a Simpson would admire. In the altar are said to lie three of the most gallant relics in the world; the keys of Acre, Rhodes, and Jerusalem. What blood was shed in defending these emblems! What faith, endurance, genius, and generosity; what pride, hatred, ambition, and savage lust of blood were roused together for their guardianship!

In the lofty halls and corridors of the governor's house, some portraits of the late grand masters still remain; a very fine one, by Caravaggio, of a knight in gilt armour, hangs in the dining-room, near a full-length of poor Louis XVI, in royal robes, the very picture of uneasy impotency. But the portrait of Vignacourt is the only one which has a respectable air;[13] the other chiefs of the famous society are pompous old gentlemen in black, with huge periwigs, and crowns round their hats, and a couple of melancholy pages in yellow and red. But pages and wigs and grand masters have almost faded out of the canvas, and are vanishing into Hades with a most melancholy indistinctness. The names of most of these gentlemen, however, live as yet in the forts

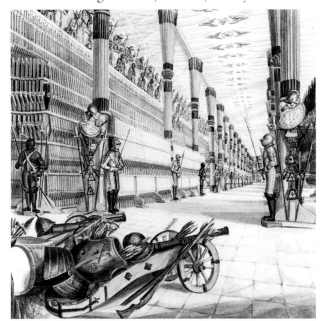

Facing Page, Top Left. *Marina of Valetta, Malta.* On landing in Malta in 1844 Thackeray would have witnessed a 'cheerful, animated and busy scene' similar to that portrayed in this etching and described in the text accompanying the plate in Fisher's then recently published *The Shores and Islands of the Mediterranean* (1840). Victoria and Albert Museum (Searight Collection).

Facing Page, Bottom Left. *Strada St Cristoforo, Valetta,* one of the streets of Malta's capital city, 'thronged with a lively comfortable looking population', that impressed Thackeray during his visit. The lithograph is by one of the Brocktorffs, a family of artists whose large lithographic business thrived in Malta during the 1840s. The Order of St John.

Left. *Armoury of the Grand Master's Palace,* watercolour by Charles Frederick de Brocktorff, 1818-19. The impressive arrangement of the Armoury displayed in this view, with row-upon-row of muskets, bayonets, pikes and pistols, along with helmets, cuirasses and full suits of armour, was unchanged when Thackeray saw it in 1844. The Order of St John.

Interior View of the Cathedral Church of St John in the City of Valetta, Island of Malta,
watercolour by Charles Frederick de Brocktorff, c.1819-25. The decorative splendour of
St John's Co-Cathedral, with its painted barrel vault, gilded carving and multicoloured marble
floor, is well conveyed by this Maltese artist. The Order of St John.

of the place, which all seem to have been eager to build and
christen: so that it seems as if, in the Malta mythology, they
had been turned into freestone.

In the armoury is the very suit painted by Caravaggio, by
the side of the armour of the noble old La Valette, whose
heroism saved his island from the efforts of Mustapha and
Dragut, and an army quite as fierce and numerous as that
which was baffled before Gibraltar, by similar courage and
resolution. The sword of the last-named famous corsair (a
most truculent little scimitar), thousands of pikes and hal-
berts, little old cannons and wall pieces, helmets and
cuirasses, which the knights or their people wore, are trimly
arranged against the wall, and, instead of spiking Turks or
arming warriors, now serve to point morals and adorn tales.
And here likewise are kept many thousand muskets, swords,
and boarding pikes, for daily use, and a couple of ragged old
standards of one of the English regiments, who pursued
and conquered in Egypt the remains of the haughty and
famous French republican army, at whose appearance the
last Knights of Malta flung open the gates of all their for-
tresses, and consented to be extinguished without so much
as a remonstrance, or a kick, or a struggle.[14]

We took a drive into what may be called the country;
where the fields are rocks, and the hedges are stones – passing by the stone gardens of the Florian, and wondering at
the number and handsomeness of the stone villages and
churches rising everywhere among the stony hills. Handsome villas were passed everywhere, and we drove for a long
distance along the sides of an aqueduct, quite a royal work
of the Caravaggio in gold armour, the grand master
de Vignacourt. A most agreeable contrast to the arid rocks
of the general scenery, was the garden at the governor's
country house; with the orange trees and water, its beautiful golden grapes, luxuriant flowers, and thick cool
shrubberies. The eye longs for this sort of refreshment,
after being seared with the hot glare of the general country;
and St Antonio was as pleasant after Malta, as Malta was
after the sea.

We paid the island a subsequent visit in November, passing seventeen days at an establishment called Fort Manuel
there, and by punsters the *Manuel des Voyageurs*, where
government accommodates you with quarters; where the
authorities are so attentive as to scent your letters with aro-

matic vinegar before you receive them, and so careful of your health as to lock you up in your room every night lest you should walk in your sleep, and so over the battlements into the sea; if you escaped drowning in the sea, the sentries on the opposite shore would fire at you, hence the nature of the precaution. To drop, however, this satirical strain; those who know what quarantine is, may fancy that the place somehow becomes unbearable in which it has been endured.[15] And though the November climate of Malta is like the most delicious May in England, and though there is every gaiety and amusement in the town, a comfortable little opera, a good old library filled full of good old books (none of your works of modern science, travel, and history, but good old *useless* books of the last two centuries), and nobody to trouble you in reading them; and though the society of Valetta is most hospitable, varied, and agreeable, yet somehow one did not feel *safe* in the island, with perpetual glimpses of Fort Manuel from the opposite shore; and, lest the quarantine authorities should have a fancy to fetch one back again, on a pretext of posthumous plague, we made our way to Naples by the very first opportunity – those who remained that is, of the little Eastern expedition. They were not all there. The Giver of life and death had removed two of our company: one was left behind to die in Egypt, with a mother to bewail his loss; another we buried in the dismal lazaretto cemetery.

*   *   *   *   *

One is bound to look at this, too, as a part of our journey. Disease and death are knocking perhaps at your next cabin door. Your kind and cheery companion has ridden his last ride and emptied his last glass beside you. And while fond hearts are yearning for him far away, and his own mind, if conscious, is turning eagerly towards the spot of the world whither affection or interest call it – the Great Father summons the anxious spirit from earth to himself, and ordains that the nearest and dearest shall meet here no more.

Such an occurrence as a death in a lazaretto, mere selfishness renders striking. We were walking with him but two days ago on deck. One has a sketch of him, another his card, with the address written yesterday, and given with an invitation to come and see him at home in the country, where his children are looking for him. He is dead in a day, and buried in the walls of the prison. A doctor felt his pulse by deputy – a clergyman comes from the town to read the last service over him – and the friends, who attend his funeral, are marshalled by lazaretto-guardians, so as not to touch each other. Every man goes back to his room and applies the lesson to himself. One would not so depart without seeing again the dear, dear faces. We reckon up those

we love; they are but very few, but I think one loves them better than ever now. Should it be your turn next? – and why not? Is it pity or co- mfort to think of that affection which watches and survives you?

The Maker has linked together the whole race of man with this chain of love. I like to think that there is no man but has had kindly feelings for some other, and he for his neighbour, until we bind together the whole family of Adam. Nor does it end here. It joins Heaven and earth together. For my friend or my child of past days is still my friend or my child to me here, or in the home prepared for us by the Father of all. If identity survives the grave, as our faith tells us, is it not a consolation to think that there may be one or two souls among the purified and just, whose affection watches us invisible, and follows the poor sinner on earth?

View of the Entrance to the Quarantine harbour, taken from St Michael's bastion, with the H. E. Frederick Ponsonby's Monument, watercolour by Louis Taffien, 1840s. Travellers from the East returning to Europe were obliged to spend time in quarantine at Fort Manoel in Marsamxett Harbour, on the north-west side of Valletta. In the centre of the view is the spire of the recently completed St Paul's Anglican Cathedral in Valletta. The Order of St John.

Chapter V: ATHENS

NOT feeling any enthusiasm myself about Athens, my bounden duty of course is clear, to sneer and laugh heartily at all who have. In fact, what business has a lawyer, who was in Pump Court this day three weeks, and whose common reading is law reports or the newspaper, to pretend to fall in love for the long vacation with mere poetry, of which I swear a great deal is very doubtful, and to get up an enthusiasm quite foreign to his nature and usual calling in life? What call have ladies to consider Greece 'romantic,' they who get their notions of mythology from the well-known pages of *Tooke's Pantheon* ?[1] What is the reason that blundering Yorkshire squires, young dandies from Corfu regiments, jolly sailors from ships in the harbour, and yellow old Indians returning from Bundelcund, should think proper to be enthusiastic about a country of which they know nothing; the mere physical beauty of which they cannot, for the most part, comprehend; and because certain characters lived in it two thousand four hundred years ago?[2] What have these people in common with Pericles, what have these ladies in common with Aspasia (O fie)? Of the race of Englishmen who come wondering about the tomb of Socrates, do you think the majority would not have voted to hemlock him? Yes; for the very same superstition which leads men by the nose now, drove them onward in the days when the lowly husband of Xantippe died for daring to think simply and to speak the truth.[3] I know of no quality more magnificent in fools than their faith: that perfect consciousness they have, that they are doing virtuous and meritorious actions, when they are performing acts of folly, murdering Socrates, or pelting Aristides with holy oyster shells,[4] all for Virtue's sake; and a *History of Dullness in all Ages of the World*, is a book which a philosopher would surely be hanged, but as certainly blessed, for writing.

If papa and mamma (honour be to them!) had not followed the faith of their fathers, and thought proper to send away their only beloved son (afterwards to be celebrated under the name of Titmarsh) into ten years' banishment of infernal misery, tyranny, annoyance; to give over the fresh feelings of the heart of the little Michael Angelo to the discipline of vulgar bullies, who, in order to lead tender young children to the Temple of Learning (as they do in the spelling-books), drive them on with clenched fists and low abuse; if they fainted, revived them with a thump, or assailed them with a curse; if they were miserable, consoled them with a brutal jeer – if, I say, my dear parents, instead of giving me the inestimable benefit of a ten years' classical education, had kept me at home with my dear thirteen sisters, it is probable I should have liked this country of Attica, in sight of the blue shores of which the present pathetic letter is written; but I was made so miserable in youth by a classical education, that all connected with it is disagreeable in my eyes; and I have the same recollection of Greek in youth that I have of castor oil.

So in coming in sight of the promontory of Sunium,[5] where the Greek muse, in an awful vision, came to me, and said in a patronizing way, 'Why, my dear,' (she always, the old spinster, adopts this high and mighty tone), 'Why, my dear, are you not charmed to be in this famous neighbourhood, in this land of poets and heroes, of whose history your classical education ought to have made you a master; if it did not, you have woefully neglected your opportunities, and your dear parents have wasted their money in sending you to school.' I replied, 'Madam, your company in youth was made so laboriously disagreeable to me, that I can't at present reconcile myself to you in age. I read your poets, but it was in fear and trembling; and a cold sweat is but an ill accompaniment to poetry. I blundered through your histories; but history is so dull (saving your presence) of herself, that when the brutal dullness of a schoolmaster is superadded to her own slow conversation, the union becomes intolerable: hence I have not the slightest pleasure in renewing my acquaintance with a lady who has been the source of so much bodily and mental discomfort to me.' To make a long story short, I am anxious to apologise for a want of enthusiasm in the classical line, and to excuse an ignorance which is of the most undeniable sort.

This is an improper frame of mind for a person visiting the land of Æschylus and Euripides; add to which, we have been abominably overcharged at the inn: and what are the blue hills of Attica, the silver calm basin of Peiræus, the heathery heights of Pentelicus, and yonder rocks crowned by the Doric columns of the Parthenon, and the thin Ionic shafts of the Erechtheum, to a man who has had little rest, and is bitten all over by bugs? Was Alcibiades bitten by bugs, I wonder; and did the brutes crawl over him as he lay in the rosy arms of Phryne? I wished all night for Socrates' hammock or basket, as it is described in the *Clouds*,[6] in which resting place, no doubt, the abominable animals kept per force clear of him.

A French man-of-war, lying in the silvery little harbour, sternly eyeing out of its stern port-holes a saucy little English corvette beside, began playing sounding marches as a crowd of boats came paddling up to the steamer's side to convey us travellers to shore. There were Russian schooners and Greek brigs lying in this little bay; dumpy little windmills whirling round on the sunburnt heights round about it; an improvised town of quays and marine taverns has sprung up on the shore; a host of jingling barouches, more miserable than any to be seen even in Germany, were

collected at the landing-place; and the Greek drivers (how queer they looked in skull-caps, shabby jackets with profuse embroidery of worsted, and endless petticoats of dirty calico!) began, in a generous ardour for securing passen-

gers, to abuse each other's horses and carriages in the regular London fashion.

Satire could certainly hardly caricature the vehicle in which we were made to journey to Athens; and it was only by thinking that, bad as they were, these coaches were much more comfortable contrivances than any Alcibiades or Cymon ever had, that we consoled ourselves along the road. It was flat for six miles along the plain to the city: and you see for the greater part of the way the purple mount on which the Acropolis rises, and the gleaming houses of the town spread beneath. Round this wide, yellow, barren plain,- a stunt district of olive-trees is almost the only vegetation visible – there rises, as it were, a sort of chorus of the most beautiful mountains; the most elegant, gracious, and noble the eye ever looked on. These hills did not appear at all lofty or terrible, but superbly rich and aristocratic. The clouds were dancing round about them; you could see their rosy, purple shadows sweeping round the clear, serene summits of the hills. To call a hill aristocratic seems affected or absurd; but the difference between these hills and the others, is the difference between Newgate Prison and the Travellers' Club, for instance: both are buildings; but the one stern, dark, and coarse; the other rich, elegant, and festive. At least, so I thought.

With such a stately palace as munificent Nature had built for these people, what could they be themselves but lordly, beautiful, brilliant, brave, and wise? We saw four Greeks on donkeys on the road (which is a dust-whirlwind where it is not a puddle); and other four were playing with a dirty pack of cards, at a barrack that English poets have christened the half-way house. Does external nature and beauty influence the soul to good? You go about Warwickshire, and fancy that from merely being born and wandering in those sweet sunny plains and fresh woodlands, Shakespeare must have drunk in a portion of that frank, artless sense of beauty, which lies about his works like a bloom or dew; but a Coventry ribbon maker, or a slang Leamington squire, are looking on those very same landscapes too, and what do they profit? You theorise about the influence which the climate and appearance of Attica must have had in ennobling those who were born there; yonder dirty swindling ragged blackguards, lolling over greasy cards three hours before noon, quarrelling and shrieking, armed to the teeth and

The drive to Athens, wood engraving by William Thackeray.

afraid to fight, are bred out of the same land which begot the philosophers and heroes. But the half-way house is past by this time, and behold we are in the capital of King Otho.[7]

I swear solemnly that I would rather have two hundred a year in Fleet Street, than be King of the Greeks, with Basileus written before my name round their beggarly coin; with the bother of perpetual revolutions in my huge plaster of Paris palace, with no amusement but a drive in the afternoon over a wretched arid country, where roads are not

King Otho being greeted on his arrival in Athens, watercolour by Alfred Beaumont, 1834. Prince Otho, the young son of King Ludwig I of Bavaria, was enthroned as King of Greece in 1834.
Museum of the City of Athens.
Photograph: The Fine Art Society.

made, with ambassadors (the deuce knows why, for what good can the English, or the French, or the Russian party get out of such a bankrupt alliance as this?) perpetually pulling and tugging at me, away from honest Germany, where there is beer and aesthetic conversation, and operas at a small cost. The shabbiness of this place actually beats Ireland, and that is a strong word. The palace of the Basileus is an enormous edifice of plaster, in a square containing six houses, three donkeys, no roads, no fountains (except in the picture of the inn); backwards it seems to look straight to the mountain – on one side is a beggarly garden – the king goes out to drive (revolutions permitting) at five – some four-and-twenty black- guards saunter up to the huge sandhill of a terrace, as his majesty passes by in a gilt barouche and an absurd fancy dress; the gilt barouche goes plunging down the sandhills: the two dozen soldiers, who have been presenting arms, slouch off to their quarters: the vast barrack of a palace remains entirely white, ghastly, and lonely: and save the braying of a donkey now and then (which long-eared minstrels are more active and sonorous in Athens than in any place I know), all is entirely silent round Basileus's palace. How could people who knew Leopold fancy he would be so 'jolly green' as to take such a berth? It was only a *gobemouche*

of a Bavarian that could ever have been induced to accept it.[8]

I beseech you to believe that it was not the bill and the bugs at the inn which induced the writer hereof to speak so slightingly of the residence of Basileus. These evils are now cured and forgotten. This is written off the leaden flats and mounds which they call the Troad. It is stern justice alone which pronounces this excruciating sentence. It was a farce to make this place into a kingly capital; and I make no manner of doubt that King Otho, the very day he can get away unperceived, and get together the passage-money, will be off for dear old Deutschland, Fatherland, Beerland!

I have never seen a town in England which may be compared to this; for though Herne Bay is a ruin now, money was once spent upon it and houses built; here, beyond a few score of mansions comfortably laid out, the town is little better than a rickety agglomeration of larger and smaller huts, tricked out here and there with the most absurd cracked ornaments, and cheap attempts at elegance. But neatness is the elegance of poverty, and these people despise such a homely ornament. I have got a map with squares, fountains, theatres, public gardens, and Places d'Othon marked out; but they could only exist in the paper capital – the wretched, tumble-down, wooden one boasts of none.

One is obliged to come back to the old disagreeable comparison of Ireland. Athens may be about as wealthy a place as Carlow or Killarney – the streets swarm with idle crowds, the innumerable little lanes flow over with dirty little children, they are playing and paddling about in the dirt everywhere, with great big eyes, yellow faces, and the queerest little gowns and skull caps. But in the outer man, the Greek has far the advantage of the Irishman; most of them are well and decently dressed (if five-and-twenty yards of petticoat may not be called decent, what may?); they swagger to and fro with huge knives in their girdles. Almost all the men are handsome, but live hard, it is said, in order to decorate their backs with those fine clothes of theirs. I have seen but two or three handsome women, and these had the great drawback which is common to the race – I mean, a sallow, greasy, coarse complexion, at which it was not advisable to look too closely.

And on this score I think we English may pride ourselves on possessing an advantage (by we, I mean the lovely ladies to whom this is addressed with the most respectful

Athens: The Acropolis and Mount Hymettus, lithograph forming part of Frederick Stademann's 'all-round' view of Athens, *Panorama von Athen,* published in Munich in 1841 and dedicated to King Otho I. *Photograph:* The Fine Art Society.

The Parthenon and Erechtheum, watercolour by George Chiewitz, 1834-40. Thackeray did not share the conventional veneration that Athens's classical associations aroused in his contemporaries, but he could not help admiring the 'astonishing grace, severity, elegance, completeness of the Parthenon'.
Photograph: The Fine Art Society.

compliments) over the most classical country in the world. I don't care for beauty which will only bear to be looked at from a distance like a scene in a theatre. What is the most beautiful nose in the world, if it be covered with a skin of the texture and colour of coarse whitey-brown paper; and if Nature has made it as slippery and shining as though it had been anointed with pomatum? They may talk about beauty, but would you wear a flower that had been dipped in a grease-pot? No; give me a fresh, dewy, healthy rose out of Somersetshire; not one of those superb, tawdry, unwholesome exotics, which are only good to make poems about. Lord Byron wrote more cant of this sort than any poet I know of. Think of 'the peasant girls with dark blue eyes' of the Rhine – the brown-faced, flat-nosed, thick-lipped, dirty wenches! Think of 'filling high a cup of Samian wine'; small beer is nectar compared to it, and Byron himself always drank gin. That man never wrote from his heart. He got up rapture and enthusiasm with an eye to the public; but this is dangerous ground, even more dangerous than to look Athens full in the face, and say that your eyes are not dazzled by its beauty. The Great Public admires Greece and Byron; the

public knows best. Murray's 'Guide Book' calls the latter 'our native bard'.[9] Our native bard! *Mon Dieu! He* Shakespeare's, Milton's, Keat's, Scott's native bard! Well, woe be to the man who denies the public gods!

The truth is, then, that Athens is a disappointment; and I am angry that it should be so. To a skilled antiquarian, or an enthusiastic Greek scholar, the feelings created by a sight of the place of course will be different; but you who would be inspired by it must undergo a long preparation of reading, and possess, too, a particular feeling; both of which, I suspect, are uncommon in our busy commercial newspaper-reading country. Men only say they are enthusiastic about the Greek and Roman authors and history, because it is considered proper and respectable. And we know how gentlemen in Baker Street have editions of the classics handsomely bound in the library, and how they use them. Of course they don't retire to read the newspaper; it is to look over a favourite ode of Pindar, or to discuss an obscure passage in Athenæus! Of course country magistrates and members of Parliament are always studying Demosthenes and Cicero; we know it from their continual habit of quoting the Latin grammar in Parliament. But it is agreed that the classics are respectable; therefore we are to be enthusiastic about them. Also let us admit that Byron is to be held up as 'our native bard'.

I am not so entire a heathen as to be insensible to the beauty of those relics of Greek art, of which men much more learned and enthusiastic have written such piles of descriptions. I thought I could recognise the towering beauty of the prodigious columns of the temple of Jupiter; and admire the astonishing grace, severity, elegance, completeness of the Parthenon. The little temple of Victory, with its fluted Corinthian shafts, blazed under the sun almost as fresh as it must have appeared to the eyes of its founders; I saw nothing more charming and brilliant, more graceful, festive, and aristocratic than this sumptuous little building. The Roman remains which lie in the towns below, look like the works of barbarians beside these perfect structures. They jar strangely on the eye, after it has been accustoming itself to perfect harmony and proportions. If, as the schoolmaster tells us, the Greek writing is as complete as the Greek art; if an ode of Pindar is as glittering and pure as the temple of Victory; or a discourse of Plato as polished and calm as yonder mystical portico of the Erectheum; what treasures of the senses and delights of the imagination have those lost to whom the Greek books are as good as sealed!

And yet one meets with very dull first-class men. Genius won't transplant from one brain to another, or is ruined in the carriage like fine Burgundy. Sir Robert Peel and Sir John Hobhouse are both good scholars;[10, 11] but their poetry in Parliament does not strike one as fine. Muzzle, the schoolmaster, who is bullying poor trembling little boys, was a fine scholar when he was a sizar, and a ruffian then and ever since. Where is the great poet, since the days of Milton, who has improved the natural offshoots of his brain by grafting it from the Athenian tree?

I had a volume of Tennyson in my pocket, which somehow settled that question, and ended the querulous dispute between me and conscience, under the shape of the neglected and irritated Greek muse, which had been going on ever since I had commenced my walk about Athens. The old spinster saw me wince at the idea of the author of Dora and Ulysses, and tried to follow up her advantage by further hints of time lost, and precious opportunities thrown away – 'You might have written poems like them', said she; 'or, no, not like them perhaps, but you might have done a neat prize poem, and pleased your papa and mamma. You might have translated Jack and Jill into Greek iambics, and been a credit to your college.' I turned testily away from her, 'Madam,' says I, 'because an eagle houses on a mountain, or soars to the sun, don't you be angry with a sparrow that perches on a garret-window, or twitters on a twig. Leave me to myself; look, my beak is not aquiline by any means.'

And so, my dear friend, you who have been reading this last page in wonder, and who, instead of a description of Athens, have been accommodated with a lament on the part of the writer, that he was idle at school, and does not know Greek, excuse this momentary outbreak of egotistic despondency. To say truth, dear Jones, when one walks among the nests of eagles, and sees the prodigious eggs they laid, a certain feeling of discomfiture must come over us smaller birds. You and I could not invent, it even stretches our minds painfully to try and comprehend part of the beauty of the Parthenon – ever so little of it – the beauty of a single column, – a fragment of a broken shaft lying under the astonishing blue sky there, in the midst of that unrivalled

landscape. There may be grand aspects of nature, but none more deliciously beautiful. The hills rise in perfect harmony, and fall in the most exquisite cadences, – the sea seems brighter, the islands more purple, the clouds more light and rosy than elsewhere. As you look up through the open roof, you are almost oppressed by the serene depth of the blue overhead. Look even at the fragments of the marble, how soft and pure it is, glittering and white like fresh snow! 'I was all beautiful,' it seems to say, 'even the hidden parts of me were spotless, precious, and fair' – and so, musing over this wonderful scene, perhaps I get some feeble glimpse or idea of that ancient Greek spirit which peopled it with sublime races of heroes and gods;* and which I never could get out of a Greek book, – no, not though Muzzle flung it at my head.

*Saint Paul speaking from the *Areopagus*, and rebuking these superstitions away, yet speaks tenderly to the people before him, whose devotions he had marked; quotes their poets, to bring them to think of the God unknown, whom they had ignorantly worshipped; and says, that the times of this ignorance *God winked at*, but that now it was time to repent. No rebuke can surely be more gentle than this delivered by the upright Apostle.

The Temple of Olympian Zeus with the Acropolis in the distance, watercolour by Edmund Thomas Parris. Thackeray referred to this as the temple of Jupiter, and, despite his jaded response to Athens in general, even he was impressed by the grandeur of its gigantic columns.
Photograph: The Fine Art Society.

Smyrna, watercolour by Maria Mathias, 1857. As travelling became easier, more ordinary tourists from the middle classes were able to venture beyond Europe. Mrs Mathias, who visited Egypt and the eastern Mediterranean in the mid-1850s, *Murray's Guide* in one hand, sketch-book in the other, was one of these. Victoria and Albert Museum (Searight Collection).

I AM glad that the Turkish part of Athens was extinct, so that I should not be balked of the pleasure of entering an eastern town by an introduction to any garbled or incomplete specimen of one. Smyrna seems to me the most eastern of all I have seen;[1] as Calais will probably remain to the Englishman the most French town in the world. The jack-boots of the postilions don't seem so huge elsewhere, or the tight stockings of the maid-servants so Gallic. The churches and the ramparts, and the little soldiers on them, remained for ever impressed upon your memory; from which larger temples

and buildings, and whole armies have subsequently disappeared: and the first words of actual French heard spoken, and the first dinner at Quillacq's, remain after twenty years as clear as on the first day. Dear Jones, can't you remember the exact smack of the white hermitage, and the toothless old fellow singing *Largo al factotum?*

The first day in the East is like that. After that there is nothing. The wonder is gone, and the thrill of that delightful shock, which so seldom touches the nerves of plain men of the world, though they seek for it everywhere. One such

Facing Page. *P&O Steamship Tagus,* oil painting by S. D. Skillet, 1837. When the *Tagus* was launched in 1837, P&O claimed her and another of their new steamships to be the 'largest and most powerful that have yet been put afloat'. Thackeray transferred to her at Gibraltar.
The Peninsular and Oriental Steam Navigation Company.

looked out at Smyrna from our steamer, and yawned without the least excitement, and did not betray the slightest emotion, as boats with real Turks on board came up to the ship. There lay the town with minarets and cypresses, domes and castles; great guns were firing off, and the blood-red flag of the Sultan flaring over the fort ever since sun-rise; woods and mountains came down to the gulf's edge, and as you looked at them with the telescope, there peeped out of the general mass a score of pleasant episodes of Eastern life – there were cottages with quaint roofs; silent cool kiosks, where the chief of the eunuchs brings down the ladies of the harem. I saw Hassan, the fisherman, getting his nets; and Ali Baba going off with his donkey to the great forest for wood. Smith looked at these wonders quite unmoved; and I was surprised at his apathy: but he had been at Smyrna before. A man only sees the miracle once; though you yearn after it ever so, it won't come again. I saw nothing of Ali Baba and Hassan the next time we came to Smyrna, and had some doubts (recollecting the badness of the inn) about landing at all. A person who wishes to understand France and the East should come in a yacht to Calais or Smyrna, land for two hours, and never afterwards go back again.

But those two hours are beyond measure delightful. Some of us were querulous up to that time, and doubted of the wisdom of making the voyage. Lisbon, we owned, was a failure; Athens a dead failure. Malta very well, but not worth the trouble and sea sickness; in fact, Baden Baden or Devonshire would be a better move than this; when Smyrna came, and rebuked all mutinous cockneys into silence. Some men may read this who are in want of a sensation. If they love the odd and picturesque, if they loved the *Arabian Nights* in their youth,[2] let them book themselves on board one of the Peninsula and Oriental vessels, and try one *dip* into Constantinople or Smyrna. Walk into the bazaar, and the East is unveiled to you; how often and often have you tried to fancy this, lying out on a summer holiday at school! It is wonderful, too, how *like* it is; you may imagine that you have been in the place before, you seem to know it so well!

The beauty of that poetry is, to me, that it was never too handsome; there is no fatigue of sublimity about it. Shaccabac[3] and the little barber play as great a part in it as the heroes; there are no uncomfortable sensations of terror; you may be familiar with the great Afreet,[4] who was going to

execute the travellers for killing his son with a date-stone. Morgiana,[5] when she kills the forty robbers with boiling oil, does not seem to hurt them in the least; and though King Schahriar makes a practice of cutting off his wives' heads,[6] yet you fancy they have got them on again in some of the back rooms of the palace, where they are dancing and playing on dulcimers. How fresh, easy, good-natured, is all this! How delightful is that notion of the pleasant Eastern people about knowledge, where the height of science is made to consist in the answering of riddles! and all the mathematicians and magicians bring their great beards to bear on a conundrum!

When I got into the bazaar among this race, somehow I felt as if they were all friends. There sat the merchants in their little shops, quiet and solemn, but with friendly looks. There was no smoking, it was the *Ramazan*;[7] no eating, the fish and meats fizzing in the enormous pots of the cook-shops are only for the Christians. The children abounded; the law is not so stringent upon them, and many wandering merchants were there selling figs (in the name of the prophet, doubtless,) for their benefit, and elbowing onwards with baskets of grapes and cucumbers. Countrymen passed bristling over with arms, each with a huge bellyful of pistols and daggers in his girdle; fierce, but not the least dangerous. Wild swarthy Arabs, who had come in with caravans, walked solemnly about, very different in look and demeanour from the sleek inhabitants of the town. Greeks and Jews squatted and smoked, their shops tended by sallow-faced boys, with large eyes, who smiled and welcomed you in; negroes bustled about in gaudy colours; and women, with black nose-bags and shuffling yellow slippers, chattered and bargained at the doors of the little shops.

There was the rope quarter and the sweetmeat quarter, and the pipe bazaar and the arm bazaar, and the little turned up shoe quarter and the shops where ready-made jackets and pelisses were swinging, and the region where, under the ragged awnings, regiments of tailors were at work. The sun peeps through these awnings of mat or canvas, which are hung over the narrow lanes of the bazaar, and ornaments them with a thousand freaks of light and shadow. Cogia Hassan Alhabbal's shop is in a blaze of light; while his neighbour, the barber and coffee-house keeper, has his premises, his low seats and narghiles,[8] his queer pots and basins, in the shade. The cobblers are always good-natured; there was one who, I am sure, has been revealed to me in my dreams, in a dirty old green turban, with a pleasant wrinkled face like an apple, twinkling his little grey eyes as he held them up to talk to the gossips, and smiling under a delightful old grey beard, which did the heart good to see. You divine the conversation between him and the cucumber-man, as the Sultan used to understand the language of birds. Are any of those cucumbers stuffed with pearls, and is that Armenian with the black square turban Harun Alraschid in disguise,[9] standing yonder by the fountain where the children are drinking – the gleaming marble fountain, chequered all over with light and shadow, and engraved with delicate Arabesques and sentences from the Koran?

But the greatest sensation of all is when the camels come. Whole strings of real camels, better even than in the procession of *Bluebeard*, with soft rolling eyes and bended necks, swaying from one side of the bazaar to the other to and fro, and treading gingerly with their great feet. O, you fairy dreams of boyhood! O, you sweet meditations of half-holidays, here you are realized for half-an-hour! The genius which presides over youth led us to do a good action that day. There was a man sitting in an open room, ornamented with fine long-tailed sentences of the Koran; some in red, some in blue; some written diagonally over the paper; some so shaped as to represent ships, dragons, or mysterious animals. The man squatted on a carpet in the middle of this room, with folded arms, waggling his head to and fro, swaying about, and singing through his nose choice phrases from the sacred work. But from the room above came a clear noise of many little shouting voices, much more musical than that of Naso in the matted parlour,[10] and the guide told us it was a school, so we went upstairs to look.

I declare, on my conscience, the master was in the act of bastinadoing a little mulatto boy; his feet were in a bar, and the brute was laying on with a cane; so we witnessed the howling of the poor boy, and the confusion of the brute who was administering the correction. The other children were made to shout, I believe, to drown the noise of their little comrade's howling; but the punishment was instantly discontinued as our hats came up over the stair-trap, and the boy cast loose, and the bamboo huddled into a corner, and the schoolmaster stood before us abashed. All the small

scholars in red caps, and the little girls in gaudy handkerchiefs, turned their big wondering dark eyes towards us; and the caning was over for *that* time, let us trust. I don't envy some schoolmasters in a future state. I pity that poor little blubbering Mahometan; he will never be able to relish the *Arabian Nights* in the original, all his life long.

From this scene we rushed off somewhat discomposed, to make a breakfast off red mullets and grapes, melons, pomegranates, and Smyrna wine, at a dirty little comfortable inn, to which we were recommended; and from the windows of which we had a fine cheerful view of the gulf and its busy craft, and the loungers and merchants along the shore. There were camels unloading at one wharf, and piles of melons much bigger than the Gibraltar cannon-balls at another. It was the fig season, and we passed through several alleys encumbered with long rows of fig-dressers, children and women for the most part, who were packing the fruit diligently into drums, dipping them in salt-water first, and spreading them neatly over with leaves; while the figs and leaves are drying, large white worms crawl out of them, and swarm over the decks of the ships which carry them to Europe and to England, where small children eat

Bridge at Smyrna, watercolour by Max Schmidt, 1844. Thackeray judged many of the scenes he saw on his journey with a painter's eye. Extraordinarily, this German artist, travelling at the same time, has depicted the bridge over which camel caravans passed to and from the town of Smyrna almost exactly as Thackeray described it.
Photograph: Christie's.

Camels, Smyrna, watercolour by William James Müller, 1843. Thackeray could not have been aware that his call to painters for 'faithful transcripts of everyday Oriental life' had already been answered by Müller when he visited Smyrna and Lycia (south-west Turkey) almost exactly a year before.
Tate Gallery.

them with pleasure – I mean the figs, not the worms – and where they are still served at wine parties at the Universities. When fresh they are not better than elsewhere; but the melons are of admirable flavour, and so large, that Cinderella might almost be accommodated with a coach made of a big one, without any very great distention of its original proportions.

Our guide, an accomplished swindler, demanded two dollars as the fee for entering the mosque, which others of our party subsequently saw for sixpence, so we did not care to examine that place of worship. But there were other cheaper sights, which were to the full as picturesque, for which there was no call to pay money, or, indeed, for a day scarcely to move at all. I doubt whether a man who would

smoke his pipe on a bazaar counter all day, and let the city flow by him, would not be almost as well employed as the most active curiosity hunter.

To be sure he would not see the women. Those in the bazaar were shabby people for the most part, whose black masks nobody would feel a curiosity to remove. You could see no more of their figures than if they had been stuffed in bolsters; and even their feet were brought to a general splay uniformity by the double yellow slippers which the wives of true believers wear. But it is in the Greek and Armenian quarters, and among those poor Christians who were pulling figs, that you see the beauties; and a man of a generous disposition may lose his heart half a dozen times a day in Smyrna. There was the pretty maid at work at a tambour-

frame in an open porch, with an old duenna spinning by her side, and a goat tied up to the railings of the little court-garden; there was the nymph who came down the stair with the pitcher on her head, and gazed with great, calm eyes, as large and stately as Juno's; there was the gentle mother, bending over a queer cradle, in which lay a small crying bundle of infancy. All these three charmers were seen in a single street

in the Armenian quarter, where the house doors are all open, and the women of the families sit under the arches in the court. There was the fig-girl, beautiful beyond all others, with an immense coil of deep black hair twisted round a head of which Raphael was worthy to draw the outline, and Titian to paint the colour. I wonder the Sultan has not swept her off, or that the Persian merchants, who come with

Fontaine du Khan des Chameaux, Smyrne, lithograph by Eugène-Napoléon Flandin from *L'Orient* (1853-76). The camel market attracted the attention of several artists and writers during the 1840s. Victoria and Albert Museum (Searight Collection).

Disputing Accounts, watercolour by John Frederick Lewis, 1863. It is likely that Lewis saw and made sketches of this Persian merchant in 1841, either in Constantinople, or in Smyrna where his ship may well have stopped during the journey to Alexandria. *Photograph:* Christie's.

silks and sweetmeats, have not kidnapped her for the Shah of Tehran.

We went to see the Persian merchants at their Khan, and purchased some silks there from a swarthy black-bearded man, with a conical cap of lamb's wool. Is it not hard to think that silks bought of a man in a lamb's-wool cap, in a caravanserai, brought hither on the backs of camels, should have been manufactured after all at Lyons? Others of our party bought carpets, for which the town is famous; and there was one who absolutely laid in a stock of real Smyrna figs; and purchased three or four real Smyrna sponges for his carriage; so strong was his passion for the genuine article.

I wonder that no painter has given us familiar views of the East: not processions, grand sultans, or magnificent landscapes; but faithful transcripts of everyday Oriental life, such as each street will supply to him. The camels afford endless motives, couched in the market-places, lying by thousands in the camel square, snorting and bubbling after their manner, the sun blazing down on their backs, their slaves and keepers lying behind them in the shade: and the caravan-bridge, above all, would afford a painter subjects for a dozen of pictures. Over this Roman arch, which crosses the Meles river, all the caravans pass on their entrance to the town. On one side, as we sat and looked at it, was a great row of plane trees; on the opposite bank a deep wood of tall cypresses: in the midst of which rose up innumerable grey tombs, surmounted with the turbans of the defunct believers. Beside the stream, the view was less gloomy. There was under the plane-trees a little coffee-house, shaded by a trellis work, covered over with a vine, and ornamented with many rows of shining pots and water-pipes, for which there was no use at noon-day now, in the time of *Ramazan*.

Hard by the coffee-house was a garden and a bubbling marble fountain, and over the stream was a broken summer-house, to which amateurs may ascend, for the purpose of examining the river; and all round the plane-trees plenty of stools for those who were inclined to sit and drink sweet thick coffee, or cool lemonade made of fresh green citrons. The master of the house, dressed in a white turban, and light blue pelisse, lolled under the coffee-house awning; the slave, in white, with a crimson-striped jacket, his face as black as ebony, brought us pipes and lemonade again, and returned to his station at the coffee-house, where he curled his black legs together, and began singing out of his flat nose, to the thrumming of a long guitar with wire strings. The instrument was not bigger than a soup ladle, with a long straight handle, but its music pleased the performer; for his eyes rolled shining about, and his head wagged, and he grinned with an innocent intensity of enjoyment that did one good to look at. And there was a friend to share his pleasure: a Turk, dressed in scarlet, and covered all over with daggers and pistols, sat leaning forward on his little stool, rocking about, and grinning quite as eagerly as the black minstrel. As he sang and we listened, figures of women bearing pitchers went passing over the Roman bridge, which we saw between the large trunks of the planes; or grey forms of camels were seen stalking across it, the string preceded by the little donkey, who is always here their long-eared conductor.

These are very humble incidents of travel. Wherever the steamboat touches the shore adventure retreats into the interior, and what is called romance vanishes. It won't bear the vulgar gaze; or rather the light of common day puts it out, and it is only in the dark that it shines at all. There is no cursing and insulting of *Giaours* now.[11] If a cockney looks or behaves in a particularly ridiculous way, the little Turks come out and laugh at him. A Londoner is no longer a spittoon for true believers: and now that dark Hassan sits in his divan and drinks champagne, and Selim has a French watch, and Zuleikha perhaps takes Morrison's pills, Byronism becomes absurd instead of sublime, and is only a foolish expression of cockney wonder. They still occasionally beat a man for going into a mosque, but this is almost the only sign of ferocious vitality left in the Turk of the Mediterranean coast, and strangers may enter scores of mosques without molestation. The paddle-wheel is the great conqueror. Wherever the captain cries 'Stop her', Civilization stops, and lands in the ship's boat, and makes a permanent acquaintance with the savages on shore. Whole hosts of crusaders have passed and died, and butchered here in vain. But to manufacture European iron into pikes and helmets was a waste of metal: in the shape of piston-rods and furnace-pokers it is irresistible; and I think an allegory might be made showing how much stronger commerce is than chivalry, and finishing with a grand image of Mahomet's crescent being extinguished in Fulton's boiler.[12]

This I thought was the moral of the day's sights and adventures. We pulled off to the steamer in the afternoon- the Inbat blowing fresh, and setting all the craft in the gulf dancing over its blue waters. We were presently underway again, the captain ordering his engines to work only at half power, so that a French steamer which was quitting Smyrna at the same time might come up with us, and fancy she could beat the irresistible *Tagus*. Vain hope! Just as the Frenchman neared us, the *Tagus* shot out like an arrow, and the discomfited Frenchman went behind. Though we all relished the joke exceedingly, there was a French gentleman on board who did not seem to be by any means tickled with it; but he had received papers at Smyrna, containing news of Marshal Bugeaud's victory at Isley,[13] and had this land victory to set against our harmless little triumph at sea.

That night we rounded the island of Mitylene: and the next day the coast of Troy was in sight, and the tomb of Achilles[14] - a dismal looking mound that rises in a low dreary barren shore – less lively and not more picturesque than the Scheldt or the mouth of the Thames. Then we passed Tenedos and the forts and town at the mouth of the Dardanelles: the weather was not too hot: the water as smooth as at Putney; and everybody happy and excited at the thought of seeing Constantinople to-morrow. We had music on board all the way from Smyrna. A German *commis-voyageur*, with a guitar, who had passed unnoticed until that time, produced his instrument about mid-day, and began to whistle waltzes. He whistled so divinely that the ladies left their cabins, and men laid down their books. He whistled a polka so bewitchingly that two young Oxford men began whirling round the deck, and performed that popular dance with much agility until they sank down tired. He still continued an unabated whistling, and as nobody would dance, pulled off his coat, produced a pair of castanets, and whistling a mazurka, performed it with tremendous agility. His whistling made everybody gay and happy – made those acquainted who had not spoken before, and inspired such a feeling of hilarity in the ship, that that night, as we floated over the sea of Marmora, a general vote was expressed for broiled bones and a regular supper party. Punch was brewed and speeches were made, and, after a lapse of fifteen years, I heard the *Old English Gentleman* and *Bright Chanticleer Proclaims the Morn*, sung in such style, that you would almost fancy the proctors must hear, and send us all home.

Constantinople: From the Entrance to the Golden Horn, watercolour by C. F. Buckley, 1840s. Vessels of various types throng the entrance to the Golden Horn, one of the finest natural harbours in the world. Victoria and Albert Museum (Searight Collection).

Chapter VII: CONSTANTINOPLE

WHEN we rose at sunrise to see the famous entry to Constantinople, we found, in the place of the city and the sun, a bright white fog, which hid both from sight, and which only disappeared as the vessel advanced towards the Golden Horn. There the fog cleared off as it were by flakes; and as you see gauze curtains lifted away, one by one, before a great fairy scene at the theatre, this will give idea enough of the fog; the difficulty is to describe the scene afterwards, which was in truth the great fairy scene, than which it is impossible to conceive anything more brilliant and magnificent. I can't go to any more romantic place than Drury Lane to draw my similes from – Drury Lane, such as we used to see it in our youth, when to our sight, the grand last pictures of the melodrama or pantomime were as magnificent as any objects of nature we have seen with maturer eyes. Well, the view of Constantinople is as fine as any of Stanfield's best theatrical pictures, seen at the best period of youth, when fancy had all the bloom on her – when all the heroines who danced before the scene appeared as ravishing beauties, when there shone an unearthly splendour about Baker and Diddear[1] – and the sound of the bugles and fiddles, and the cheerful clang of the cymbals, as the scene unrolled, and the gorgeous procession meandered triumphantly through it – caused a thrill of pleasure, and awakened an innocent fullness of sensual enjoyment that is only given to boys.

The above sentence contains the following propositions: the enjoyments of boyish fancy are the most intense and delicious in the world. Stanfield's panorama used to be the realization of the most intense youthful fancy. I puzzle my brains and find no better likeness for the place. The view of Constantinople resembles the *ne plus ultra* of a Stanfield diorama, with a glorious accompaniment of music, spangled *houris*, warriors, and winding processions, feasting the eyes and the soul with light, splendour, and harmony. If you were never in this way during your youth ravished at the

play-house, of course the whole comparison is useless: and you have no idea, from this description, of the effect which Constantinople produces on the mind. But if you were never affected by a theatre, no words can work upon your fancy, and typographical attempts to move it are of no use. For, suppose we combine mosque, minaret, gold, cypress, water, blue, *caïques*, seventy-four, Galata, Tophana, *Ramazan, Backallum*, and so forth, together, in ever so many ways, your imagination will never be able to depict a city out of them. Or, suppose I say the Mosque of St. Sophia is four hundred and seventy-three feet in height, measuring from the middle nail of the gilt crescent, surmounting the dome, to the ring in the centre stone; the circle of the dome is one hundred and twenty-three feet in diameter, the windows ninety-seven in number – and all this may be true, for

Panorama of Constantinople from the Suleymaniye Camii, oil painting by Hubert Sattler, 1844. A stupendous view, painted in microscopic detail, extending over the rooftops of the city out to the Bosphorus and Sea of Marmara.
Photograph: The Fine Art Society.

esquely disposed at a fair, you don't suppose that they are all faultless beauties, or that the men's coats have no rags, and the women's gowns are made of silk and velvet: the wild ugliness of the interior of Constantinople or Pera has a charm of its own, greatly more amusing than rows of red bricks or drab stones, however symmetrical. With brick or stone they could never form those fantastic ornaments, railings, balconies, roofs, galleries, which jut in and out of the rugged houses of the city. As we went from Galata to Pera up a steep hill, which new comers ascend with some difficulty, but which a porter, with a couple of hundred weight on his back, paces up without turning a hair, I thought the wooden houses far from being disagreeable objects, sights quite as surprising and striking as the grand one we had just left.

I do not know how the Custom House of his Highness is made to be a profitable speculation. As I left the ship, a man pulled after my boat, and asked for backsheesh, which was given him to the amount of about twopence. He was a Custom House officer, but I doubt whether this sum which he levied ever went to the revenue.

I can fancy the scene about the quays somewhat to resemble the river of London in olden times, before coal smoke had darkened the whole city with soot, and when according to the old writers, there really was bright weather. The fleets of *caïques* bustling along the shore, or scudding over the blue water, are beautiful to look at; in Hollar's print London river is so studded over with wherry boats, which bridges and steamers have since destroyed.[2] Here the *caïque* is still in full perfection: there are thirty thousand boats of the kind playing between the cities; every boat is neat and trimly carved and painted; and I scarcely saw a man pulling in one of them that was not a fine specimen of his race, brawny and brown, with an open chest and a handsome face. They wear a thin shirt of exceedingly light cotton, which leaves their fine brown limbs full play; and with a purple sea for a back ground, every one of these dashing boats forms a brilliant and glittering picture. Passengers squat in the inside of the boat; so that as it passes, you see little more than the heads of the true believers, with their red fez and blue tassel, and that placid gravity of expression which the sucking of a tobacco pipe is sure to give to a man.

The Bosphorus is enlivened by a multiplicity of other

anything I know to the contrary; yet who is to get an idea of St. Sophia's from dates, proper names, and calculations with a measuring line? It can't be done by giving the age and measurement of all the buildings along the river, the names of all the boatmen who ply on it. Has your fancy, which pooh poohs a simile, faith enough to build a city with a footrule? Enough said about descriptions and similes (though whenever I am uncertain of one, I am naturally most anxious to fight for it): it is a scene not perhaps sublime, but charming, magnificent, and cheerful beyond any I have ever seen – the most superb combination of city and gardens, domes and shipping, hills and water, with the healthiest breeze blowing over it, and above it the brightest and most cheerful sky.

It is proper they say to be disappointed on entering the town, or any of the various quarters of it; because the houses are not so magnificent on inspection and seen singly, as they are when beheld *en masse* from the waters. But why form expectations so lofty? If you see a group of peasants pictur-

Left. *A Greek Boatman*, watercolour by Amadeo Preziosi, c.1843. Victoria and Albert Museum.

Right. *Quay at Top-Hané*, lithograph by Camille Rogier, 1846. One of the picturesque quays, bustling with fleets of *caïques*, that Thackeray described. Victoria and Albert Museum (Searight Collection).

Facing Page, Top. *View of Constantinople from the Terrace of a Turkish House in Pera*, watercolour by Amadeo Preziosi, 1856. The master of the house smokes his *çubuk*, with one of his wives and a black slave serving coffee, in attendance. The scene is characteristic of the many picturesque views painted by Preziosi, a Maltese artist who lived and worked in Constantinople from 1842 for forty years. *Photograph*: Christie's.

Facing Page, Bottom. *Petit champ des morts*, watercolour by Alfred de Courville, 1851-54 *(detail)*. This shows the edge of one of the Muslim cemeteries in Pera, a district on the far side of the Golden Horn, with a street lined of old wooden houses that Thackeray found agreeable to the eye. *Photograph*: Christie's.

kinds of craft. There are the dirty men-of-war's boats of the Russians, with unwashed mangy crews; the great ferry-boats carrying hundreds of passengers to the villages; the melon boats piled up with enormous golden fruit; his Excellency the Pasha's boat, with twelve men bending to their oars; and his Highness's own *caïque*, with a head like a serpent, and eight- and-twenty tugging oarsmen, that goes shooting by amidst the thundering of the cannon. Ships and steamers, with black sides and flaunting colours, are moored everywhere, showing their flags, Russian and English, Austrian, American and Greek; and along the quays country ships from the Black Sea or the islands, with high carved poops and bows, such as you see in the pictures of the shipping of the seventeenth century. The vast groves and towers, domes and quays, tall minarets and spired spreading mosques of the three cities, rise all around in endless magnificence and variety, and render this water street a scene of such delightful liveliness and beauty, that one never tires of looking at it. I lost a great number of the sights in and round Constantinople, through the beauty of this admirable scene: but what are sights after all? And isn't that the best sight which makes you most happy?

We were lodged at Pera at Misseri's hotel,[3] the host of which has been made famous ere this time, by the excellent book *Eothen*,[4] a work for which all the passengers on board our ship had been battling, and which had charmed all – from our great statesman, our polished lawyer, our young Oxonian, who sighed over certain passages that he feared were wicked, down to the writer of this, who, after perusing it with delight, laid it down with wonder, exclaiming, '*Aut*

[65]

diabolus aut'⁵ – a book which has since (greatest miracle of all) excited a feeling of warmth and admiration in the bosom of the godlike, impartial, stony Athenæum. Misseri, the faithful and chivalrous Tartar, is transformed into the most quiet and gentlemanlike of landlords, a great deal more gentlemanlike in manner and appearance than most of us, who sat at his table, and smoked cool pipes on his house top, as we looked over the hill and the Russian palace to the water,

The Sultan's Barge approaching the Quay in front of the Nusretiye Camii, watercolour by Amadeo Preziosi, c.1843-50. Soldiers on the quay stand in readiness to receive the Sultan as he disembarks in order to participate in Friday prayers at the mosque.
Victoria and Albert Museum.

and the Seraglio gardens shining in the blue. We confronted Misseri, *Eothen* in hand, and found, on examining him, that it *was* '*aut diabolus aut amicus*'⁵ – but the name is a secret; I will never breath it, though I am dying to tell it.

The last good description of a Turkish bath, I think, was Lady Mary Wortley Montague's,⁶ which voluptuous picture must have been painted at least a hundred and thirty years ago; so that another sketch may be attempted by a humbler artist in a different manner. The Turkish bath is certainly a novel sensation to an Englishman, and may be set down as a most queer and surprising event of his life. I made the *valet de place* or dragoman⁷ (it is rather a fine thing to have a

dragoman in one's service) conduct me forthwith to the best appointed *hummums* in the neighbourhood; and we walked to a house at Tophana,⁸ and into a spacious hall lighted from above, which is the cooling room of the bath.

The spacious hall has a large fountain in the midst, a painted gallery running round it; and many ropes stretched from one gallery to another, ornamented with profuse draperies of towels and blue cloths, for the use of the frequenters of the place. All round the room and the galleries were matted enclosures, fitted with numerous neat beds and cushions for reposing on, where lay a dozen of true believers smoking, or sleeping, or in the happy half-dozing state. I was led up to one of these beds to rather a retired corner, in consideration of my modesty; and to the next bed presently came a dancing dervish, who forthwith began to prepare for the bath.

When the dancing dervish had taken off his yellow sugar-loaf cap, his gown, shawl, etc., he was arrayed in two large blue cloths; a white one being thrown over his shoulders, and another in the shape of a turban plaited neatly round his head; the garments of which he divested himself were folded up in another linen, and neatly put by. I beg leave to state I was treated in precisely the same manner as the dancing dervish.

The reverend gentleman then put on a pair of wooden pattens, which elevated him about six inches from the ground; and walked down the stairs, and paddled across the moist marble floor of the hall, and in at a little door, by the which also Titmarsh entered. But I had none of the professional agility of the dancing dervish; I staggered about very ludicrously upon the high wooden pattens; and should have been down on my nose several times, had not the dragoman and the master of the bath supported me down the stairs and across the hall. Dressed in three large cotton napkins, with a white turban round my head, I thought of Pall Mall with a sort of despair. I passed the little door, it was closed behind me – I was in the dark – I couldn't speak the language – in a white turban – *Mon Dieu!* what was going to happen?

The dark room was the tepidarium, a moist oozing arched den, with a light faintly streaming from an orifice in the domed ceiling. Yells of frantic laughter and song came booming and clanging through the echoing arches, the doors clapped to with loud reverberations. It was the laughter of the followers of Mahound,[9] rollicking and taking their pleasure in the public bath. I could not go into that place: I swore I would not; they promised me a private room, and the dragoman left me. My agony at parting from that Christian cannot be described.

When you get into the Sudarium, or hot room, your first sensations only occur about half a minute after entrance, when you feel that you are choking. I found myself in that state, seated on a marble slab; the bath man was gone; he had taken away the cotton turban and shoulder shawl: I saw I was in a narrow room of marble, with a vaulted roof, and a fountain of warm and cold water; the atmosphere was in a steam, the choking sensation went off, and I felt a sort of pleasure presently in a soft boiling simmer, which, no doubt, potatoes feel when they are steaming. You are left in this state for about ten minutes; it is warm certainly, but odd and pleasant, and disposes the mind to reverie.

But let any delicate mind in Baker Street fancy my horror, when, on looking up out of this reverie, I saw a great brown wretch extended before me, only half dressed, standing on pattens, and exaggerated by them and the steam until he looked like an ogre, grinning in the most horrible way, and waving his arm, on which was a horsehair glove. He spoke in his unknown nasal jargon, words which echoed through the arched room; his eyes seemed astonishingly large and bright, his ears stuck out, and his head was all shaved, except a bristling top-knot, which gave it a demoniac fierceness.

This description, I feel, is growing too frightful; ladies who read it will be going into hysterics, or saying, 'Well, upon my word, this is the most singular, the most extraordinary kind of language. Jane, my love, you will not read that odious book' – and so I will be brief. This grinning man belabours the patient violently with the horse brush. When he has completed the horsehair part, and you lie expiring under a squirting fountain of warm water, and fancying all is done, he reappears with a large brass basin, containing a quantity of lather, in the midst of which is something like old Miss MacWhirter's flaxen wig that she is so proud of, and that we have all laughed at.[10] Just as you are going to remonstrate, the thing like the wig is dashed into your face and eyes, covered over with soap, and for five minutes you are drowned in lather; you can't see, the suds are frothing over your eyeballs; you can't hear, the soap is whizzing into your

ears; you can't gasp for breath, Miss MacWhirter's wig is down your throat with half a pailful of suds in an instant – you are all soap. Wicked children in former days have jeered you, exclaiming, 'How are you off for soap?' You little knew what saponacity was till you entered a Turkish bath.

When the whole operation is concluded, you are led – with what heartfelt joy I need not say – softly back to the cooling-room, having been robed in shawls and turbans as

before. You are laid gently on the reposing bed; somebody brings a narghile, which tastes as tobacco must taste in Mahomet's Paradise; a cool sweet dreamy languor takes possession of the purified frame; and half an hour of such delicious laziness is spent over the pipe as is unknown in Europe, where vulgar prejudice has most shamefully maligned indolence, calls it foul names, such as the father of all evil, and the like; in fact, does not know how to educate idleness as those honest Turks do, and the fruit which, when properly cultivated, it bears.

The after-bath state is the most delightful condition of

laziness I ever knew, and I tried it wherever we went afterwards on our little tour. At Smyrna the whole business was much inferior to the method employed in the capital. At Cairo, after the soap, you are plunged into a sort of stone coffin, full of water, which is all but boiling. This has its charms; but I could not relish the Egyptian shampooing. A hideous old blind man (but very dexterous in his art) tried to break my back and dislocate my shoulders, but I could not see the pleasure of the practice; and another fellow began tickling the soles of my feet, but I rewarded him with a kick that sent him off the bench. The pure idleness is the best, and I shall never enjoy such in Europe again.

Victor Hugo,[11] in his famous travels on the Rhine, visiting Cologne, gives a learned account of what he didn't see there. I have a remarkable catalogue of similar objects at Constantinople. I didn't see the dancing dervishes, it was *Ramazan*; nor the howling dervishes at Scutari, it was *Ramazan*; nor the interior of Saint Sophia, nor the women's apartment of the seraglio, nor the fashionable promenade at the Sweet Waters,[12] always because it was *Ramazan*; during which period the dervishes dance and howl but rarely, their legs and lungs being unequal to much exertion during a fast of fourteen hours. On account of the same holy season, the royal palaces and mosques are shut; and though the valley of the Sweet Waters is there, no one goes to walk; the people remaining asleep all day, and passing the night in feasting and carousing. The minarets are illuminated at this season; even the humblest mosque at Jerusalem, or Jaffa, mounted a few circles of dingy lamps; those of the capital were handsomely lighted with many festoons of lamps, which had a fine effect from the water. I need not mention other and constant illuminations of the city, which innumerable travellers have described – I mean the fires. There were three in Pera during our eight days' stay there; but they did not last long enough to bring the Sultan out of bed to come and lend his aid.[13] Mr. Hobhouse (quoted in the guide book) says, if a fire lasts an hour, the Sultan is bound to attend it in person; and that people having petitions to present, have often set houses on fire for the purpose of forcing out this royal trump. The Sultan can't lead a very 'jolly life', if this rule be universal. Fancy His Highness, in the midst of his moon-faced beauties, handkerchief in hand, and obliged to tie it round his face, and go out of his warm harem at midnight at the cursed cry of '*Yang en Var!*'.

We saw His Highness in the midst of his people and their petitions, when he came to the mosque at Tophana; not the largest, but one of the most picturesque of the public buildings of the city. The streets were crowded with people watching for the august arrival, and lined with the squat military in their bastard European costume; the sturdy police, with bandeliers and brown *surtouts*, keeping order, driving off the faithful from the railings of the Esplanade through which their emperor was to pass, and only admitting (with a very unjust partiality I thought) us Europeans into that reserved space. Before the august arrival, numerous officers collected, colonels and pashas went by with their attendant running footmen; the most active, insolent, and hideous of these great men, as I thought, being His Highness's black eunuchs, who went prancing through the crowd, which separated before them with every sign of respect.

The common women were assembled by many hundreds, the *yakmac*, a muslin chin cloth which they wear, makes almost every face look the same; but the eyes and noses of these beauties are generally visible, and, for the most part, both these features are good. The jolly negresses wear the same white veil, but they are by no means so particular about hiding the charms of their good-natured black faces, and they let the cloth blow about as it lists, and grin unconfined. Wherever we went the negroes seemed happy. They have the organ of child-loving; little creatures were always prattling on their shoulders, queer little things in night-gowns of yellow dimity, with great flowers, and pink, or red, or yellow shawls, with great eyes glistening underneath. Of such the black women seemed always the happy guardians. I saw one at a fountain, holding one child in her arms, and giving another a drink – a ragged little beggar – a sweet and touching picture of a black charity.

I am almost forgetting His Highness the Sultan. About a hundred guns were fired off at clumsy intervals from the esplanade facing the Bosphorus, warning us that the monarch had set off from his summer palace, and was on the way to his grand canoe. At last that vessel made its appearance; the band struck up his favourite air; his caparisoned horse was led down to the shore to receive him; the eunuchs, fat pashas, colonels, and officers of state gathering round as the commander of the faithful mounted. I had the indescribable happiness of seeing him at a very short distance. The

Padishah, or Father of all the Sovereigns on earth, has not that majestic air which some sovereigns possess, and which makes the beholder's eyes wink, and his knees tremble under him: he has a black beard, and a handsome well-bred face, of a French cast; he looks like a young French *roué* worn out by debauch; his eyes bright, with black rings round them; his cheeks pale and hollow. He was lolling on his horse as if he could hardly hold himself on the saddle: or, as if his cloak, fastened with a blazing diamond clasp on his breast, and falling over his horse's tail, pulled him back. But the handsome sallow face of the Refuge of the World looked decidedly interesting and intellectual. I have seen many a young Don Juan at Paris, behind a counter, with such a beard and countenance; the flame of passion still burning in his hollow eyes, while on his damp brow was stamped the fatal mark of premature decay. The man we saw cannot live

many summers. Women and wine are said to have brought the Zilullah to this state; and it is whispered by the dragomans, or *Laquais de Place*, (from whom travellers at Constantinople generally get their political information), that the Sultan's mother and his ministers conspire to keep him plunged in sensuality, that they may govern the kingdom, according to their own fancies. Mr Urquhart,[14] I am sure, thinks that Lord Palmerston has something to do with the business, and drugs the Sultan's champagne for the benefit of Russia.

As the Pontiff of Mussulmans passed into the mosque, a shower of petitions was flung from the steps where the crowd was collected, and over the heads of the *gendarmes* in brown. A general cry, as for justice, rose up; and one old, ragged woman came forward, and burst through the throng, howling, and flinging about her lean arms, and baring her old, shrunken breast. I never saw a finer action of tragic woe, or heard sounds more pitiful than those old, passionate groans of hers. What was your prayer, poor old wretched soul? The *gendarmes* hemmed her round, and hustled her away, but rather kindly. The Padishah went on quite impassible – the picture of debauch and *ennui*.

I like pointing morals, and inventing for myself cheap consolations, to reconcile me to that state of life into which it has pleased heaven to call me; and as the Light of the World disappeared round the corner, I reasoned pleasantly with myself about His Highness, and enjoyed that secret selfish satisfaction a man has, who sees he is better off than his neighbour. 'Michael Angelo,' I said, 'you are still (by courtesy) young: if you had five hundred thousand a year, and were a great prince, I would lay a wager that men would discover in you a magnificent courtesy of demeanour, and a majestic presence that only belongs to the sovereigns of the world. If you had such an income, you think you could spend it with splendour; distributing genial hospitalities, kindly alms, soothing misery, bidding humility be of good heart, rewarding desert. If you had such means of purchasing pleasure, you think, you rogue, you could relish it with gusto. But fancy being brought to the condition of the poor Light of the Universe, yonder; and reconcile yourself with the idea that you are only a farthing rushlight. The cries of the poor widow fall as dead upon him, as the smiles of the brightest eyes out of Georgia. He can't stir abroad but those

His Imperial Majesty the Sultan Abdul Meedgid, lithograph after Sir David Wilkie, 1840-43. Wilkie's sympathetic portrayal of the young Ottoman Sultan is in stark contrast to Thackeray's diatribe: while Wilkie's ruler is a westernised and forward-looking head of state, Thackeray's is a cruel despot and debauched *roué*.
Victoria and Albert Museum (Searight Collection).

Dolmabahçe Palace on the Shores of the Bosphorus, watercolour by Joseph Schranz, 1850s. Thackeray described Topkapi Saray in its last years as the principal residence of the Ottoman Sultan. Ten years later, Abdul Mecid moved into his gleaming new palace on the Bosphorus.
The Peninsular and Oriental Steam Navigation Company.

abominable cannon begin roaring and deafening his ears. He can't see the world but over the shoulders of a row of fat pashas, and eunuchs, with their infernal ugliness. His ears can never be regaled with a word of truth, or blessed with an honest laugh. The only privilege of manhood left to him, he enjoys but for a month in the year, at this time of *Ramazan*, when he is forced to fast for fifteen hours; and, by consequence, has the blessing of feeling hungry.' Sunset during Lent appears to be his single moment of pleasure; they say the poor fellow is ravenous by that time, and as the gun fires the dish covers are taken off, so that for five minutes a day he lives and is happy over *pillau*, like another mortal.

And yet, when floating by the summer palace, a barbaric edifice of wood and marble, with gilded suns blazing over the porticoes, and all sorts of strange ornaments and trophies figuring on the gates and railings – when we passed a long row of barred and filigreed windows, looking on the water – when we were told that those were the apartments of His Highness's ladies, and actually heard them whispering and laughing behind the bars – a strange feeling of curiosity

came over some ill-regulated minds – just to have one peep, one look at all those wondrous beauties, singing to the dulcimers, paddling in the fountains, dancing in the marble halls, or lolling on the golden cushions, as the gaudy black slaves brought pipes and coffee. This tumultuous movement was calmed, by thinking of that dreadful statement of travellers, that in one of the most elegant halls there is a trapdoor, on peeping below which, you may see the Bosphorous running underneath, into which some luckless beauty is plunged occasionally, and the trap-door is shut, and the dancing and the singing, and the smoking and the laughing go on as before. They say it is death to pick up any of the sacks thereabouts, if a stray one should float by you. There were none any day when I passed, *at least, on the surface of the water.*

It has been rather a fashion of our travellers to apologise for Turkish life, of late, and paint glowing, agreeable pictures, of many of its institutions. The celebrated author of *Palm Leaves*[15] (his name is famous under the date-trees of the Nile, and uttered with respect beneath the tents of

the Bedawee) has touchingly described Ibraham Pasha's[16] paternal fondness, who cut off a black slave's head for having dropped and maimed one of his children; and has penned a melodious panegyric of *The Harem*, and of the fond and beautiful duties of the inmates of that place of love, obedience, and seclusion. I saw, at the Mausoleum of the late Sultan Mahmoud's family, a good subject for a *Ghazul*, in the true new Oriental manner.

These royal burial-places are the resort of the pious Moslems. Lamps are kept burning there; and in the antechambers, copies of the Koran are provided for the use of believers; and you never pass these cemeteries but you see Turks washing at the cisterns,[17] previous to entering for prayer, or squatted on the benches, chanting passages from the sacred volume. Christians, I believe, are not admitted, but may look through the bars, and see the coffins of the defunct monarchs and children of the royal race. Each lies in his narrow sarcophagus, which is commonly flanked by huge candles, and covered with a rich embroidered pall. At the head of each coffin rises a slab, with a gilded inscription;

for the princesses, the slab is simple, not unlike our own monumental stones. The headstones of the tombs of the defunct princes are decorated with a turban, or, since the introduction of the latter article of dress, with the red fur. That of Mahmoud is decorated with the imperial aigrette.

In this dismal but splendid museum, I remarked two little tombs with little red fezzes, very small, and for very young heads evidently, which were lying under the little embroidered palls of state. I forget whether they had candles too; but their little flame of life was soon extinguished, and there was no need of many pounds of wax to typify it. These were the tombs of Mahmoud's grandsons, nephews of the present Light of the Universe, and children of his sister, the wife of Halil Paça. Little children die in all ways; these of the much-maligned Mahometan royal race perished by the bowstring. Sultan Mahmoud (may he rest in glory!) strangled the one;[18] but, having some spark of human feeling, was so moved by the wretchedness and agony of the poor bereaved mother, his daughter, that his royal heart relented towards her, and he promised that, should she ever have

Left. *Lady playing a Lute inside a Harem*, watercolour by Amadeo Preziosi, c.1845. *Photograph:* Sotheby's.

Right. *Interior of a Harem*, watercolour by Amadeo Preziosi, 1851. By the mid-19th century in Constantinople, it was fashionable to decorate interiors in the French style, especially a degenerate form of the rococo. Victoria and Albert Museum (Searight Collection).

[71]

another child, it should be allowed to live. He died; and Abdul Medjid (may his name be blessed!), the debauched young man whom we just saw riding to the mosque, suc-

The Atmeidan, or Hippodrome, with the Sultan Ahmed Camii or Blue Mosque, and in the background the Egyptian Obelisk, the Serpentine Column and the so-called Column of Constantine or Colossus. The etching is one of the plates from drawings by Thomas Allom published in *Fisher's Illustrations of Constantinople and its Environs,* 1838-40, one of several books on the Near East popular at this time.

Victoria and Albert Museum (Searight Collection).

ceeded. His sister, whom he is said to have loved, became again a mother, and had a son. But she relied upon her father's word and her august brother's love, and hoped that this little one should be spared. The same accursed hand tore this infant out of its mother's bosom, and killed it. The poor woman's heart broke outright at this second calamity, and she died. But on her death-bed she sent for her brother, rebuked him as a perjurer and an assassin, and expired calling down the divine justice on his head. She lies now by the side of the two little fezzes.

Now, I say this would be a fine subject for an oriental poem. The details are dramatic and noble, and could be grandly touched by a fine artist. If the mother had borne a daughter, the child would have been safe; that perplexity might be pathetically depicted as agitating the bosom of the young wife, about to become a mother. A son is born: you can see her despair and the pitiful look she casts on the child, and the way in which she hugs it every time the curtains of her door are removed. The Sultan hesitated probably; he allowed the infant to live for six weeks. He could not bring his royal soul to inflict pain. He yields at last; he is a martyr – to be pitied, not to be blamed. If he melts at his daughter's agony, he is a man and a father. There are men and fathers too in the much-maligned Orient.

Then comes the second act of the tragedy. The new hopes, the fond yearnings, the terrified misgivings, the timid belief, and weak confidence; the child that is born – and dies smiling prettily – and the mother's heart is rent so, that it can love, or hope, or suffer no more. Allah is God! She sleeps by the little fezzes. Hark! the guns are booming over the water, and His Highness is coming from his prayers.

After the murder of that little child, it seems to me one can never look with anything but horror upon the butcherly Herod who ordered it. The death of the seventy thousand Janissaries ascends to historic dignity, and takes rank as war. But a great prince and Light of the Universe, who procures abortions and throttles little babies, dwindles away into such a frightful insignificance of crime, that those may respect him who will. I pity their excellencies the ambassadors, who are obliged to smirk and cringe to such a rascal. To do the Turks justice – and two days' walk in Constantinople will settle this fact as well as a year's residence in the city – the people do not seem in the least animated by this Herodian spirit. I never saw more kindness to children than among all classes, more fathers walking about with little solemn Mahometans in red caps and big trousers, more business going on than in the toy quarter – and in the Atmeidan,[19] although you may see there the Thebaic stone set up by the Emperor Theodosius, and the bronze column of serpents which Murray says was brought from Delphi, but which my guide informed me was the very one exhibited by Moses in the wilderness: yet I found the examination of these antiquities much less pleasant than to look at the many troops of children assembled on the plain to play; and to watch them as they were dragged about in little queer *arobas,* or painted carriages, which are there kept for hire. I have a picture of one of them now in my eyes: a little green oval machine, with flowers rudely painted round the window, out of which two smiling heads are peeping, the picture of happiness. An old, good-humoured, grey-bearded Turk is tugging the cart; and behind it walks a lady in a *yakmac* and yellow slippers,

and a black female slave, grinning as usual, towards whom the little coach-riders are looking. A small, sturdy, bare-footed Mussulman is examining the cart with some feelings of envy: he is too poor to purchase a ride for himself and the round-faced puppy-dog, which he is hugging in his arms as young ladies in our country do dolls.

All the neighbourhood of the Atmeidan is exceedingly picturesque – the mosque court and cloister, where the Persians have their stalls of sweetmeats and tobacco; a superb sycamore tree grows in the middle of this, overshadowing aromatic fountain: great flocks of pigeons are settling in corners of the cloister, and barley is sold at the gates, with which the good-natured people feed them. From the Atmeidan you have a fine view of Saint Sophia: and here stands a mosque which struck me as being much more picturesque and sumptuous – the mosque of Sultan Achmed,[20] with its six gleaming white minarets, and its beautiful courts and trees. Any infidels may enter the court without molestation, and, looking through the barred windows of the mosque, have a view of its airy and spacious interior. A small audience of women was collected there when I looked in, squatted on the mats, and listening to a preacher, who was walking among them, and speaking with great energy. My drago-man interpreted to me the sense of a few words of his sermon: he was warning them of the danger of gadding about to public places, and of the immorality of too much

talking; and, I dare say, we might have had more valuable information from him, regarding the follies of womankind, had not a tall Turk clapped my interpreter on the shoulder, and pointed him to be off.

Although the ladies are veiled, and muffled with the ug-liest dresses in the world, yet it appears their modesty is alarmed in spite of all the coverings which they wear. One day, in the bazaar, a fat old body, with diamond rings on her fingers, that were tinged with *henné*,[21] of a logwood colour, came to the shop where I was purchasing slippers, with her son, a young aga of six years of age, dressed in a braided frock coat, with a huge tassel to his fez, exceeding fat, and of a most solemn demeanour. The young aga came for a pair of shoes, and his contortions were so delightful as he tried them, that I remained looking on with great pleasure, wishing for Leech to be at hand to sketch his lordship and his fat mamma,[22] who sat on the counter. That lady fancied I was looking at her, though, as far as I could see, she had the fig-ure and complexion of a roly-poly pudding; and so, with quite a premature bashfulness, she sent me a message by the shoemaker, ordering me to walk away if I had made my purchases, for that ladies of her rank did not choose to be stared at by strangers; and I was obliged to take my leave, though with sincere regret, for the little lord had just squeezed himself into an attitude than which I never saw anything more ludicrous in General Tom Thumb. When the ladies of the seraglio come to that bazaar with their *cortège* of infernal black eunuchs, strangers are told to move on briskly. I saw a bevy of about eight of these, with their *aides-de-camp*; but they were wrapped up, and looked just as vulgar and ugly as the other women, and were not, I sup-pose, of the most beautiful sort. The poor devils are allowed to come out, half a dozen times in the year, to spend their little wretched allowance of pocket-money in purchasing trinkets and tobacco; all the rest of the time they pursue the beautiful duties of their existence in the walls of the sacred harem.

Though strangers are not allowed to see the interior of the cage in which these birds of Paradise are confined; yet many parts of the seraglio are free to the curiosity of visitors, who choose to drop a *backsheesh* here and there. I landed one morning at the seraglio point from Galata, close by an ancient pleasure-house of the defunct Sultan; a vast broad-

a

c

e

b

[74]

d

f

brimmed pavilion, that looks agreeable enough to be a dancing-room for ghosts now: there is another summer-house, the guide book cheerfully says, whither the Sultan goes to sport with his women and mutes.[23] A regiment of infantry, with their music at their head, were marching to exercise in the outer grounds of the seraglio; and we followed them, and had an opportunity of seeing their evolutions, and hearing their bands, upon a fine green plain under the seraglio walls, where stands one solitary column, erected in memory of some triumph of some Byzantian emperor.

There were three battalions of the Turkish infantry exercising here; and they seemed to perform their evolutions in a very satisfactory manner: that is, they fired altogether, and charged and halted in very straight lines, and bit off imaginary cartridge-tops with great fierceness and regularity, and made all their ramrods ring to measure, just like so many Christians. The men looked small, young, clumsy, and ill-built; uncomfortable in their shabby European clothes; and about the legs, especially, seemed exceedingly weak and ill-formed. Some score of military invalids were lolling in the sunshine, about a fountain and a marble summer-house, that stand on the ground, watching their comrades' manoeuvres (as if they could never have enough of that delightful pastime); and these sick were much better cared for than their healthy companions. Each man had two dressing-gowns, one of white cotton, and an outer wrapper of warm brown woollen. Their heads were accommodated with wadded cotton nightcaps; and it seemed to me from their condition, and from the excellent character of the military hospitals, that it would be much more wholesome to be ill than to be well in the Turkish service.

Facing this green esplanade, and the Bosphorus shining beyond it, rise the great walls of the outer seraglio gardens; huge masses of ancient masonry, over which peep the roofs of numerous kiosks and outhouses, amongst thick ever-greens, planted so as to hide the beautiful frequenters of the place from the prying eyes and telescopes. We could not catch a glance of a single figure moving in these great pleasure grounds. The road winds round the walls; and the outer park, which is likewise planted with trees, and diversified by garden plots and cottages, had more the air of the outbuildings of a homely English park, than of a palace which we must all have imagined to be the most stately in the world. The most commonplace water carts were passing here and there; roads were being repaired in the Macadamite manner; and carpenters were mending the park palings, just as they do in Hampshire. The next thing you might fancy would

Watercolours by
Amadeo Preziosi

a. *Negresses in the Slave Market*, c.1843. Several westerners commented on the cheerful demeanor of the women in the slave markets in both Constantinople and Cairo.
Victoria and Albert Museum.

b. *Two Jewesses in Outdoor Dress*, 1844. The presence in Constantinople of men and women of many different races and creeds, from all over the Ottoman Empire, gave it its cosmopolitan character.
Photograph: Sotheby's.

c. *Ladies at a Sebil or Street-Fountain*, c.1845. All western visitors were intrigued by the women they saw in the streets, with their faces and figures completely encased in a white muslin veil *(yaşmak)* and a voluminous outer gown *(ferice)*. Preziosi has depicted three of them at a street-fountain: a wealthy lady lowers her veil to drink, while her black slave – one of the good-natured and child-loving negresses noted by Thackeray – holds her richly-dressed son.
Victoria and Albert Museum (Searight Collection).

d. *Ladies and a Child in an Araba*, 1850. Turkish women spent much of their time in the seclusion of their houses, but they would also go on outings in gaily decorated carriages.
Photograph: Sotheby's.

e. *Turkish Lady*, c.1843.
Victoria and Albert Museum.

f. *Armenian Lady*, 1844.
Photograph: Sotheby's.

g. *The Baghdad Kiosk, in the Fourth Court of Topkapi Saray*, 1853. This elaborately decorated kiosk stands at the north end of the terrace overlooking the Golden Horn.
Photograph: Sotheby's.

be the Sultan walking out with a spud and a couple of dogs, on the way to meet the post-bag and the *Saint James's Chronicle*.

The palace is no palace at all. It is a great town of pavilions, built without order, here and there, according to the fancy of succeeding Lights of the Universe, or their favourites. The only row of domes which looked particularly regular or stately, were the kitchens. As you examined the buildings they had a ruinous, dilapidated look, – they are not furnished, it is said, with particular splendour, – not a bit more elegantly than Miss Jones's seminary for young ladies, which we may be sure is much more comfortable than the extensive establishment of His Highness Abdul Medjid.

In the little stable I thought to see some marks of royal magnificence, and some horses worthy of the King of all Kings. But the Sultan is said to be a very timid horseman: the animal that is always kept saddled for him did not look to be worth twenty pounds; and the rest of the horses in the shabby, dirty stalls, were small, ill kept, common-looking brutes. You might see better, it seemed to me, at a country inn stable of any market day.

The kitchens are the most sublime part of the seraglio. There are nine of these great halls, for all ranks, from His Highness downwards; where many hecatombs are roasted daily, according to the accounts; and where cooking goes on with a savage Homeric grandeur. Chimneys are despised in these primitive halls; so that the roofs are black with the smoke of hundreds of furnaces, which escapes through apertures in the domes above. These, too, give the chief light in the rooms, which streams downwards, and thickens and mingles with the smoke, and so murkily lights up hundreds of swarthy figures busy about the spits and the cauldrons. Close to the door by which we entered, they were making pastry for the Sultanas; and the chief pastrycook, who knew my guide, invited us courteously to see the process, and partake of the delicacies prepared for those charming lips. How those sweet lips must shine after eating these puffs! First, huge sheets of dough are rolled out till the paste is about as thin as silver paper: then an artist forms the dough-muslin into a sort of drapery, curling it round and round in many fanciful and pretty shapes, until it is all got into the circumference of a round metal tray in which it is baked. Then the cake is drenched in grease most profusely; and, finally, a quantity of syrup is poured over it, when the delectable mixture is complete. The moon-faced ones are said to devour immense quantities of this wholesome food; and, in fact, are eating grease and sweetmeats from morning till night. I don't like to think what the consequences may be, or allude to the agonies which the delicate creatures must inevitably suffer.

The good-natured chief pastrycook filled a copper basin with greasy puffs; and, dipping a dubious ladle into a large cauldron, containing several gallons of syrup, poured a liberal portion over the cakes, and invited us to eat. One of the tarts was quite enough for me: and I excused myself on the plea of ill-health from imbibing any more grease and sugar. But my companion, the dragoman, finished some forty puffs in a twinkling. They slipped down his opened jaws as the sausages go down clown's throats in a pantomime. His moustachios shone with grease, and it dripped down his beard and fingers. We thanked the smiling chief pastrycook, and rewarded him handsomely for the tarts. It is something to have eaten of the dainties prepared for the ladies of the harem; but I think Mr. Cockle ought to get the names of the chief Sultanas among the exalted patrons of his Antibilious Pills.

From the kitchens we passed into the second court of the seraglio, beyond which is death. The guide book only hints at the dangers which would befall a stranger caught prying in the mysterious *first* court of the palace. I have read *Bluebeard*, and don't care for peeping into forbidden doors; so that the second court was quite enough for me; the pleasure of beholding it being heightened, as it were, by the notion of the invisible danger sitting next door, with uplifted scimitar ready to fall on – present though not seen.

A cloister runs along one side of this court; opposite is the hall of the divan, 'large but low, covered with lead, and gilt, after the Moorish manner, plain enough.' The Grand Vizir sits in this place, and the ambassadors used to wait here, and be conducted hence on horseback, attired with robes of honour. But the ceremony is now, I believe, discontinued; the English envoy, at any rate, is not allowed to receive any *backsheesh*, and goes away as he came, in the habit of his own nation. On the right is a door leading into the interior of the seraglio; *none pass through it but such as are sent for*, the guide book says: it is impossible to top the terror of that description.

About this door lads and servants were lolling, ichoglans[24] and pages, with lazy looks and shabby dresses; and among them, sunning himself sulkily on a bench, a poor old, fat, wrinkled, dismal white eunuch, with little fat white hands, and a great head sunk into his chest, and two sprawling little legs that seemed incapable to hold up his bloated old body. He squeaked out some surly reply to my friend the dragoman, who, softened and sweetened by the tarts he had just been devouring, was, no doubt, anxious to be polite: and the poor worthy fellow walked away rather crestfallen at this return of his salutation, and hastened me out of the place.

The palace of the seraglio, the cloister with marble pillars, the hall of the ambassadors, the impenetrable gate guarded by eunuchs and ichoglans, has a romantic look in print; but not so in reality. Most of the marble is wood, almost all the gilding is faded, the guards are shabby, the foolish perspectives painted on the walls are half cracked off. The place looks like Vauxhall in the daytime.[25]

We passed out of the second court under THE SUBLIME PORTE,[26] which is like a fortified gate of a German town of the middle ages, into the outer court, round which are public offices, hospitals, and dwellings of the multifarious servants of the palace. This place is very wide and picturesque; there is a pretty church[27] of Byzantine architecture at the further end and in the midst of the court a magnificent plane tree, of prodigious dimensions and fabulous age, according to the guides; Saint Sophia tower, in the further distance: and from here, perhaps, is the best view of its light swelling domes and beautiful proportions. The Porte itself, too, forms an excellent subject for the sketcher, if the officers of the court will permit him to design it. I made the attempt and a couple of Turkish beadles looked on very good-naturedly for some time at the progress of the drawing; but a good number of other spectators speedily joined them, and made a crowd, which is not permitted, it would seem, in the seraglio; so I was told to pack up my portfolio, and remove the cause of the disturbance, and lost my drawing of the Ottoman Porte.

I don't think I have anything more to say about the city, which has not been much better told by graver travellers. I

Fontaine de Sainte Sophie, watercolour by Alfred de Courville, 1851-54 *(detail)*. Two Turks draw water from the street fountain of Ahmed III, one of the most splendid examples of Turkish rococo architecture in Constantinople, situated near Haghia Sophia (Aya Sofya). *Photograph:* Christie's.

with them could see (perhaps it was the preaching of the politicians that warned me of the fact) that we are looking on at the last days of an empire; and heard many stories of weakness, disorder, and oppression. I even saw a Turkish lady drive up to Sultan Achmet's mosque *in a brougham.* Is not that a subject to moralize upon? And might one not draw endless conclusions from it, that the knell of the Turkish dominion is rung; that the European spirit and institutions once admitted can never be rooted out again; and that the scepticism prevalent amongst the higher orders must descend ere very long to the lower; and the cry of the *muezim* from the mosque become a mere ceremony?

But as I only stayed eight days in this place, and knew not a syllable of the language, perhaps it is as well to pretermit any disquisitions about the spirit of the people. I can only say that they looked to be very good-natured, handsome, and lazy; that the women's yellow slippers are very ugly; that the kabobs at the shop, hard by the rope bazaar, are very hot and good; and that at the Armenian cook-shops they serve you delicious fish, and a stout raisin wine of no small merit. There came in, as we sat and dined there at sunset, a good old Turk, who called for a penny fish, and sat down under a tree very humbly, and ate it with his own bread. We made that jolly old mussulman happy with a quart of the raisin wine; and his eyes twinkled with every fresh glass, and he wiped his old beard delighted, and talked and chirped a good deal, and, I dare say, told us the whole state of the empire. He was the only mussulman with whom I attained any degree of intimacy during my stay in Constantinople; and you will see that, for obvious reasons, I cannot divulge the particulars of our conversation.

'You have nothing to say, and you own it,' says somebody: 'then why write?' That question perhaps (between ourselves) I have put likewise; and yet, my dear sir, there are

The Kibab Shop, Scutari, Asia Minor, watercolour by John Frederick Lewis, 1858. Lewis's kebab shop, though in Scutari (now Üsküdar), on the opposite side of the Bosphorus to Constantinople, was presumably similar in its layout and clientele to the one that Thackeray visited in the city. Lewis had spent a year in and around Constantinople in 1840-41. *Photograph:* Sotheby's.

Turk asleep, wood engraving by William Thackeray.

some things worth remembering even in this brief letter: that woman in the brougham is an idea of significance: that comparison of the seraglio to Vauxhall in the daytime, is a true and real one; from both of which your own great soul and ingenious philosophic spirit may draw conclusions, that I myself have modestly foreborne to press. You are too clever to require a moral to be tacked to all the fables you read, as it is done for children in the spelling books; else I would tell you that the government of the Ottoman Porte seems to be as rotten, as wrinkled, and as feeble as the old eunuch I saw crawling about it in the sun; that when the lady drove up in a brougham to Sultan Achmet, I felt that the schoolmaster was really abroad; and that the crescent will go out before that luminary, as meekly as the moon does before the sun.

[78]

Chapter VIII: RHODES

The Harbour at Rhodes, oil painting by William Müller, 1845. In the mid-19th century, Rhodes was an ordinary Turkish port, but Thackeray was keenly aware of its noble past as the headquarters of the Knights of St John of Jerusalem.
Photograph: The Fine Art Society.

THE sailing of a vessel direct for Jaffa, brought a great number of passengers together, and our decks were covered with Christian, Jew, and Heathen. In the cabin we were Poles and Russians, Frenchmen, Germans, Spaniards, and Greeks; on the deck were squatted several little colonies of people of different race and persuasion. There was a Greek papa, a noble figure with a flowing and venerable white beard, who had been living on bread and water for I don't know how many years, in order to save a little money to make the pilgrimage to Jerusalem. There were several families of Jewish rabbis, who celebrated their 'feast of tabernacles' on board; their chief men performing worship twice or thrice a day, dressed in their pontifical habits, and

bound with phylacteries: and there were Turks, who had their own ceremonies and usages, and wisely kept aloof from their neighbours of Israel.

The dirt of these children of captivity exceeds all possibility of description; the profusion of stinks which they raised, the grease of their venerable garments and faces, the horrible messes cooked in the filthy pots, and devoured with the nasty fingers, the squalor of mats, pots, old bedding, and foul carpets of our Hebrew friends, could hardly be painted by Swift, in his dirtiest mood, and cannot be, of course, attempted by my timid and genteel pen. What would they say in Baker Street to some sights with which our new friends favoured us? What would your ladyship have said if

Top Left. *Isaac, a Karaite Jew from Hasköy near Constantinople,* watercolour by Amadeo Preziosi, 1852.
Victoria and Albert Museum.

Top Right. *A Greek Priest,* watercolour by Amadeo Preziosi, c.1843.
Victoria and Albert Museum.

Oriental figures on board ship, pencil drawing by Sir David Wilkie, 1841 *(detail).* Three years before Thackeray, Wilkie had made the same journey by sea from Constantinople to Jaffa, and encountered a similar mix of races among his fellow passengers, many of them pilgrims bound for Jerusalem and Mecca.
Victoria and Albert Museum (Searight Collection).

you had seen the interesting Greek nun combing her hair over the cabin – combing it with the natural fingers, and averse to slaughter, flinging the delicate little intruders, which she found in the course of her investigation, gently into the great cabin? Our attention was a good deal occupied in watching the strange ways and customs of the various comrades of ours.

The Jews were refugees from Poland, going to lay their bones to rest in the valley of Jehoshaphat, and performing with exceeding rigour the offices of their religion. At morning and evening you were sure to see the chiefs of the families, arrayed in white robes, bowing over their books, at

prayer. Once a week, on the eve before the Sabbath, there was a general washing in Jewry, which sufficed until the ensuing Friday. The men wore long gowns and caps of fur, or else broad-brimmed hats, or in service time, bound on their heads little iron boxes, with the sacred name engraved on them. Among the lads there were some beautiful faces; and among the women your humble servant discovered one who was a perfect rose-bud of beauty, when first emerging from her Friday's toilette, and for a day or two afterwards, until each succeeding day's smut darkened those fresh and delicate cheeks of hers. We had some very rough weather in the cou-rse of the passage from Constantinople to Jaffa, and the sea washed over and over our Israelite friends and their baggages and bundles; but though they were said to

be rich, they would not afford to pay for cabin shelter. One father of a family, finding his progeny half drowned in a squall, vowed he would pay for a cabin; but the weather was somewhat finer the next day, and he could not squeeze out his dollars, and the ship's authorities would not admit him except upon payment.

This unwillingness to part with money is not only found amongst the followers of Moses, but in those of Mahomet, and Christians too. When we went to purchase in the bazaars, after offering money for change, the honest fellows would frequently keep back several piastres, and when urged to refund, would give most dismally: and begin doling out penny by penny, and utter pathetic prayers to their customer not to take any more. I bought five or six pounds worth of Broussa silks for the womankind,[1] in the bazaar at Constantinople, and the rich Armenian who sold them, begged for three-halfpence to pay his boat to Galata. There is something naïf and amusing in this exhibition of cheatery – this simple cringing and wheedling, and passion, for two-pence-halfpenny. It was pleasant to give a millionaire beggar an alms, and laugh in his face, and say, 'There, Dives, there's a penny for you: be happy, you poor old swindling scoundrel, as far as a penny goes.' I used to watch these Jews on shore, and making bargains with one another as soon as they came on board; the battle between vendor and purchaser was an agony – they shrieked, clasped hands, appealed to one another passionately; their handsome, noble faces assumed a look of woe – quite an heroic eagerness and sadness about a farthing.

Ambassadors from our Hebrews descended at Rhodes to buy provisions, and it was curious to see their dealings: there was our venerable rabbi, who, robed in white and silver, and bending over his book at the morning service, looked like a patriarch, and whom I saw chaffering about a fowl with a brother Rhodian Israelite. How they fought over the body of that lean animal! The street swarmed with Jews – goggling eyes looked out from the old carved casements – hooked noses issued from the low, antique doors – Jew boys driving donkeys--Hebrew mothers nursing children; dusky, tawdry, ragged young beauties – and most venerable grey-bearded fathers – were all gathered round about the affair of the hen! And at the same time that our rabbi was arranging the price of it, his children were in-

An Oriental Jew, wood engraving by William Thackeray.

structed to procure bundles of green branches to decorate the ship during their feast. Think of the centuries during which these wonderful people have remained unchanged; and how, from the days of Jacob downwards, they have believed and swindled!

The Rhodian Jews, with their genius for filth, have made their quarter of the noble, desolate old town, the most ruinous and wretched of all. The escutcheons of the proud old knights are still carved over the doors, whence issue these miserable greasy hucksters and pedlars. The Turks respected these emblems of the brave enemies whom they had overcome, and left them untouched; when the French seized Malta they were by no means so delicate. They effaced armorial bearings with their usual hot-headed eagerness; and a few years after they had torn down the coats of arms of the gentry, the heroes of Malta and Egypt were busy devising heraldry for themselves, and were wild to be barons and counts of the empire.

The chivalrous relics at Rhodes are very superb. I know of no buildings, whose stately and picturesque aspect seems to correspond better with one's notions of their proud founders. The towers and gates are warlike and strong, but beautiful and aristocratic: you see that they must have been high-bred gentlemen who built them. The edifices appear in almost as perfect a condition as when they were in the occupation of the noble Knights of St John;[2] and they have this advantage over modern fortifications, that they are a thousand times more picturesque. Ancient war condescended to ornament itself, and built fine carved castles and vaulted gates: whereas, to judge from Gibraltar and Malta, nothing can be less romantic than the modern military architecture; which sternly regards the fighting, without in the least heeding the war-paint. Some of the huge artillery, with which the place was defended, still lies in the bastions; and the touch-holes of the guns are preserved by being covered with rusty old corslets, worn by defenders of the fort three hundred years ago.

The Turks, who battered down chivalry, seem to be waiting their turn of destruction now. In walking through Rhodes one is strangely affected by witnessing the signs of this double decay. For instance, in the streets of the knights, you see noble houses, surmounted by noble escutcheons of superb knights, who lived there, and prayed,

A Street in Rhodes, watercolour by William Müller, 1844.
Private Collection.

and quarrelled, and murdered the Turks; and were the most gallant pirates of the inland seas; and made vows of chastity, and robbed and ravished; and, professing humility, would admit none but nobility into their order; and died recommending themselves to sweet St John, and calmly hoping for heaven in consideration of all the heathen they had slain. When this superb fraternity was obliged to yield to courage as great as theirs, faith as sincere, and to robbers even more dexterous and audacious than the noblest knight who ever sang a canticle to the Virgin, these halls were filled by magnificent pashas and agas, who lived here in the intervals of war, and, having conquered its best champions, despised Christendom and chivalry pretty much as an Englishman despises a Frenchman. Now the famous house is let to a shabby merchant, who has his little beggarly shop in the bazaar; to a small officer, who ekes out his wretched pension by swindling, and who gets his pay in bad coin. Mahometanism pays in pewter now, in place of silver and

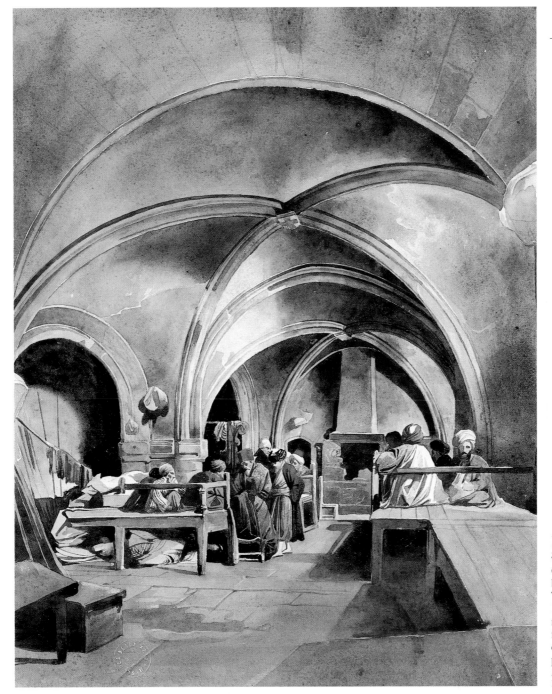

Palace of the Knights, now a Coffee-shop, Rhodes, watercolour by Charles Gleyre, 1834. Rhodes had been taken by the Ottoman Turks in 1522, and by the 19th century much of its fine medieval architecture had fallen into ruin or been taken over for more mundane purposes, as seen here.
Musée cantonal des Beaux-Arts, Lausanne.

gold. The lords of the world have run to seed. The powerless old sword frightens nobody now – the steel is turned to pewter too, somehow, and will no longer shear a Christian head off any shoulders. In the Crusades my wicked sympathies have always been with the Turks. They seem to me the best Christians of the two; more humane, less brutally presumptuous about their own merits, and more generous in esteeming their neighbours. As far as I can get at the authentic story, Saladin is a pearl of refinement compared to the brutal beef-eating Richard – about whom Sir Walter Scott has led all the world astray.[3]

When shall we have a real account of those times and heroes – no good-humoured pageant, like those of the Scott romances – but a real authentic story to instruct and frighten honest people of the present day, and make them thankful that the grocer governs the world now in place of the baron? Meanwhile a man of tender feelings may be pardoned for twaddling a little over this sad spectacle of the decay of two of the great institutions of the world. Knighthood is gone – Amen; it expired with dignity, its face to the foe: and old Mahometanism is lingering, just about ready to drop. But it is unseemly to see such a Grand Potentate in such a state of decay: the son of Bajazet Ilderim insolvent;[4] the descendants of the Prophets bullied by Calmucs[5] and English and whippersnapper Frenchmen; the Fountain of Magnificence done up, and obliged to coin pewter! Think of the poor dear houris in Paradise, how sad they must look as the arrivals of the Faithful become less and less frequent every day. I can fancy the place beginning to wear the fatal Vauxhall look of the seraglio, and which has pursued me ever since I saw it: the fountains of eternal wine are beginning to run rather dry, and of a questionable liquor; the ready-roasted meat trees may cry 'Come, eat me', every now and then, in a faint voice, without any gravy in it – but the Faithful begin to doubt about the quality of the victuals. Of nights you may see the *houris* sitting sadly under them, darning their faded muslins: Ali, Omar, and the Imaums are reconciled and have gloomy consultations: and the Chief of the Faithful himself, the awful camel driver, the supernatural husband of Kadisheh,[6] sits alone in a tumble-down kiosk, thinking moodily of the destiny that is impending over him; and of the day when his gardens of bliss shall be as vacant as the bankrupt Olympus.

All the town of Rhodes has this appearance of decay and ruin, except a few consuls' houses planted on the seaside, here and there, with bright flags flaunting in the sun; fresh paint; English crockery; shining mahogany, etc., – so many emblems of the new prosperity of *their* trade, while the old inhabitants were going to rack – the fine church of St John, converted into a mosque, is a ruined church, with a ruined mosque inside; the fortifications are mouldering away, as much as time will let them. There was considerable bustle and stir about the little port; but it was a bustle of people, who looked for the most part to be beggars; and I saw no shop in the bazaar, that seemed to have the value of a pedlar's pack.

I took, by way of guide, a young fellow from Berlin, a journeyman shoemaker, who had just been making a tour in Syria, and who professed to speak both Arabic and Turkish quite fluently, which I thought he might have learned when he was a student at college, before he began his profession of shoemaking; but I found he only knew about three words of Turkish, which were produced on every occasion, as I walked under his guidance through the desolate streets of the noble old town. We went out upon the lines of fortification, through an ancient gate and guard-house, where once a chapel probably stood, and of which the roofs were richly carved and gilded. A ragged squad of Turkish soldiers lolled about the gate now – a couple of boys on a donkey; a grinning slave on a mule; a pair of women flapping along in yellow papooshes; a basket-maker sitting under an antique carved portal, and chanting or howling as he platted his osiers; a peaceful well of water, at which knights' chargers had drunk, and at which the double-buoyed donkey was now refreshing himself – would have made a pretty picture for a sentimental artist. As he sits, and endeavours to make a sketch of this plaintive little comedy, a shabby dignitary of the island comes clattering by on a thirty-shilling horse, and two or three of the ragged soldiers leave their pipes to salute him as he passes under the Gothic archway.

The astonishing brightness and clearness of the sky under which the island seemed to bask, struck me as surpassing anything I had seen – not even at Cadiz, or the Peiræus, had I seen sands so yellow, or water so magnificently blue. The houses of the people along the shore were but poor tenements, with humble courtyards and gardens; but every fig-tree was gilded and bright, as if it were in a Hesperian orchard; the palms, planted here and there, rose with a sort of halo of light round about them; the creepers on the walls quite dazzled with the brilliancy of their flowers and leaves; the people lay in the cool shadows, happy and idle, with handsome solemn faces; nobody seemed to be at work; they only talked a very little, as if idleness and silence were a condition of the delightful shining atmosphere in which they lived.

We went down to an old mosque by the seashore, with a cluster of ancient domes hard by it, blazing in the sunshine, and carved all over with names of Allah, and titles of old pirates and generals who reposed there. The guardian of the mosque sat in the garden-court, upon a high wooden pulpit, lazily wagging his body to and fro, and singing the praises of the prophet gently through his nose, as the breeze stirred through the trees overhead, and cast chequered and changing shadows over the paved court, and the little fountains, and the nasal psalmist on his perch. On one side was the mosque, into which you could see, with its white walls and cool matted floor, and quaint carved pulpit and ornaments, and nobody at prayers. In the middle distance rose up the noble towers and battlements of the knightly town, with the deep sea-line behind them.

It really seemed as if everybody was to have a sort of sober cheerfulness, and must yield to indolence under this charming atmosphere. I went into the courtyard by the seashore (where a few lazy ships were lying, with no one on board), and found it was the prison of the place. The door was as wide open as Westminster Hall. Some prisoners, one or two soldiers and functionaries, and some prisoners' wives, were lolling under an arcade by a fountain; other criminals were strolling about here and there, their chains clinking quite cheerfully: and they and the guards and officials came up chatting quite friendly together, and gazed languidly over the portfolio, as I was endeavouring to get the likeness of one or two of these comfortable malefactors. One old and wrinkled she-criminal, whom I had selected on account of the peculiar hideousness of her countenance, covered it up with a dirty cloth, at which there was a general roar of laughter among this good-humoured auditory of cut-throats, pickpockets, and policemen. The only symptom of a prison about the place was a door, across which a couple of sentinels were stretched, yawning; while within

Turkish Merchants on the Quay at Rhodes, oil painting by William Müller, 1844-45. Müller called in at Rhodes in 1843 and 1844 on his way to and from Lycia in south-west Turkey.
Photograph: Christie's.

lay three freshly caught pirates, chained by the leg. They had committed some murders of a very late date, and were awaiting sentence; but their wives were allowed to communicate freely with them: and it seemed to me, that if half a dozen friends would set them free, and they themselves had energy enough to move, the sentinels would be a great deal too lazy to walk after them.

The combined influence of Rhodes and *Ramazan,* I suppose, had taken possession of my friend, the *schustergesell* from Berlin. As soon as he received his fee, he cut me at once, and went and lay down by a fountain near the port, and ate grapes out of a dirty pocket-handkerchief. Other Christian idlers lay near him, dozing, or sprawling in the boats, or listlessly munching water-melons. Along the coffee-houses of the quay sat hundreds more, with no better employment; and the captain of the *Iberia* and his officers, and several of the passengers in that famous steamship, were in this company, being idle with all their might. Two or three adventurous young men went off to see the valley where the dragon was killed; but others more susceptible of the real influence of the island, I am sure would not have moved, though we had been told that the Colossus himself was taking a walk half a mile off.

On deck, beneath the awning,
I dozing lay and yawning;
It was the grey of dawning,
  Ere yet the sun arose;
And above the funnel's roaring,
And the fitful wind's deploring,
I heard the cabin snoring
  With universal nose.
I could hear the passengers snorting,
I envied their disporting,
Vainly I was courting
  The pleasure of a doze.

So I lay, and wondered why light
Came not, and watched the twilight
And the glimmer of the skylight,
  That shot across the deck;
And the binnacle pale and steady,
And the dull glimpse of the dead-eye,
And the sparks in fiery eddy,
  That whirled from the chimney neck:
In our jovial floating prison
There was sleep from fore to mizen,
And never a star had risen
  The hazy sky to speck.

To starboard Turks and Greeks were,
Whiskered, and brown their cheeks were,
Enormous wide their breeks were,
  Their pipes did puff alway;
Each on his mat allotted,
In silenced smoked and squatted,
Whilst round their children trotted,
  In pretty, pleasant play.

He can't but smile who traces
The smiles on those brown faces,
And the pretty prattling graces
  Of those small heathens gay.
And so the hours kept tolling,
And through the ocean rolling,
Went the brave *Iberia* bowling
  Before the break of day ——

When A SQUALL upon a sudden,
Came o'er the waters scudding;
And the clouds began to gather,
And the sea was lashed to lather,
And the lowering thunder grumbled,
And the lightning jumped and tumbled,
And the ship, and all the ocean,
Woke up in wild commotion.
Then the wind set up a howling,
And the poodle-dog a yowling,
And the cocks began a crowing,
And the old cow raised a lowing,
As she heard the tempest blowing;
And fowls and geese did cackle,
And the cordage and the tackle
Began to shriek and crackle;
And the spray dashed o'er the funnels,
And down the deck in runnels;
And the rushing water soaks all,
From the seamen in the fo'ksal,
To the stokers, whose black faces
Peer out of their bed-places;
And the captain he was bawling,
And the sailors pulling, hauling;
And the quarter-deck tarpauling
Was shivered in the squalling;

And the passengers awaken,
Most pitifully shaken;
And the steward jumps up, and hastens
For the necessary basins.

  Then the Greeks they groaned and quivered,
And they knelt, and moaned, and shivered,
As the plunging waters met them,
And splashed and overset them;
And they call in their emergence
Upon countless saints and virgins;
And their marrowbones are bended,
And they think the world is ended.

  And the Turkish women for'ard
Were frightened and behorror'd;
And, shrieking and bewildering,
The mothers clutched their children;
The men sung, 'Allah Illah
Mashallah Bismillah!'
As the warring waters doused them,
And splashed them and soused them;
And they called upon the Prophet,
And thought but little of it.

  This was the White Squall famous,
Which latterly o'ercame us,
And which all will well remember
On the 28th September;
When a Prussian captain of Lancers
(Those tight-laced, whiskered prancers)
Came on the deck astonished,
By that wild squall admonished,
And wondering cried, '*Potz tausend,
Wie ist der Stürm jetzt brausend?*

A Glimpse of the Sun, wood engraving from *The Graphic*, 10 April 1875. A storm at sea, witnessed by passengers and crew on board a later and larger steamship than those on which Thackeray travelled. The Peninsular and Oriental Steam Navigation Company.

And looked at Captain Lewis,
Who calmly stood and blew his
Cigar in all the bustle,
And scorned the tempest's tussle.
And oft we've thought hereafter
How he beat the storm to laughter;
For well he knew his vessel

With that vain wind could wrestle;
And when a wreck we thought her
And doomed ourselves to slaughter,
How gaily he fought her,
And through the hubbub brought her,
And, as the tempest caught her,
Cried, 'GEORGE! SOME BRANDY AND WATER !'

And when, its force expended,
The harmless storm was ended,
And, as the sunrise splendid
    Came blushing o'er the sea;
I thought, as day was breaking,
My little girls were waking,
And smiling, and making
    A prayer at home for me.

THERE should have been a poet in our company to describe that charming little Bay of Glaucus,[1] into which we entered on the 26th September, in the first steamboat that ever disturbed its beautiful waters. You can't put down in prose that delicious episode of natural poetry; it ought to be done in a symphony, full of sweet melodies and swelling harmonies; or sung in a strain of clear crystal iambics, such as Milnes knows how to write.[2] A mere map, drawn in words, gives the mind no notion of that exquisite nature. What do mountains become in type, or rivers in Mr Vizetelly's best brevier?[3] Here lies the sweet bay, gleaming peaceful in the rosy sunshine: green islands dip here and there in its waters: purple mountains swell circling round it; and towards them, rising from the bay, stretches a rich green plain, fruitful with herbs and various foliage, in the midst of which the white houses twinkle. I can see a little minaret, and some spreading palm trees; but, beyond these, the description would answer as well for Bantry Bay as well as Makri. You could write so far, nay, much more particularly and grandly, without seeing the place at all, and after reading Beauforts's *Caramania*,[4] which gives you not the least notion of it.

Suppose the great hydrographer of the Admiralty himself can't describe it, who surveyed the place; suppose Mr Fellowes,[5] who discovered it afterwards – suppose I say Sir John Fellowes, Knt. – can't do it (and I defy any man of imagination to get an impression of Telmessus from his book)- -can you, vain man, hope to try? The effect of the artist, as I take it, ought to be, to produce upon his hearer's mind, by his art, an effect something similar to that produced on his own, by the sight of the natural object. Only music, or the best poetry, can do this. Keats' *Ode to a Grecian Urn* is the best description I know of that sweet, old, silent ruin of Telmessus[6]. After you have once seen it, the remembrance remains with you, like a tune from Mozart, which he seems to have caught out of Heaven, and

which rings sweet harmony in your ears for ever after! It's a benefit for all after life! You have but to shut your eyes, and think, and recall it, and the delightful vision comes smiling back, to your order! – the divine air – the delicious little pageant, which nature set before you on this lucky day.

Here is the entry made in the note book on the eventful day: – In the morning steamed into the Bay of Glaucus – landed at Makri[7] – cheerful old desolate village – theatre by the beautiful sea-shore – great fertility, oleanders – a palm tree in the midst of the village, spreading out like a sultan's aigrette – sculptured caverns, or tombs, up the mountain – camels over the bridge.

Perhaps it is best for a man of fancy to make his own landscape out of these materials: to group the couched camels under the plane trees; the little crowd of wandering, ragged heathens come down to the calm water, to behold the nearing steamer; to fancy a mountain, in the sides of which some scores of tombs are rudely carved; pillars and porticos, and Doric entablatures. But it is of the little theatre that he must make the most beautiful picture – a charming little place of festival, lying out on the shore, and looking over the sweet bay and the swelling purple islands. No theatre-goer ever looked out on a fairer scene. It encourages poetry, idleness, delicious sensual reverie. O, Jones! friend of my heart! would you not like to be a white-robed Greek, lolling languidly on the cool benches here, and pouring compliments (in the Ionic dialect) into the rosy ears of Neæra? Instead of Jones, your name should be Ionides; instead of a silk hat, you should wear a chaplet of roses in your hair: you would not listen to the choruses they were singing on the stage, for the voice of the fair one would be whispering a rendezvous for the *mesonuktiais horais*, and my Ionides would have no ear for aught beside. Yonder, in the mountain, they would carve a Doric cave temple, to receive your urn when all was done; and you would be accompanied thither by a dirge of the surviving Ionidæ. The caves of the dead are empty now, however, and their place knows them not any more among the festal haunts of the living. But, by way of supplying the choric melodies, sung here in old time, one of our companions mounted on the scene and spouted,

'My name is Norval.'

On the same day we lay to for a while at another ruined theatre, that of Antiphilos.[8] The Oxford men, fresh with recollections of the little-go, bounded away up the hill on which it lies to the ruin, measured the steps of the theatre, and calculated the width of the scene; while others, less active, watched them with telescopes from the ship's sides, as they plunged in and out of the stones and hollows.

Two days after, the scene was quite changed. We were out of sight of the classical country, and lay in St George's Bay,[9] behind a huge mountain, upon which St George fought the dragon, and rescued the lovely lady Sabra, the King of Babylon's daughter. The Turkish fleet was lying about us, commanded by that Halil Paçha, whose two children the two last Sultans murdered. The crimson flag, with the star and crescent, floated at the stern of his ship. Our diplomatist put on his uniform and cordons, and paid His Excellency a visit. He spoke in rapture, when he returned, of the beauty and order of the ship, and the urbanity of the infidel admiral. He sent us bottles of ancient Cyprus wine to drink: and the captain of Her Majesty's Ship, *Trump*,[10] alongside which we were lying, confirmed that good opinion of the Capitan Pasha, which the reception of the above present led us to entertain, by relating many instances of his friendliness and hospitalities. Captain G. —— said, the Turkish ships were as well manned, as well kept, and as well manoeuvred, as any vessels in any service; and intimated a desire to command a Turkish seventy-four, and a perfect willingness to fight her against a French ship of the same size. But I heartily trust he will neither embrace the Mahometan opinions, nor be called upon to engage any seventy-four whatever. If he do, let us hope he will have his own men to fight with. If the crew of the *Trump* were all like the crew of the captain's boat, they need fear no two hundred and fifty men out of any country, with any Joinville at their head. We were carried on shore by this boat. For two years, during which the *Trump* had been lying off

Beyrout, none of the men but these eight had ever set foot on shore. Mustn't it be a happy life? We were landed at the busy quay of Beyrout, flanked by the castle that the fighting old commodore half battered down.

Along the Beyrout quays civilization flourishes under the flags of the consul, which are streaming out over the yellow buildings in the clear air. Hither she brings from England her produce of marine stores and woollens, her crockeries, her portable soups, and her bitter ale. Hither she has brought politeness, and the last modes from Paris.

They were exhibited in the person of a pretty lady, superintending the great French store, and who seeing a stranger sketching on the quay, sent forward a man with a chair, to accommodate that artist, and greeted him with a bow and a smile, such as only can be found in France. Then she fell to talking with a young French officer, with a beard, who was greatly smitten with her. They were making love just as they do on the Boulevard. An Arab porter left his bales, and the camel he was unloading, to come and look at the sketch. Two stumpy, flat-faced Turkish soldiers, in red caps and white undresses, peered over the paper. A noble little Lebanese girl, with a deep yellow face, and curly dun-coloured hair, and a blue tattooed chin, and for all clothing, a little ragged shift of blue cloth, stood by like a little statue, holding her urn, and stared with wondering brown eyes. How

of an amethyst colour. The French officer and the lady went on chattering quite happily about love, the last new bonnet, or the battle of Isly, or the *Juif Errant*; how neatly her gown and sleeves fitted her pretty little person! We had not seen a woman for a month, except honest Mrs Flanigan, the stewardess, and the ladies of our party, and the tips of the noses of the Constantinople beauties, as they passed by leering from their *yakmacs*, waddling and plapping in their odious yellow papooses.

And this day is to be marked with a second white stone; for having giving the lucky writer of the present, occasion to behold a second beauty. This was a native Syrian damsel, who bore the sweet name of Mariam. So it was, she stood as two of us (I mention the number for fear of scandal) took her picture.

Beirut, watercolour by Max Schmidt, 1843-44.
Private Collection.

'Mariam', a Syrian Girl, with her Negro cook, wood engraving by William Thackeray.

magnificently blue the water was! – how bright the flags and buildings as they shone above it, and the lines of the rigging tossing in the bay! The white crests of the blue waves jumped and sparkled like quick-silver; the shadows were as broad and cool as the lights were brilliant and rosy; the battered old towers of the commodore looked quite cheerful in the delicious atmosphere; and the mountains beyond were

So it was, that the good-natured black cook looked behind her young mistress, with a benevolent grin, that only the admirable Leslie could paint.[11]

Mariam was the sister of the young guide, whom we hired to show us through the town; and to let us be cheated in the purchase of gilt scarfs and handkerchiefs, which strangers think proper to buy. And before the above authentic

[90]

Beirut from the Sea, watercolour by Amadeo Preziosi, 1862. 'Along the Beyrout quays civilisation flourishes under the flags of the consul, which are streaming out over the yellow buildings in the clear air.' Thackeray and many other western travellers responded enthusiastically to Beirut, which was very different to some of the wilder parts of the Ottoman Empire that they had experienced.

Connoisseur Gallery. *Photograph*: Christie's.

Druse Women, pen and ink drawing by an unknown English artist, 1820-30. The distinctive horned head-dress, or *tantour*, worn by the local women, attracted the curiosity of many visitors to Lebanon.
Victoria and Albert Museum (Searight Collection).

drawing could be made, many were the stratagems the wily artists were obliged to employ, to subdue the shyness of the little Mariam. In the first place, she would stand behind the door (from which in the darkness her beautiful black eyes gleamed out like penny tapers); nor could the entreaties of her brother and mamma, bring her from that hiding place. In order to conciliate the latter, we began by making a picture of her too – that is, not of her, who was an enormous old fat woman in yellow, quivering all over with strings of pearls, and necklaces of sequins, and other ornaments, the which descended from her neck, and down her ample stomach – we did not depict that big old woman, who would have been frightened at an accurate representation of her own enormity; but an ideal being, all grace and beauty, dressed in her costume, and still simpering before me in my sketch-book, like a lady in a book of fashions.

This portrait was shown to the old woman, who handed it over to the black cook, who, grinning, carried it to little Mariam – and the result is, that the young creature stepped forward, and submitted; and has come over to Europe, as you see.

A very snug and happy family did this of Mariam's appear to be. If you could judge by all the laughter and giggling, by the splendour of the women's attire, by the neatness of the little house, prettily decorated with arabesque paintings, neat mats, and gay carpets; they were a family well to do in the Beyrout world, and lived with as much comfort as any Europeans. They had one book; and, on the wall of the principal apartment, a black picture of the Virgin, whose name is borne by pretty Mariam.

The camels and the soldiers, the bazaars and khans, the fountains and awnings, which chequer, with such delightful variety of light and shade, the alleys and markets of an oriental town, are to be seen in Beyrout in perfection; and an artist might here employ himself for months with advantage and pleasure. A new costume was here added to the motley and picturesque assembly of dresses. This was the dress of the blue-veiled women from the Lebanon,[12] stalking solemnly through the markets, with huge horns, near a yard high, on their foreheads. For thousands of years since the time the Hebrew prophets wrote, these horns have so been exalted in the Lebanon.

At night Captain Lewis gave a splendid ball and supper to the *Trump*. We had the *Trump*'s band to perform the music; and a grand sight it was to see the captain himself enthusiastically leading on the drum. Blue lights and rockets were burned from the yards of our ship; which festive signals were answered presently from the *Trump*, and from another English vessel in the harbour.

They must have struck the Capitan Pasha with wonder, for he sent his secretary on board of us to inquire what the fireworks meant. And the worthy Turk had scarcely put his foot on the deck, when he found himself seized round the waist by one of the *Trump*'s officers, and whirling round the deck in a waltz, to his own amazement, and the huge delight of the company. His face of wonder and gravity, as he went on twirling, could not have been exceeded by that of a dancing dervish at Scutari; and the manner in which he managed to *enjamber* the waltz excited universal applause.

I forget whether he accommodated himself to European ways so much further as to drink champagne at supper time; to say that he did would be telling tales out of school, and might interfere with the future advancement of that jolly dancing Turk.

We made acquaintance with another of the Sultan's subjects, who, I fear, will have occasion to doubt of the honour of the English nation, after the foul treachery with which he was treated.

Among the occupiers of the little bazaar watchboxes, venders of embroidered handkerchiefs and other articles of showy Eastern haberdashery, was a good-looking, neat young fellow, who spoke English very fluently, and was particularly attentive to all the passengers on board our ship. This gentleman was not only a pocket-handkerchief merchant in the bazaar, but earned a further livelihood by letting out mules and donkeys; and he kept a small lodging house, or inn, for travellers, as we were informed.

No wonder he spoke good English, and was exceedingly polite and well bred; for the worthy man had passed some time in England, and in the best society too. That humble haberdasher at Beyrout had been a lion here, at the very best houses of the great people, and had actually made his appearance at Windsor, where he was received as a Syrian Prince, and treated with great hospitality by royalty itself.

I don't know what waggish propensity moved one of the officers of the *Trump* to say that there was an equerry of His Royal Highness the Prince on board, and to point me out as the dignified personage in question. So the Syrian Prince was introduced to the royal equerry, and a great many compliments passed between us. I even had the audacity to state, that on my very last interview with my royal master, His Royal Highness had said, 'Colonel Titmarsh, when you go to Beyrout, you will make special inquiries regarding my interesting friend Cogia Hassan.'

Poor Cogia Hassan (I forget whether that was his name, but it is as good as another) was overpowered with this royal message; and we had an intimate conversation together, at which the waggish officer of the *Trump* assisted with the greatest glee.

But see the consequences of deceit! The next day, as we were getting under way, who should come on board but my friend the Syrian Prince, most eager for a last interview with the Windsor equerry; and he begged me to carry his protestations of unalterable fidelity to the gracious consort of her Majesty. Nor was this all. Cogia Hassan actually pro- duced a great box of sweetmeats, of which he begged excellency to accept, and a little figure of a doll, dresse the costume of Lebanon. Then the punishment of imp ture began to be felt severely by me. How to accep poor devil's sweetmeats? How to refuse them? And a know that one fib leads to another, so I was obliged to port the first falsehood by another; and putting o dignified air – 'Cogia Hassan,' says I, 'I am surprised y don't know the habits of the British court better, and a not aware that our gracious master solemnly forbids h servants to accept any sort of *backsheesh* upon our travels.'

So Prince Cogia Hassan went over the side with his chest of sweetmeats, but insisted on leaving the doll, which may be worth twopence-halfpenny; of which, and of the cos- tume of the women of Lebanon, the following is an accurate likeness.

Chapter XI: A DAY AND NIGHT IN SYRIA

WHEN, after being for five whole weeks at sea, with a general belief that at the end of a few days the marine malady leaves you for good, you find that a brisk wind and a heavy rolling swell create exactly the same inward effects which they occasioned at the very commencement of the voyage – you begin to fancy that you are unfairly dealt with: and I, for my part, had thought of complaining to the company of this atrocious violation of the rules of their prospectus; but we were perpetually coming to anchor in various ports, at which intervals of peace and good humour were restored to us.

On the 3rd of October our cable rushed with a huge rattle into the blue sea before Jaffa, at a distance of considerably more than a mile of the town, which lay before us very clear, with the flags of the consuls flaring in the bright sky,[1] and making a cheerful and hospitable show. The houses a great heap of sun-baked stones, surmounted here and there by minarets and countless little white-washed domes; a few date trees spread out their fan-like heads over these dull looking buildings; long sands stretched away on either side, with low purple hills behind them; we could see specks of camels crawling over these yellow plains; and those persons who were about to land, had the leisure to behold the sea-spray flashing over the sands, and over a heap of black rocks which lie before the entry to the town. The swell is very great, the passage between the rocks narrow, and the danger sometimes considerable. So the guide began to entertain the ladies and other passengers in the huge country boat which brought us from the steamer, with an agreeable story of a lieutenant and eight seamen of one of Her Majesty's ships, who were upset, dashed to pieces, and drowned upon these rocks, through which two men and two boys, with a very moderate portion of clothing, each standing and pulling half an oar – there were but two oars between them – and another by way of rudder – were endeavouring to guide us.

When the danger of the rocks and surf was passed, came another danger of the hideous brutes in brown skins and the briefest shirts, who came towards the boat, straddling through the water with outstretched arms, grinning and yelling their Arab invitations to mount their shoulders. I think these fellows frightened the ladies still more than the rocks and the surf; but the poor creatures were obliged to submit, and trembling were accommodated somehow upon the mahogany backs of these ruffians, carried through the shallows, and flung up to a ledge before the city gate, where crowds more of dark people were swarming, howling after their fashion. The gentlemen, meanwhile, were having arguments about the eternal *backsheesh* with the roaring Arab boatmen; and I recall with wonder and delight especially, the curses and screams of one small and extremely loud-lunged fellow, who expressed discontent at receiving a five, instead of a six piastre piece. But how is one to know, without possessing the language? Both coins are made of a greasy pewtery sort of tin; and I thought the biggest was the most valuable: but the fellow showed a sense of their value, and a disposition seemingly to cut any man's throat who did not understand it. Men's throats have been cut for a less difference before now.

Being cast upon the ledge, the first care of our gallantry was to look after the ladies, who were scared and astonished by the naked savage brutes, who were shouldering the poor things to and fro; and bearing them through these and a dark archway, we came into a street crammed with donkeys and their packs and drivers, and towering camels with leering eyes looking into the second-floor rooms, and huge splay feet, through which *mesdames et mesdemoiselles* were to be conducted. We made a rush at the first open door, and passed comfortably under the heels of some horses gathered under the arched court, and up a stone staircase, which turned out to be that of the Russian consul's house. His people welcomed us most cordially to his abode, and the

Jaffa, watercolour by David Roberts, 1839. Jaffa, now part of the modern city of Tel-Aviv, was an important port in ancient times. In Thackeray's day, travellers arriving by sea would disembark there on their way to Jerusalem. In the foreground of Roberts's view, a party of Polish Jews in their broad-brimmed hats wait on the seashore. *Photograph:* Spink & Son, Ltd.

ladies and the luggage (objects of our solicitude) were led up many stairs and across several terraces to a most comfortable little room, under a dome of its own, where the representative of Russia sat. Women with brown faces and draggle-tailed coats and turbans, and wondering eyes, and no stays, and blue beads and gold coins hanging round their necks, came to gaze, as they passed, upon the fair neat English women; blowsy black cooks puffing over fires, and the strangest pots and pans on the terraces; children paddling about in long striped robes, interrupted their sports or labours, to come and stare; and the consul, in his cool domed chamber, with a lattice overlooking the sea, with clean mats, and pictures of the Emperor, the Virgin, and St George, received the strangers with smiling courtesies, regaling these with pomegranates and sugar, those with pipes of tobacco, whereof the fragrant tubes were three yards long.

The Russian amenities concluded, we left the ladies still under the comfortable, cool dome of the Russian consulate, and went to see our own representative. The streets of the little town are neither agreeable to horse or foot travellers. Many of the streets are mere flights of rough steps, leading abruptly into private houses; you pass under archways and passages numberless; a steep, dirty labyrinth of stone-vaulted stables and sheds occupy the ground-floor of the habitations; and you pass from flat to flat of the terraces; at various irregular corners of which, little chambers, with little private domes, are erected, and the people live seemingly as much upon the terrace as in the room.

We found the English consul in a queer little arched chamber, with a strange old picture of the king's arms to decorate one side of it: and here the consul, a demure old man, dressed in red flowing robes, with a feeble janissary, bearing a shabby tin-mounted staff, or mace, to denote his office, received such of our nation as came to him for hospitality. He distributed pipes and coffee to all and everyone; he made us a present of his house and all his beds for the night, and went himself to lie quietly on the terrace; and for all this hospitality he declined to receive any reward from us, and said he was but doing his duty in taking us in. This worthy man, I thought, must doubtless be very well paid by our government for making such sacrifices; but it appears, that he does not get one single farthing, and that the greater number of our Levant consuls are paid at a similar rate of easy remuneration. If we have bad consular agents, have we a right to complain? If the worthy gentlemen cheat occasionally, can we reasonably be angry? But in travelling through these countries, English people, who don't take into consideration the miserable poverty and scanty resources of their country, and are apt to brag and be proud of it, have their vanity hurt by seeing the representatives of every nation but their own well and decently maintained, and feel ashamed at sitting down under the shabby protection of our mean consular flag.

The active young men of our party had been on shore long before us, and seized upon all the available horses in the town; but we relied upon a letter from Halil Paçha, enjoining all governors and pachas to help us in all ways: and hearing we were the bearers of this document, the Cadi and Vice Governor of Jaffa came to wait upon the head of our party,[2] declared that it was his delight and honour to set eyes upon us; that he would do everything in the world to serve us; that there were no horses, unluckily, but he would send and get some in three hours; and so left us with a world of grinning bows and many choice compliments, from one side to the other, which came to each filtered through an obsequious interpreter. But hours passed, and the clatter of horses' hoofs was not heard. We had our dinner of eggs and flaps of bread, and the sunset gun fired: we had our pipes and coffee again, and the night fell. Is this man throwing dirt upon us? we began to think. Is he laughing at our beards, and are our mother's graves ill-treated by this smiling, swindling Cadi? We determined to go and seek in his own den this shuffling dispenser of infidel justice. This time we would be no more bamboozled by compliments; but we would use the language of stern expostulation, and, being roused, would let the rascal hear the roar of the indignant British lion: so we rose up in our wrath. The poor consul got a lamp for us with a bit of wax candle, such as I wonder his means could afford; the shabby janissary marched ahead with his tin mace, the two *laquais de place*, that two of our company had hired, stepped forward, each with an old sabre, and we went clattering and stumbling down the streets of the town, in order to seize upon this Cadi in his own divan. I was glad, for my part (though outwardly majestic and indignant in demeanor), that the horses had not come, and that we had a chance of seeing this little, queer glimpse of oriental life, which the magistrate's faithlessness procured for us.

As piety forbids the Turks to eat during the weary daylight hours of the *Ramazan*, they spend their time profitably in sleeping until the welcome sunset, when the town wakens: all the lanterns are lighted up; all the pipes begin to puff, and the narghiles to bubble; all the sour-milk-and-sherbet men begin to yell out the excellence of their wares; all the frying pans in the little, dirty cook-shops begin to friz, and the pots to send forth a steam: and through this dingy, ragged, bustling, beggarly, cheerful scene, we began now to march towards the Bow Street of Jaffa. We bustled through a crowded narrow archway which led to the Cadi's police office, entered the little room, atrociously perfumed with musk, and passing by the rail-board, where the common sort stood, mounted up the stage upon which his worship and friends sat, and squatted down on the divans in stern and silent dignity. His honour ordered us coffee, his countenance evidently showing considerable alarm. A black slave, whose duty seemed to be to prepare this beverage in a side-room with a furnace, prepared for each of us about a teaspoonful of the liquor: his worship's clerk, I presume, a tall Turk of a noble aspect, presented it to us, and having lapped up the little modicum of drink, the British lion began to speak.

All the other travellers (said the lion with perfect reason) have good horses and are gone; the Russians have got horses, the Spaniards have horses, the English have horses, but we, we vizirs in our country, coming with letters of Halil Paçha are laughed at, spit upon! Are Halil Paçha's letters dirt, that you attend to them in this way? Are British lions dogs that you treat them so? – and so on. This speech with many variations was made on our side for a quarter of an hour; and we finally swore, that unless the horses were forthcoming, we would write to Halil Paçha the next morning, and to His Excellency the English Minister at the Sublime Porte. Then you should have heard the chorus of Turks in reply: a dozen voices rose up from the divan, shouting, screaming, ejaculating, expectorating (the Arabic spoken language seems to require a great employment of the two latter oratorial methods), and uttering what the meek interpreter did not translate to us, but what I dare say were by no means complimentary phrases towards us and our nation. Finally, the palaver concluded by the Cadi declaring that by the will of Heaven horses should be forthcoming at three o'clock in the morning; and that if not, why then we might write to Halil Paçha.

This posed us, and we rose up and haughtily took leave. I should like to know that fellow's real opinion of us lions very much: and especially to have had the translation of the speeches of a huge-breeched turbaned roaring infidel, who looked and spoke as if he would have liked to fling us all into the sea, which was hoarsely murmuring under our windows an accompaniment to the concert within.

We then marched through the bazaars, that were lofty and grim, and pretty full of people. In a desolate broken building, some hundreds of children were playing and singing; in many corners sat parties over their water-pipes, one of whom every now and then would begin twanging out a most queer chant; others there were playing at casino[3] – a crowd squatted around the squalling gamblers, and talking and looking on with eager interest. In one place of the bazaar we found a hundred people at least listening to a storyteller, who delivered his tale with excellent action, voice and volubility: in another they were playing a sort of thimblerig with coffee cups,[4] all intent upon the game, and the player himself very wild lest one of our party, who had discovered where the pea lay, should tell the company. The devotion and energy with which all these pastimes were pursued, struck me as much as anything. These people have been playing thimblerig and casino; that storyteller has been shouting his tale of Antar,[5] for forty years; and they are just as happy with this amusement now as when first they tried it. Is there no *ennui* in the Eastern countries, and are blue devils not allowed to go abroad there?

From the bazaars we went to see the house of Mustapha, said to be the best house and the greatest man of Jaffa. But the great man had absconded suddenly, and had fled into Egypt. The Sultan had made a demand upon him for sixteen thousand purses, £80,000 – Mustapha retired – the Sultan pounced down upon his house, and his goods, his horses and his mules. His harem was desolate. Mr Milnes could have written six affecting poems, had he been with us, on the dark loneliness of that violated sanctuary. We passed from hall to hall, terrace to terrace – a few fellows were slumbering on the naked floors, and scarce turned as we went by them.

Bazaar at Jaffa, after William Bartlett. Merchants sell their wares beside a public fountain in the courtyard of a khan. The etching is among those illustrating *Syria, the Holy Land, Asia Minor, &c*, published by Fisher in 1836-38, and one of the most popular topographical books of its day.
Victoria and Albert Museum (Searight Collection).

We entered Mustapha's particular divan – there was the raised floor, but no bearded friends squatting away the night of *Ramazan*; there was the little coffee furnace, but where was the slave and the coffee and the glowing embers of the pipes? Mustapha's favourite passages from the Koran were still painted up on the walls, but nobody was the wiser for them. We walked over a sleeping negro, and opened the windows which looked into his gardens. The horses and donkeys, the camels and mules were picketed there below, but where is the said Mustapha? From the frying pan of the Porte, has he not fallen into the fire of Mehemet Ali? And which is best, to broil or to fry? If it be but to read the *Arabian Nights* again on getting home, it is good to have made this little voyage and seen these strange places and faces.

Then we went out through the arched lowering gateway of the town into the plain beyond, and that was another famous and brilliant scene of the *Arabian Nights*. The heaven shone with a marvellous brilliancy – the plain disappeared far in the haze – the towers and battlements of the town rose black against the sky – old outlandish trees rose up here and there- -clumps of camels were couched in the rare herbage – dogs were baying about – groups of men lay sleeping under their *haicks* round about[6] – round about the tall gates many lights were twinkling – and they brought us water-pipes and sherbet – and we wondered to think that London was only three weeks off.

Then came the night at the consul's. The poor demure old gentleman brought out his mattresses; and the ladies sleeping round on the divans, we lay down quite happy; and I for my part intended to make as delightful dreams as Alnaschar; but- lo, the delicate mosquito sounded his horn: the active flea jumped up, and came to feast on Christian flesh (the Eastern flea bites more bitterly than the most savage bug in Christendom), and the bug – oh, the accursed! Why was he made? What duty has that infamous ruffian to perform in the world, save to make people wretched? Only Bulwer in his most pathetic style could describe the miseries of that night – the moaning, the groaning, the cursing, the tumbling, the blistering, the infamous despair and degradation! I heard all the cocks in Jaffa crow; the children crying, and the mothers hushing them; the donkeys braying fitfully in the moonlight; at last, I heard the clatter of hoofs below, and the hailing of men. It was three o'clock, the horses were actually come; nay, there were camels likewise; asses and mules, pack-saddles and drivers, all bustling together under the moonlight in the cheerful street – and the first night in Syria was over.

Chapter XII: FROM JAFFA TO JERUSALEM

I took an hour or more to get our little caravan into marching order, to accommodate all the packs to the horses, the horses to the riders; to see the ladies comfortably placed in their litter, with a sleek and large black mule fore and aft, a groom to each mule, and a tall and exceedingly good-natured and mahogany-coloured infidel to walk by the side of the carriage, to balance it as it swayed to and fro, and to offer his back as a step to the inmates whenever they were minded to ascend or alight. These three fellows, fasting through the *Ramazan*, and over as rough a road, for the greater part, as ever shook mortal bones, performed their fourteen hours' walk of near forty miles with the most admirable courage, alacrity, and good humour. They once or twice drank water on the march, and so far infringed the rule; but they refused all bread or edible refreshment offered to them, and tugged on with an energy that the best camel, and I am sure the best Christian, might envy. What a lesson of good-humoured endurance it was to certain Pall Mall Sardanapaluses,[1] who grumble if club sofa cushions are not soft enough!

If I could write sonnets at leisure, I would like to chronicle in fourteen lines my sensations on finding myself on a high Turkish saddle, with a pair of fire-shovel stirrups and worsted reins, red padded saddle cloth, and innumerable tags, fringes, glass beads, ends of rope, to decorate the harness of the horse, the gallant steed on which I was about to gallop into Syrian life. What a figure we cut in the moonlight, and how they would have stared in the Strand! Aye, or in Leicestershire, where I warrant such a horse and rider are not often visible! The shovel stirrups are deucedly short; the clumsy leathers cut the shins of some equestrians abominably; you sit over your horse as it were on a tower, from which the descent would be very easy, but for the big peak of the saddle. A good way for the inexperienced is to put a stick or umbrella across the saddle peak again, so that it is next to impossible to go over your horse's neck. I found this a vast

comfort in going down the hills, and recommend it conscientiously to other dear simple brethren of the city.

Peaceful men, we did not ornament our girdles with pistols, *yataghans*,[2] etc., such as some pilgrims appeared to bristle all over with; and as a lesson to such rash people, a story may be told which was narrated to us at Jerusalem, and carries a wholesome moral. The Honourable Hoggin Armer,[3] who was lately travelling in the East, wore about his stomach two brace of pistols, of such exquisite finish and make, that a Sheikh, in the Jericho country, robbed him merely for the sake of the pistols. I don't know whether he has told the story to his friends at home.

Another story about Sheikhs may here be told apropos. That celebrated Irish Peer, Lord Oldgent,[3] (who was distinguished in the Buckinghamshire Dragoons), having paid a sort of blackmail to the Sheikh of Jericho country, was suddenly set upon by another Sheikh, who claimed to be the real Jericho governor; and these twins quarrelled over the body of Lord Oldgent, as the widows for the innocent baby before Solomon. There was enough for both – but these digressions are interminable.

The party got underway at near four o'clock: the ladies in the litter, the French *femme de chambre* manfully caracoling on a grey horse; the cavaliers, like your humble servant, on their high saddles; the domestics, flunkeys, guides, and grooms, on all sorts of animals – some fourteen in all. Add to these, two most grave and stately Arabs in white beards, white turbans, white *haicks* and raiments; sabres curling round their military thighs, and immense long guns at their backs. More venerable warriors I never saw; they went by the side of the litter soberly prancing. When we emerged from the steep clattering streets of the city into the grey plains, lighted by the moon and starlight, these militaries rode onward, leading the way through the huge avenues of strange diabolical looking prickly pears (plants that look as

Arab Muleteer, watercolour by Sir David Wilkie, 1841. Three years before Thackeray, Wilkie visited the Near East with the intention of finding authentic subjects for biblical paintings. His muleteer, observed on the same journey between Jaffa and Jerusalem, has therefore been invested with the gravitas suitable for his purpose, whereas Thackeray's description of the mule drivers that accompanied his party is characteristically down-to-earth.
National Gallery of Scotland, Edinburgh.

if they had grown in Tartarus), by which the first mile or two of route from the city is bounded; and as the dawn arose before us, exhibiting first a streak of grey, then of green, then of red in the sky, it was fine to see these martial figures defined against the rising light. The sight of that little cavalcade and of the nature around it, will always remain with me, I think, as one of the freshest and most delightful sensations I have enjoyed since the day I first saw Calais pier. It was full day when they gave their horses a drink at a large pretty oriental fountain, and then presently we entered the open plain – the famous plain of Sharon[4] – so fruitful in roses once, now hardly cultivated, but always beautiful and noble.

Here presently, in the distance, we saw another cavalcade pricking over the plain. Our two white warriors spread to the right and left, and galloped to reconnoitre. We too, put our steeds to the canter, and handling our umbrellas as Richard did his lance against Saladin,[5] went undaunted to challenge this caravan. The fact is, we could distinguish that it was formed of the party of our pious friends the Poles, and we hailed them with cheerful shouting, and presently the two caravans joined company, and scoured the plain at the rate of near four miles per hour. The horse-master, a courier of this company, rode three miles for our one. He was a broken-nosed Arab, with pistols, a sabre, a *fusée*, a yellow Damascus cloth flapping over his head, and his nose ornamented with diachylon.[6] He rode a hog-necked grey Arab, bristling over with harness, and jumped, and whirled, and reared, and halted, to the admiration of all.

Scarce had the diachylonian Arab finished his evolutions, when, lo! yet another cloud of dust was seen, and another party of armed and glittering horsemen appeared. They, too, were led by an Arab, who was followed by two Janissaries, with silver maces shining in the sun. 'Twas the party of the new American Consul General of Syria and Jerusalem,[7] hastening to that city, with the inferior consuls of Ramleh and Jaffa to escort him. He expects to see the millenium in three years, and has accepted the office of consul at Jerusalem, so as to be on the spot in readiness.

When the Diachylon Arab saw the American Arab, he straightway galloped his steed towards him, took his pipe, which he delivered at his adversary in guise of a *jereed*,[8] and galloped round and round, and in and out, and there and back again, as in a play of war. The American replied in a

similar playful ferocity – the two warriors made a little tournament for us there on the plains before Jaffa, in the which Diachylon, being a little worsted, challenged his adversary to a race, and fled away on his grey, the American following on his bay. Here poor sticking-plaster was again worsted, the Yankee contemptuously riding round him, and then declining further exercise.

What more could mortal man want? A troop of knights and paladins could have done no more. In no page of Walter Scott have I read a scene more fair and sparkling. The sober warriors of our escort did not join in the gambols of the young men. There they rode soberly, in their white turbans, by their ladies' litter, their long guns rising up behind them.

There was no lack of company along the road: donkeys numberless, camels by twos and threes; now a mule driver, trudging along the road, chanting a most queer melody; now a lady, in white veil, black mask, and yellow papooshes, bestriding her ass, and followed by her husband, – met us on the way; and most people gave a salutation. Presently we saw Ramleh, in a smoking mist, on the plain before us, flanked to the right by a tall lonely tower, that might have held the bells of some *moustier* of Caen or Evreux. As we entered, about three hours and a half after starting, among the white domes and stone houses of the little town, we passed the place of tombs. Two women were sitting on one of them, – the one bending her head towards the stone, and rocking to and fro, and moaning out a very sweet, pitiful lamentation.

The American Consul invited us to breakfast at the house of his subaltern, the hospitable one-eyed Armenian, who represents the United States at Jaffa. The stars and stripes were flaunting over his terraces, to which we ascended, leaving our horses to the care of a multitude of roaring, ragged Arabs beneath, who took charge of and fed the animals, though I can't say in the least why; but, in the same way as getting off my horse on entering Jerusalem, I gave the rein into the hand of the first person near me, and have never heard of the worthy brute since. At the American Consul's we were served first with rice soup in *pishpash*, flavoured with cinnamon and spice; then with boiled mutton, then with stewed ditto and tomatoes; then with fowls swimming in grease; then with brown ragoûts belaboured with onions;

then with a smoking pilaff of rice: several of which dishes I can pronounce to be of excellent material and flavour. When the gentry had concluded this repast it was handed to a side table, where the commonalty speedily discussed it. We left them licking their fingers as we hastened away upon the second part of the ride.

And as we quitted Ramleh, the scenery lost that sweet and peaceful look which characterises the pretty plain we had traversed; and the sun, too, rising in the heaven, dissipated all those fresh, beautiful tints in which God's world is clothed of early morning, and which city people have so sel-

dom the chance of beholding. The plain over which we rode looked yellow and gloomy; the cultivation little or none; the land across the roadside fringed, for the most part, with straggling wild carrot plants; a patch of green only here and there. We passed several herds of lean, small, well-conditioned cattle; many flocks of black goats, tended now and then by a ragged negro shepherd, his long gun slung over his back, his hand over his eyes to shade them as he stared at our little cavalcade. Most of the half naked country folks we met, had this dismal appendage to Eastern rustic life; and the weapon could hardly be one of mere defence, for,

Ramla, lithograph after David Roberts. On the journey between Jaffa and Jerusalem, travellers often stopped at Ramlah. Roberts's view of the town, with classical remains in the foreground, is more appealing than the bleak landscape that Thackeray describes. Victoria and Albert Museum (Searight Collection).

beyond the faded skull cap, or tattered coat of blue or dirty white, the brawny, brown-chested, solemn looking fellows had nothing seemingly to guard. As before, there was no lack of travellers on the road: more donkeys trotted by, looking sleek and strong; camels singly and by pairs, laden with a little humble ragged merchandise, on their way between the two towns. About noon we halted eagerly at a short distance from an Arab village and well, where all were glad of a drink of fresh water. A village of beavers, or a colony of ants, make habitations not unlike these dismal huts piled together on the plain here. There were no single huts along the whole line of road; poor and wretched as they are, the *fellahs*[9] huddle all together for protection from the other thieves, their neighbours. The government (which we restored to them) has no power to protect them, and is only strong enough to rob them. The women with their long blue gowns and ragged veils, came to and fro with pitchers on their heads. Rebecca had such an one when she brought drink to the lieutenant of Abraham. The boys came staring round, bawling after us with their fathers for the inevitable *backsheesh*. The village dogs barked round the flocks, as they were driven to water or pasture.

We saw a gloomy, not very lofty-looking ridge of hills in front of us; the highest of which the guide pointing out to us, told us that from it we should see Jerusalem. It looked very near, and we all set up a trot of enthusiasm to get into this hill country.

But that burst of enthusiasm (it may have carried us nearly a quarter of a mile in three minutes) was soon destined to be checked by the disagreeable nature of the country we had to traverse. Before we got to the real mountain district, we were in a manner prepared for it, by the mounting and descent of several lonely outlying hills, up and down which our rough stony track wound. Then we entered the hill district, and our path lay through the clattering bed of an ancient stream, whose brawling waters have rolled away into the past, along with the fierce and turbulent race who once inhabited these savage hills. There may have been cultivation here two thousand years ago. The mountains, or huge stony mounds environing this rough path, have level ridges all the way up to their summits; on these parallel ledges there is still some verdure and soil: when water flowed here and the country was thronged with that extraordinary population, which, according to the Sacred Histories, was crowded into the region, these mountain steps may have been gardens and vineyards, such as we see now thriving along the hills of the Rhine. Now the district is quite deserted, and you ride among what seem to be so many petrified waterfalls. We saw no animals moving among the stony brakes; scarcely even a dozen little birds in the whole course of the ride. The sparrows are all at Jerusalem, among the house tops, where there ceaseless chirping and twittering forms the most cheerful sound of the place.

The company of Poles, the company of Oxford men, and the little American army, travelled too quick for our caravan, which was made to follow the slow progress of the ladies' litter, and we had to make the journey through the mountains in a very small number. Not one of our party had a single weapon more dreadful than an umbrella; and a couple of Arabs, wickedly inclined, might have brought us all to the halt, and rifled every carpet bag and pocket belonging to us. Nor can I say that we journeyed without certain qualms of fear. When swarthy fellows, with girdles full of pistols and *yataghans*, passed us without unslinging their long guns; when scowling camel-riders, with awful long bending lances, decorated with tufts of rags, or savage plumes of scarlet feathers, went by without molestation, I think we were rather glad that they did not stop and parley; for after all, a British lion with an umbrella is no match for an Arab with his infernal long gun. What, too, would have become of our women? So we tried to think that it was entirely out of anxiety for them that we were inclined to push on.

There is a shady resting-place and village in the midst of the mountain district where the travellers are accustomed to halt for an hour's repose and refreshment; and the other caravans were just quitting this spot, having enjoyed its cool shades and waters when we came up. Should we stop? Regard for the ladies (of course no other earthly consideration) made us say, 'No!' What admirable self-denial and chivalrous devotion! So our poor devils of mules and horses got no rest and no water, our panting litter-men no breathing time, and we staggered desperately after the procession ahead of us. It wound up the mountain in front of us: the Poles with their guns and attendants, the American with his janissaries; fifty or sixty all riding slowly like the procession in *Bluebeard*.

But alas, they headed us very soon; when we got up the weary hill they were all out of sight; perhaps thoughts of Fleet Street did cross the minds of some of us then, and a vague desire to see a few policemen. The district now seemed peopled, and with an ugly race. Savage personages peered at us out of huts, and grim holes in the rocks. The mules began to loiter most abominably – water the muleteers must have – and, behold, we came to a pleasant looking village of trees standing on a hill; children were shaking figs from the trees – women were going about – before us was the mosque of a holy man – the village, looking like a collection of little forts, rose up on the hill to our right, with a long view of the fields and gardens stretching from it, and camels arriving with their burdens. Here we must stop; Paolo the chief servant knew the Sheikh of the village – he very good man – give him water and supper – water very good here – in fact we began to think of the propriety of halting here for the night, and making our entry into Jerusalem on the next day.

A man on a handsome horse dressed in red came prancing up to us, looking hard at the ladies in the litter, and passed away. Then two others sauntered up, one handsome, and dressed in red too, and he stared into the litter without ceremony, began to play with a little dog that lay there, asked if we were Inglees, and was answered by me in the affirmative. Paolo had brought the water, the most delicious draught in the world. The gentlefolks had had some, the poor muleteers were longing for it. The French maid, the courageous Victoire (never since the days of Joan of Arc has there surely been a more gallant and virtuous female of France) refused the drink; when suddenly a servant of the party scampers up to his master and says: 'Abou Gosh says the ladies must get out and show themselves to the women of the village.'

It was Abou Gosh himself, the redoubted robber Sheikh about whom we had been laughing and crying 'Wolf' all day. Never was seen such a skurry – 'March!' was the instant order given. When Victoire heard who it was and the message, you should have seen how she changed countenance; trembling for her virtue in the ferocious clutches of a Gosh: '*Un verre d'eau pour l'amour de Dieu!*' gasped she, and was ready to faint on her saddle. '*Ne buvez plus, Victoire!*' screamed a little fellow of our party. 'Push on, push on!' cried one

and all. 'What's the matter!' exclaimed the ladies in the litter, as they saw themselves suddenly jogging on again. But we took care not to tell them what had been the designs of the redoubtable Abou Gosh. Away then we went – Victoire was saved – and her mistresses rescued from dangers they knew not of, until they were a long way out of the village.

Did he intend insult or good will? Did Victoire escape the odious chance of becoming Madame Abou Gosh? Or did the mountain chief simply propose to be hospitable after his fashion? I think the latter was his desire; if the former had been his wish, a half a dozen of his long guns could have been up with us in a minute, and had all our party at their mercy. But now, for the sake of the mere excitement, the incident was, I am sorry to say, rather a pleasant one than otherwise; especially for a traveller, who is in the happy condition of being able to sing before robbers, as is the case with the writer of the present.

A little way out of the land of Goshen we came upon a long stretch of gardens and vineyards, slanting towards the setting sun, which illuminated numberless golden clusters of the most delicious grapes, of which we stopped and partook. Such grapes were never before tasted; water so fresh as that which a countryman fetched for us from a well, never sluiced parched throats before. It was the ride, the sun, and above all Abou Gosh, who made that refreshment so sweet, and hereby I offer him my best thanks. Presently in the midst of a most diabolical ravine, down which our horses went sliding, we heard the evening gun; it was fired from Jerusalem. The twilight is brief in this country, and in a few minutes the landscape was grey round about us, and the sky lighted up by a hundred thousand stars, which made the night beautiful.

Under this superb canopy we rode for a couple of hours to our journey's end. The mountains round about us dark, lonely, and sad; the landscape as we saw it at night (it is not more cheerful in the day time), the most solemn and forlorn I have ever seen. The feelings of almost terror, with which riding through the night we approached this awful place, the centre of the world's past and future history, have no need to be noted down here. The recollection of those sensations must remain with a man as long as his memory lasts; and he should think of them as often, perhaps, as he should talk of them little.

THE ladies of our party found excellent quarters in readiness for them at the Greek convent in the city; where airy rooms, and plentiful meals, and wines and sweetmeats delicate and abundant, were provided to cheer them after the fatigues of their journey. I don't know whether the worthy fathers of the convent share in the good things which they lavish on their guests; but they look as if they do. Those whom we saw bore every sign of easy conscience and good living; there were a pair of strong, rosy, greasy, lazy lay-brothers, dawdling in the sun on the convent terrace, or peering over the parapet into the street below, whose looks gave one a notion of anything but asceticism.

In the principal room of the stranger's house (the lay traveller is not admitted to dwell in the sacred interior of the convent), and over the building, the Russian double-headed eagle is displayed. The place is under the patronage of the Emperor Nicholas: an imperial Prince has stayed in these rooms: the Russian Consul performs a great part in the city; and a considerable annual stipend is given by the Emperor towards the maintenance of the great establishment in Jerusalem.[1] The Great Chapel of the Church of the Holy Sepulchre is by far the richest, in point of furniture, of all the places of worship under that roof. We were in Russia, when we came to visit our friends here; under the protection of the Father of the Church and the Imperial Eagle! This butcher and tyrant, who sits on his throne only through the crime of those who held it before him – every step in whose pedigree is stained by some horrible mark of murder, parricide, adultery – this padded and whiskered pontiff – who rules in his jack-boots over a system of spies and soldiers, of deceit, ignorance, dissoluteness, and brute force, such as surely the history of the world never told of before – has a tender interest in the welfare of his spiritual children: in the Eastern Church ranks after divinity, and is worshipped by millions of men. A pious exemplar of Christianity, truly! and of the condition to which its union with politics has brought it! Think of the rank to which he pretends, and gravely believes that he possesses, no doubt! – think of those who assumed the same ultra-sacred character before him! – and then of the Bible and the Founder of the Religion, of which the Emperor assumes to be the chief priest and defender!

We had some Poles of our party; but these poor fellows went to the Latin convent, declining to worship after the Emperor's fashion. The next night after our arrival, two of them passed in the Sepulchre. There we saw them, more than once on subsequent visits, kneeling in the Latin Church before the pictures, or marching solemnly with candles in processions, or lying flat on the stones, or passionately kissing the spots which their traditions have consecrated as the authentic places of the Saviour's sufferings. More honest or more civilized, or from opposition, the Latin fathers have long given up and disowned the disgusting mummery of the Eastern Fire – which lie the Greeks continue annually to tell.

Their travellers' house and convent, though large and commodious, are of a much poorer and shabbier condition than those of the Greeks. Both make believe not to take money; but the traveller is expected to pay in each. The Latin fathers enlarge their means by a little harmless trade in beads and crosses, and mother-of-pearl shells, on which figures of saints are engraved; and which they purchase from the manufacturers, and vend at a small profit. The English, until of late, used to be quartered in these sham inns; but last year two or three Maltese took houses for the reception of tourists, who can now be accommodated with cleanly and comfortable board, at a rate not too heavy for most pockets.

To one of these we went very gladly; giving our horses the bridle at the door, which went off of their own will to their stables, through the dark, inextricable labyrinths of streets, archways, and alleys, which we had threaded after

Facing page. *Jerusalem from the Mount of Olives, Sunrise,* oil painting by Edward Lear, 1859. All western visitors to Jerusalem in the 19th century were deeply conscious of its biblical associations. From this viewpoint, wrote Lear to his patron, could be seen 'the site of the temple & the 2 domes, and it shews the ravine of the valley of Jehoshaphat, over which the whole city looks: and Absalom's pillar (if so be it is his pillar), the village of Siloam, part of Aceldama, & Gethsemane are all included in this landscape . . . added to which there is an unlimited foreground of figs, olives, & pomegranates, not to speak of goats, sheep, & huming beings'.
Photograph: The Fine Art Society.

leaving the main street from the Jaffa gate. There, there was still some life. Numbers of persons were collected at their doors, or smoking before the dingy coffee-houses, where singing and story-telling was going on; but out of this great street everything was silent, and no sign of a light from the windows of the low houses which we passed.

We ascended from a lower floor up to a terrace, on which were several little domed chambers, or pavilions. From this terrace, whence we looked in the morning, a great part of the city spread before us: – white domes upon domes, and terraces of the same character as our own. Here and there, from among these whitewashed mounds round about, a minaret rose, or a rare date tree; but the chief part of the vegetation near was that odious tree the prickly pear, – one huge green wart growing out of another, armed with spikes, as inhospitable as the aloe, without shelter or beauty. To the right the Mosque of Omar rose; the rising sun behind it.[2] Yonder steep tortuous lane before us, flanked by ruined

View of Jerusalem, with the Dome of the Holy Rock, from the terrace of the Latin Convent, watercolour by Carl Werner, 1864. Visitors to Jerusalem in the 19th century often used to stay in one of the various convents within the city. Thackeray describes a similar view over the roof-tops from the upper terrace of a nearby house in which he was accommodated.
Photograph: Christie's.

walls on either side, has borne, time out of mind, the title of Via Dolorosa; and tradition has fixed the spots where the Saviour rested, bearing his cross to Calvary. But of the mountain, rising immediately in front of us, a few grey olive trees speckling the yellow side here and there, there can be no question. That is the Mount of Olives. Bethany lies beyond it. The most sacred eyes that ever looked on this world, have gazed on those ridges: it was there He used to walk and teach. With shame and humility one looks towards the spot where that inexpressible Love and Benevolence lived and breathed; where the great yearning heart of the Saviour interceded for all our race; and whence the bigots and traitors of His day led Him away to kill Him!

That company of Jews whom we had brought with us from Constantinople, and who had cursed every delay on the route, not from impatience to view the Holy City, but from rage at being obliged to purchase dear provisions for their maintenance on shipboard, made what bargains they best could at Jaffa, and journeyed to the Valley of Jehoshaphat at the cheapest rate. We saw the tall form of the old Polish Patriarch, venerable in filth, stalking among the stinking ruins of the Jewish quarter. The sly old rabbi, in the greasy folding hat, who would not pay to shelter his children from the storm off Beyrout, greeted us in the Bazaars; the younger rabbis were furbished up with some smartness. We met them on Sunday at the kind of promenade, by the walls of the Bethlehem gate; they were in company of some red-bearded co-religionists, smartly attired in eastern raiment; but their voice was the voice of the Jews of Berlin, and of course as we passed they were talking about so many *hundert thaler*. You may track one of the people, and be sure to hear mention of that silver calf that they worship.

The English mission has been very unsuccessful with these religionists.[3] I don't believe the Episcopal apparatus – the Chaplains, and the Colleges, and the Beadles – have succeeded in converting a dozen of them; and a sort of martyrdom is in store for the luckless Hebrew at Jerusalem who shall secede from his faith. Their old community spurn them with horror; and I heard of the case of one unfortunate man, whose wife, in spite of her husband's change of creed, being resolved, like a true woman, to cleave to him, was spirited away from him in his absence; was kept in privacy in the city, in spite of all exertions of the mission, of the Consul and the Bishop, and the Chaplains and the Beadles; was passed away from Jerusalem to Beyrout, and thence to Constantinople; and from Constantinople was whisked off into the Russian territories, where she still pines after her husband. May that unhappy convert find consolation away from her. I could not help thinking as my informant, an excellent and accomplished gentleman of the mission, told me the story, that the Jews had done only what the Christians do under the same circumstances. The woman was the daughter of a most learned rabbi, as I gathered. Suppose a daughter of the Bishop of Exeter, or Canterbury, were to marry a man who

turned Jew, would not her Right Reverend Father be justified in taking her out of the power of a person likely to hurl her soul to perdition? These poor converts should surely be sent away to England out of the way of persecution. We could not but feel a pity for them, as they sat there on their benches in the church conspicuous; and thought of the scorn and contumely which attended them without, as they passed in their European dresses and shaven beards, among their grisly, scowling, long-robed countrymen.

As elsewhere in the towns I have seen, the Ghetto of Jerusalem is pre-eminent in filth. The people are gathered round about the dung-gate of the city. Of a Friday you may hear their wailings and lamentations for the lost glories of their city. I think the Valley of Jehoshaphat is the most ghastly sight I have ever seen in the world. From all quarters they come hither to bury their dead. When his time is come yonder hoary old miser, with whom we made our voyage, will lay his carcase to rest here. To do that and to claw together money, has been the purpose of that stra-nge, long life.

We brought with us one of the gentlemen of the mission, a Hebrew convert, the Rev Mr E.—; and lest I should be supposed to speak with disrespect above, of any of the converts

of the Hebrew faith, let me mention this gentleman as the only one whom I had the fortune to meet on terms of intimacy. I never saw a man whose outward conduct was more touching, whose sincerity was more evident, and whose religious feeling seemed more deep, real, and reasonable.

Only a few feet off, the walls of the Anglican Church of Jerusalem, rise up from their foundations, on a picturesque open spot, in front of the Bethlehem Gate. The English Bishop has his church hard by: and near it is the house where the Christians of our denomination assemble and worship.

There seem to be polyglot services here. I saw books of prayer, or Scripture, in Hebrew, Greek, and German: in which latter language Dr Alexander preaches every Sunday.[4] A gentleman, who sat near me at church, used all these books indifferently; reading the first lesson from the Hebrew book, and the second from the Greek. Here we all assembled on the Sunday after our arrival: it was affecting to hear the music and language of our country sounding in this distant place; to have the decent and manly ceremonial of our service; the prayers delivered in that noble language. Even that stout anti-prelatist, the American Consul, who has left his house and fortune in America in order to witness the coming of the Millenium, who believes it to be so near that he has brought a dove with him from his native land (which bird he solemnly informed us was to survive the expected Advent), was affected by the good old words and service. He swayed about and moaned in his place at various passages; during the sermon he gave especial marks of sympathy and approbation. I never heard the service more excellently and impressively read than by the Bishop's Chaplain, Mr Veitch. But it was the music that was most touching I thought, – the sweet old songs of home.

There was a considerable company assembled: near a hundred people I should think. Our party made a large addition to the usual congregation. The Bishop's family is proverbially numerous: the Consul, and the gentlemen of the mission, have wives, and children, and English establishments. These, and the strangers, occupied places down the room, to the right and left of the desk and communion table. The converts, and the members of the college, in rather a scanty number, faced the officiating clergyman; before whom the silver maces of the Janissaries were set up, as they set up the Beadles' maces in England.

The Haram al-Sharif with the Dome of the Rock, watercolour by Max Schmidt, 1844. The Dome of the Rock, seen here on the left, is sacred in both the Muslim and the Jewish faiths. Thackeray and many of his contemporaries incorrectly called it the Mosque of Omar.
Photograph: Christie's.

Entrance to the Tomb of the Kings, watercolour by David Roberts, 1841. One of several ancient sites outside the city walls that attracted the attention of tourists. Roberts's view derives added interest from the colourfully-dressed group of local inhabitants.
Photograph: Leger Galleries.

I made many walks round the city to Olivet and Bethany, to the tombs of the kings, and the fountains sacred in story. These are green and fresh, but all the rest of the landscape seemed to me to be *frightful*. Parched mountains, with a grey bleak olive tree trembling here and there; savage ravines and valleys, paved with tombstones – a landscape unspeakably ghastly and desolate, meet the eye wherever you wander round about the city. The place seems quite adapted to the events which are recorded in the Hebrew histories. It and they, as it seems to me, can never be regarded without terror. Fear and blood, crime and punishment, follow from page to page in frightful succession.

There is not a spot at which you look, but some violent deed has been done there: some massacre has been committed, some victim has been murdered, some idol has been worshipped with bloody and dreadful rites. Not far from hence is the place where the Jewish conqueror fought for the possession of Jerusalem. 'The sun stood still, and hasted not to go down about a whole day;' so that the Jews might have daylight to destroy the Amorites, whose iniquities were full, and whose land they were about to occupy. The fugitive heathen king, and his allies, were discovered in their hiding place, and hanged: 'and the children of Judah smote Jerusalem with the edge of the sword, and set the city on fire; and

[110]

they left none remaining, but utterly destroyed all that breathed.'

I went out at the Zion gate,[5] and looked at the so-called tomb of David. I had been reading all the morning in the Psalms, and his history in Samuel and Kings. 'Bring thou down Shimei's hoar head to the grave with blood' are the last words of the dying monarch as recorded by the history. What they call the tomb, is now a crumbling old mosque; from which Jew and Christian are excluded alike. As I saw it, blazing in the sunshine, with the purple sky behind it, the glare only served to mark the surrounding desolation more clearly. The lonely walls and towers of the city rose hard by. Dreary mountains, and declivities of naked stones, were round about: they are burrowed with holes in which Christian hermits lived and died.

You see one green place far down in the valley: it is called En Rogel. Adonijah feasted there, who was killed by his brother Solomon, for asking for Abishag for wife. The valley of Hinnom skirts the hill: the dismal ravine was a fruitful garden once. Ahaz, and the idolatrous kings, sacrificed to idols under the green trees there, and 'caused their children to pass through the fire'. On the mountain opposite, Solomon, with the thousand women of his harem, worshipped the gods of all their nations, 'Ashtoreh,' and 'Milcom, and Molech, the abomination of the Ammonites'. An enormous charnel-house stands on the hill where the bodies of dead pilgrims used to be thrown; and common belief has fixed upon this spot as the Aceldama, which Judas purchased with the price of his treason. Thus you go on from one gloomy place to another, each seared with its bloody tradition. Yonder is the Temple, and you think of Titus's soldiery storming its flaming porches, and entering the city, in the savage defence of which two million human souls perished. It was on Mount Zion that Godfrey and Tancred had their camp: when the Crusaders entered the mosque, they rode knee deep in the blood of its defenders, and of the women and children who had fled thither for refuge: it was the victory of Joshua over again. Then, after three days of butchery, they purified the desecrated mosque and went to prayer. In the centre of this history of crime, rises up the Great Murder of all.

*   *   *   *   *

I need say no more about this gloomy landscape. After a man has seen it once, he never forgets it – the recollection of it seems to me to follow him like a remorse, as it were to implicate him in the awful deed which was done there. Oh! with what unspeakable shame and terror should one think of that crime, and prostrate himself before the image of that Divine Blessed Sufferer!

Of course the first visit of the traveller is to the famous Church of the Sepulchre.

In the archway, leading from the street to the court and church, there is a little bazaar of Bethlehemites, who must interfere considerably with the commerce of the Latin fathers. These men bawl to you from their stalls, and hold up for your purchase their devotional baubles, – bushels of rosaries and scented beads, and carved mother-of-pearl shells, and rude stone salt-cellars and figures. Now that inns are established, – envoys of these pedlars attend them on the arrival of strangers, squat all day on the terraces before your door, and patiently entreat you to buy of their goods. Some

Tomb of the Virgin, brown ink and wash drawing by William Bartlett, 1842-44. An indefatigable and popular topographical artist, Bartlett travelled widely in search of picturesque material. He wrote and illustrated several books, including *Walks about Jerusalem*, published in 1844, in which this drawing was reproduced.
Victoria and Albert Museum (Searight Collection).

Exterior of the Church of the Holy Sepulchre, watercolour by David Roberts, 1839. 'The first and most interesting object within the walls of the Holy City, the spot to which every pilgrim first directs his steps, is the Holy Sepulchre'. These sentiments, which accompanied the lithograph in Roberts's *Holy Land* (1842), were echoed by Thackeray, but his scepticism of the validity of many of the relics was reinforced by his abhorrence of the practices of their custodians.
Photograph: Colnaghi.

worthies there are who drive a good trade by tattooing pilgrims with the five crosses, the arms of Jerusalem; under which the name of the city is punctured in Hebrew, with the auspicious year of the Hajji's visit. Several of our fellow travellers submitted to this queer operation, and will carry to their grave, this relic of their journey. Some of them had engaged a servant, a man at Beyrout, who had served as a lad on board an English ship in the Mediterranean. Above his tattooage of the five crosses, the fellow had a picture of two hearts united, and the pathetic motto, 'Betsy, my dear.' He had parted with Betsy, my dear, five years before at Malta. He had known a little English there, but had forgotten it. Betsy, my dear, was forgotten too. Only her name remained engraved with a vain simulacrum of constancy on the faithless rogue's skin: on which was now printed another token of equally effectual devotion. The beads and the tattooing,

however, seem essential ceremonies attendant on the Christian pilgrim's visit; for many hundreds of years, doubtless, the palmers have carried off with them these simple reminiscences of the sacred city. That symbol has been engraven upon the arms of how many Princes, Knights, and Crusaders! Don't you see a moral as applicable to them as to the swindling Beyrout horseboy? I have brought you back that cheap and wholesome apologue, in lieu of any of the Bethlehemite shells and beads.

After passing through the porch of the pedlars, you come to the courtyard in front of the noble old towers of the Church of the Sepulchre, with pointed arches and gothic traceries, rude, but rich and picturesque in design. Here crowds are waiting in the sun, until it shall please the Turkish guardians of the church door to open. A swarm of beggars sit here permanently: old tattered hags with long veils, ragged children, blind old bearded beggars, who raise up a chorus of prayers for money, holding out their wooden bowls, or clattering with their sticks on the stones, or pulling your coat skirts, and moaning and whining; yonder sit a group of coal black Coptic pilgrims, with robes and turbans of dark blue, fumbling their perpetual beads. A party of Arab Christians have come up from their tents or villages: the men half naked, looking as if they were beggars, or *banditti*, upon occasion; the women have flung their head-cloths back, and are looking at the strangers under their

tattooed eyebrows. As for the strangers, there is no need to describe *them*; that figure of the Englishman, with his hands in his pockets, has been seen all the world over: staring down the crater of Vesuvius, or into a Hottentot kraal; or at a pyramid, or a Parisian coffee house, or an Eskimo hut, with the same insolent calmness of demeanour. When the gates of the church are open, he elbows in among the first, and flings a few scornful piastres to the Turkish door-keeper; and gazes round easily at the place, in which people of every other nation in the world are in tears, or in rapture, or wonder. He has never seen the place until now, and looks as indifferent as the Turkish guardian who sits in the doorway, and swears at the people as they pour in.

Indeed, I believe, it is impossible for us to comprehend the source and nature of the Roman Catholic devotion. I once went into a church at Rome at the request of a Catholic

friend, who described the interior to be so beautiful and glorious, that he thought (he said) it must be like heaven itself. I found walls hung with cheap stripes of pink and white calico, altars covered with artificial flowers, a number of wax candles, and plenty of gilt paper ornaments. The place seemed to me like a shabby theatre; and here was my friend on his knees at my side, plunged in a rapture of wonder and devotion.

I could get no better impression out of this the most famous church in the world. The deceits are too open and flagrant; the inconsistencies and contrivances too monstrous. It is hard even to sympathize with persons who receive them as genuine; and though (as I know and saw in the case of my friend at Rome) the believer's life may be passed in the purest exercise of faith and charity, it is difficult even to give him credit for honesty, so barefaced seem the impostures which he professes to believe and reverence. It costs one no small effort even to admit the possibility of a Catholic's credulity: to share in his rapture and devotion is still further out of your power; and I could get from this church no other emotions but those of shame and pain.

The legends with which the Greeks and Latins have garnished the spot, have no more sacredness for you than the hideous, unreal, barbaric pictures and ornaments which they have lavished on it. Look at the fervour with which pilgrims kiss and weep over a tawdry Gothic painting, scarcely better fashioned than an idol in a South Sea Morai. The histories, which they are called upon to reverence, are of the same period and order, – savage Gothic caricatures. In either, a saint appears in the costume of the Middle Ages, and is made to accommodate himself to the fashion of the tenth century.

The different churches battle for the possession of the various relics. The Greeks show you the Tomb of Melchisedec, while the Armenians possess the Chapel of the Penitent Thief; the poor Copts (with their little cabin of a chapel) can yet boast of possessing the thicket in which Abraham caught the Ram, which was to serve as the vicar of Isaac; the Latins point out the Pillar to which the Lord was bound. The place of the Invention of the Sacred Cross, the Fissure in the Rock of Golgotha, the Tomb of Adam himself – are all here within a few yards' space. You mount a few steps, and are told it is Calvary upon which you stand.

Beggars at the entrance to the Church of the Holy Sepulchre, wood engraving by William Thackeray.

[113]

Entrance to the Church of the Holy Sepulchre, water-colour by Thomas Allom, c.1838. 'Not far within the entrance, illuminated with lamps and lofty tapers, is the "stone of anointing" on which the body of our Saviour is believed to have been prepared for burial. Numerous worshippers are gathered around it' (J. Carne, *Syria, the Holy Land, Asia Minor,* vol. III, 1838). The traditional sites of the crucifixion, burial and resurrection of Christ were enshrined in the Church of the Holy Sepulchre.
Victoria and Albert Museum (Searight Collection).

Facing page. *Jerusalem from the North,* watercolour by David Roberts, 1839. Roberts visited Jerusalem in April 1839 during his extensive tour of Egypt and the Holy Land. This landscape, with its distant view of the city, is the most romantic of the many sketches and watercolours that he made there.
Photograph: Leger Gallery.

All this in the midst of flaring candles, reeking incense, savage pictures of Scripture story, or portraits of kings who have been benefactors to the various chapels; a din and clatter of strange people, – these weeping, bowing, kissing, – those utterly indifferent; and the priests clad in outlandish robes, snuffling and chanting incomprehensible litanies, robing, dis-robing, lighting up candles or extinguishing them, advancing, retreating, bowing with all sorts of unfamiliar genuflexions. Had it pleased the inventors of the Sepulchre topography to have fixed on fifty more spots of ground, as the places of the events of the sacred story, the pilgrim would have believed just as now. The priest's authority has so mastered his faith, that it accommodates itself to any demand upon it; and the English stranger looks on the scene, for the first time, with a feeling of scorn, bewilderment, and shame, at that grovelling credulity, those strange rites and ceremonies, that almost confessed imposture.

Jarred and distracted by these, the Church of the Holy Sepulchre, for some time, seems to an Englishman the least sacred spot about Jerusalem. It is the lies, and the legends, and the priests, and their quarrels, and their ceremonies, which keep the Holy Place out of sight. A man has not leisure to view it, for the brawling of the guardians of the spot. The Roman conquerors, they say, raised up a statue of Venus in this sacred place, intending to destroy all memory of it. I don't think the heathen was as criminal as the Christian is now. To deny and disbelieve, is not so bad as to make belief a ground to cheat upon. The liar Ananias perished for that; and yet out of these gates, where angels may have kept watch – out of the tomb of Christ – Christian priests issue with a lie in their hands. What a place to choose for imposture, good God! to sully, with brutal struggles for self-aggrandisement, or shameful schemes of gain.

The situation of the Tomb (into which, be it authentic or not, no man can enter without a shock of breathless fear, and deep and awful self-humiliation) must have struck all travellers. It stands in the centre of the arched rotunda, which is common to all denominations, and from which branch off the various chapels belonging to each particular sect. In the Coptic Chapel I saw one coal-black Copt, in blue robes, cowering in the little cabin, surrounded by dingy lamps, barbarous pictures, and cheap, faded trumpery. In the Latin Church, there was no service going on, only two fathers dusting the mouldy gew-gaws along the brown walls, and laughing to one another. The gorgeous church of the Fire imposters, hard by, was always more fully attended; as was that of their wealthy neighbours, the Armenians.

These three main sects hate each other: their quarrels are interminable: each bribes and intrigues with the heathen lords of the soil, to the prejudice of his neighbour. Now it is the Latins who interfere, and allow the common church to go to ruin, because the Greeks purpose to roof it: now the Greeks demolish a monastery on Mount Olivet, and leave the ground to the Turks, rather than allow the Armenians to possess it. On another occasion, the Greeks having mended the Armenian steps, which lead to the (so called) Cave of the Nativity at Bethlehem, the latter asked for permission to destroy the work of the Greeks, and did so. And so round this sacred spot, the centre of Christendom, the representa-

[114]

tives of the three great sects worship under one roof, and hate each other!

Above the Tomb of the Saviour, the cupola *is open*, and you see the blue sky overhead. Which of the builders was it that had the grace to leave that under the high protection of Heaven, and not confine it under the mouldering old domes and roofs, which cover so much selfishness, and uncharitableness, and imposture!

We went to Bethlehem, too; and saw the apocryphal wonders there.

Five miles' ride brings you from Jerusalem to it, over naked wavy hills; the aspect of which, however, grows more cheerful as you approach the famous village. We passed the Convent of Mar Elyas on the road, walled and barred like a fort.[6] In spite of its strength, however, it has more than once been stormed by the Arabs, and the luckless fathers within put to death. Hard by was Rebecca's Well: a dead body was lying there, and crowds of male and female mourners dancing and howling round it. Now and then a little troop of savage scowling horsemen – a shepherd driving his black sheep, his gun over his shoulder – a troop of camels – or of women, with long blue robes and white veils, bearing pitchers, and staring at the strangers with their great solemn eyes – or a company of labourers, with their donkeys, bearing grain or grapes to the city, – met us and enlivened the little ride. It was a busy and cheerful scene. The Church of the Nativity, with the adjoining Convents, forms a vast and noble Christian structure. A party of travellers were going to the Jordan that day, and scores of their followers – of the robbing Arabs, who profess to protect them, (magnificent figures some of them, with flowing haicks and turbans, with long guns and scimitars, and wretched horses, covered with gaudy trappings), were standing on the broad pavement before the little Convent gate. It was such a scene as Cattermole might paint.[7] Knights and Crusaders may have witnessed a similar one. You could fancy them issuing out of the narrow little portal, and so greeted by the swarms of swarthy clamourous women and merchants and children.

The scene within the building was of the same Gothic character. We were entertained by the Superior of the Greek Convent, in a fine refectory, with ceremonies and hospitalities that pilgrims of the middle ages might have witnessed. We were shown over the magnificent Barbaric Church, visited of course the Grotto where the Blessed Nativity is said to have taken place, and the rest of the idols set up for worship by the clumsy legend. When the visit was concluded, the party going to the Dead Sea filed off with their armed attendants; each individual traveller making as brave a show as he could, and personally accoutred with warlike swords and pistols.[8] The picturesque crowds, and the Arabs and the horsemen, in the sunshine; the noble old convent, and the grey bearded priests, with their feast; and the church, and its pictures and columns, and incense; the wide brown hills spreading round the village; with the accidents of the road, – flocks and shepherds, wells and funerals, and camel-trains, have left on my mind a brilliant, romantic, and cheerful picture. But you, Dear M. —— , without visiting the place, have imagined one far finer; and Bethlehem, where the Holy Child was born, and the angels sang, 'Glory to God in the Highest, and peace and good-will on earth,' is the most sacred and beautiful spot in the earth to you.

By far the most comfortable quarters in Jerusalem, are those of the Armenians, in their convent of St James. Wherever we have been, these Eastern quakers look grave and jolly, and sleek. Their convent at Mount Zion is big enough to contain two or three thousand of their faithful; and their church is ornamented by the most rich and hideous gifts ever devised by uncouth piety. Instead of a bell, the fat monks of the convent beat huge noises on a board, and drub the faithful into prayers. I never saw men more lazy and rosy than these reverend fathers, kneeling in their comfortable matted church, or sitting in easy devotion. Pictures, images, gilding, tinsel, wax-candles, twinkle all over the place; and ten thousand ostrich eggs (or any lesser number you may allot) dangle from the vaulted ceiling. There were great numbers of people at worship in this gorgeous church; they went on their knees, kissing the walls with much fervour, and paying reverence to the most precious relic of the convent, – the chair of St James, their Patron, the first Bishop of Jerusalem.

The chair pointed out with greatest pride in the church of the Latin Convent is that shabby red damask one appropriated to the French Consul, – the representative of the King of that nation, – and the protection which it has from time immemorial accorded to the Christians of the Latin rite in Syria.[9] All French writers and travellers speak of

Chancel of the Church of the Nativity, Bethlehem, watercolour by David Roberts, c.1843. In Bethlehem Thackeray found the internecine rivalry between the various branches of the Christian church to be as contemptible as it had been in Jerusalem.
National Museums and Galleries on Merseyside (Walker Art Gallery, Liverpool).

this protection with delightful complacency. Consult the French books of travel on the subject, and any Frenchman whom you may meet; he says, '*La France, Monsieur, de tous les temps protège les Chrétiens d'Orient*'; and the little fellow looks round the church with a sweep of the arm, and protects it accordingly. It is bon ton for them to go in processions; and you see them on such errands, marching with long candles, as gravely as may be. But I have never been able to edify myself with their devotion: and the religious outpourings of Lamartine and Chateaubriand[10] which we have all been reading apropos of the journey we are to make, have inspired me with an emotion anything but respectful. '*Voyez comme M. de Chateaubriand prie Dieu*', the Viscount's eloquence seems always to say. There is a

sanctified grimace about the little French pilgrim, which it is very difficult to contemplate gravely.

The pictures, images, and ornaments of the principal Latin Convent, are quite mean and poor, compared to the wealth of the Armenians. The convent is spacious, but squalid. Many hopping and crawling plagues are said to attack the skins of pilgrims who sleep there. It is laid out in courts and galleries, the mouldy doors of which are decorated with twopenny pictures of favourite saints and martyrs; and so great is the shabbiness and laziness, that you might fancy yourself in a convent in Italy. Brown-clad fathers, dirty, bearded, and sallow, go gliding about the corridors. The relic manufactory, before mentioned, carries on a considerable business; and dispatches bales of shells,

Bethlehem, looking towards the Dead Sea, oil painting by David Roberts, 1853. The Bethlehem that existed in the minds of Europeans as a symbol of the birth of Christ, was very different from the reality that Thackeray and contemporary travellers experienced.
Private Collection.
Photograph: Barbican Art Gallery.

crosses, and beads, to believers in Europe. These constitute the chief revenue of the convent now. *La France* is no longer the most Christian kingdom, and her protection of the Latins is not good for much since Charles X was expelled;[11] and Spain, which used likewise to be generous on occasions (the gifts, arms, candlesticks, *baldaquins,* of the Spanish Sovereigns, figure pretty frequently in the various Latin chapels), has been stingy since the late disturbances, the spoliation of the clergy, etc. After we had been taken to see the humble curiosities of the place, the Prior treated us in his wooden parlour with little glasses of pink rosolio, brought with many bows and genuflexions by his reverence, the convent butler.

After this community of holy men, the most important perhaps is the American Convent, a Protestant congregation of Independents chiefly, who deliver tracts, propose to

make converts, have meetings of their own, and also swell the little congregation that attends the Anglican service. I have mentioned our fellow-traveller, the Consul General for Syria of the United States. He was a tradesman, who had made a considerable fortune, and lived at a country house in comfortable retirement. But his opinion is that the prophecies of Scripture are about to be accomplished; that the day of the return of the Jews is at hand, and the glorification of the restored Jerusalem. He is to witness this; he and a favourite dove with which he travels; and he forsook home and comfortable country house, in order to make this journey. He has no other knowledge of Syria but what he derives from the prophecy; and this (as he takes the office gratis) has been considered a sufficient reason for his appointment by the United States' Government.

As soon as he arrived, he sent and demanded an interview

with the Pasha; explained to him his interpretation of the Apocalypse, in which he has discovered that the Five Powers and America are about to intervene in Syrian affairs, and the infallible return of the Jews to Palestine. The news must have astonished the Lieutenant of the Sublime Porte; and since the days of the Kingdom of Munster, under his Anabaptist Majesty, John of Leyden, I doubt whether any government has received or appointed so queer an ambassador. The kind, worthy, simple man, took me to his temporary Consulate House at the American Missionary Establishment;[12] and, under pretence of treating me to white wine, expounded his ideas; talked of futurity as he would about an article in *The Times*, and had no more doubt of seeing a divine kingdom established in Jerusalem, than you that there will be a *levée* next spring at St James's. The little room in which we sat, as padded with Missionary tracts, but I heard of scarce any converts – not more than are made by our own Episcopal establishment.

But if the latter's religious victories are small, and very few people are induced by the American tracts, and the English preaching and catechizing, to forsake their own manner of worshipping the Divine Being, in order to follow ours: yet surely our religious colony of men and women can't fail to do good, by the sheer force of good example, pure life, and kind offices. The ladies of the mission have numbers of clients, of all persuasions, in the town, to whom they extend their charities. Each of their houses is a model of neatness, and a dispensary of gentle kindnesses; and the ecclesiastics have formed a modest centre of civilization in the place. A dreary joke was made in the House of Commons about Bishop Alexander and the Bishopess his lady, and the Bishoplings his numerous children, who were said to have scandalised the people of Jerusalem. That sneer evidently came from the Latins and Greeks; for what could the Jews and Turks care because an English clergyman had a wife and children as their own priests have? There was no sort of ill-will exhibited towards them, as far as I could learn; and I saw the Bishop's children riding about the town as safely as they could about Hyde Park. All Europeans, indeed, seemed to me to be received with forbearance, and almost courtesy within the walls.

As I was going about making sketches, the people would look on very good-humouredly, without offering the least interruption; nay, two or three were quite ready to stand still for such a humble portrait as my pencil could make of them; and the sketch done, it was passed from one person to another, each making his comments, and signifying a very polite approval. Here are a pair of them, Fath Allah and

Ameenut Daoodee, his father, horse dealers by trade, who came and sat with us at the inn, and smoked pipes (the sun being down), while the original of the above masterpiece was made. With the Arabs outside the walls, however, and the freshly arriving country people, this politeness was not so much exhibited. There was a certain tattooed girl, with black eyes and huge silver earrings, and a chin delicately picked out with blue, who formed one of a group of women outside the great convent, whose likeness I longed to carry off; – there was a woman with a little child, with wondering eyes, drawing water at the pool of Siloam, in such an attitude and dress as Rebecca may have had when Isaac's lieutenant asked her for drink: – both of these parties standing still for half a minute, at the next cried out for *backsheesh*; and not content with the five piastres which I gave them individually, screamed out for more, and summoned their friends, who screamed out *backsheesh* too. I was pursued into the convent by a dozen howling women calling for pay, barring the door against them, to the astonishment of the worthy papa who kept it; and at Miriam's Well the women were

Left. '*Fath Allah and Ameenut Daoodee*', horse-traders *in Jerusalem*, wood engraving by William Thackeray.

Right. *A Palestinian Girl*, watercolour by an unknown English artist with the initials 'MB', 1849.
Victoria and Albert Museum (Searight Collection).

joined by a man, with a large stick, who backed their petition. But him we could afford to laugh at, for we were two, and had sticks likewise.

In the village of Siloam I would not recommend the artist to loiter. A colony of ruffians inhabit the dismal place, who have guns as well as sticks at need. Their dogs howl after the strangers as they pass through; and over the parapets of their walls you are saluted by the scowls of a villainous set of countenances, that it is not good to see with one pair of eyes. They shot a man at midday at a few hundred yards from the gates while we were at Jerusalem, and no notice was taken of the murder. Hordes of Arab robbers infest the neighbourhood of the city, with the sheikhs of whom travellers make terms when minded to pursue their journey. I never could understand why the walls stopped these warriors if they had a mind to plunder the city, for there are but a hundred and fifty men in the garrison to man the long lonely lines of defence.

I have seen only in Titian's pictures those magnificent purple shadows, in which the hills round about lay, as the dawn rose faintly behind them; and we looked at Olivet for the last time, from our terrace, where we were awaiting the arrival of the horses that were to carry us to Jaffa. A yellow moon was still blazing in the midst of countless brilliant stars overhead; the nakedness and misery of the surrounding city were hidden in that beautiful rosy atmosphere of mingling night and dawn. The city never looked so noble; the mosques, domes, and minarets rising up into the calm starlit sky.

By the gate of Bethlehem there stands one palm tree, and a house with three domes. Put these and the huge old gothic gate as a background dark against the yellowing eastern sky: the foreground is a deep grey: – as you look into it dark forms of horsemen come out of the twilight: now there came lanterns, more horsemen, a litter with mules, a crowd of Arab horseboys and dealers accompanying their beasts to the gate; all the members of our party come up by twos and threes; and, at last, the great gate opens just before sunrise, and we get into the grey plains.

O! the luxury of an English saddle! An English servant of one of the gentlemen of the mission procured it for me, on the back of a little mare, which (as I am a light weight) did not turn a hair in the course of the day's march – and after we got quit of the ugly, stony, clattering, mountainous Abou Gosh district, into the fair undulating plain, which stretches to Ramleh – carried me into the town at a pleasant hand gallop. A negro, of preternatural ugliness, in a yellow gown, with a crimson handkerchief streaming over his head, digging his shovel spurs into the lean animal he rode, and driving three others before – swaying backwards and forwards on his horse, now embracing his ears, and now almost under his belly, screaming *yallah* with the most frightful shrieks, and singing country songs – galloped along ahead of me. I acquired one of his poems pretty well, and could imitate his shriek accurately; but I shall not have the pleasure of singing it to you in England. I had forgotten the delightful dissonance two days after, both the negro's and that of a real Arab minstrel, a donkey driver accompanying our baggage, who sang and grinned with the most amusing good humour.

We halted, in the middle of the day, in a little wood of olive trees, which forms almost the only shelter between Jaffa and Jerusalem, except that afforded by the orchards in the odious village of Abou Gosh, through which we went at a double quick pace. Under the olives, or up in the branches, some of our friends took a siesta. I have a sketch of four of them so employed. Two of them were dead within a month of the fatal Syrian fever.[13] But we did not know how near fate was to us then. Fires were lighted, and fowls and eggs divided, and tea and coffee served round in tin panikins, and here we lighted pipes, and smoked and laughed at our ease. I believe everybody was happy to be out of Jerusalem. The impression I have of it now is of ten days passed in a fever.

We all found quarters in the Greek convent, at Ramleh, where the monks served us a supper on a terrace, in a pleasant sunset; a beautiful and cheerful landscape, stretching around; the land in graceful undulations, the towers and mosques rosy in the sunset, with no lack of verdure, especially of graceful palms. Jaffa was nine miles off. As we rode, all the morning we had been accompanied by the smoke of our steamer, twenty miles off at sea.

The convent is a huge caravanserai; only three or four monks dwell in it, the ghostly hotel-keepers of the place. The horses were tied up and fed in the court yard, into which we rode; above were the living rooms, where there is accommodation, not only for an unlimited number of pilgrims, but for a vast and innumerable host of hopping and crawling things, who usually persist in partaking of the traveller's bed. Let all thin-skinned travellers in the east be warned on no account to travel without the admirable invention described in Mr Fellowes' book;[14] nay possibly invented by that enterprising and learned traveller. You make a sack, of calico or linen, big enough for the body, appended to which is a closed chimney of muslin, stretched out by cane hoops, and fastened up to a beam, or against the wall. You keep a sharp eye to look out that no flea or bug is on the look out, and when assured of this, you pop into the bag, tightly closing the orifice after you. This admirable bug disappointer I tried at Ramleh, and had the only undisturbed night's rest I enjoyed in the East. To be sure it was a short night, for our party were stirring at one o'clock, and those who got up insisted on talking and keeping awake those who inclined to sleep. But I shall never forget the terror inspired in my mind, being shut up in the bug disappointer, when a facetious lay brother of the convent fell upon me and began *tickling* me. I never had the courage again to try the anti-flea contrivance, preferring the friskiness of those animals to the sports of such a greasy grinning wag as my friend at Ramleh.

In the morning, and long before sunrise, our little caravan was in marching order again. We went out with lanterns, and shouts of *yallah* through the narrow streets, and issued into the plain, where, though there was no moon, there were blazing stars shining steadily overhead. They become friends to a man who travels, especially under the clear eastern sky; whence they look down as if protecting you, solemn, yellow, and refulgent. They seem *nearer* to you than in Europe; larger and more awful. So we rode on till the dawn rose, and Jaffa came in view. The friendly ship was lying out in waiting for us; the horses were given up to their owners: and in the midst of a crowd of naked beggars, and a perfect storm of curses and yells for *backsheesh*, our party got into their boats, and to the ship, where we were welcomed by the very best captain that ever sailed upon this maritime globe, namely, Captain Samuel Lewis, of the Peninsular and Oriental Company's Service.

Chapter XIV: FROM JAFFA TO ALEXANDRIA

Facing page *Alexandria*, watercolour attributed to Henry Fitzcook, for *The Route of The Overland Mail to India*, 1850-52. In the early 19th century, Alexandria's maritime importance was revived, mainly through the reopening of the Mahmudiyyah Canal, linking it to the Nile. By 1844 it had also become a staging post on the 'Overland Route' to India.
The Peninsular and Oriental Steam Navigation Company.

[From the Provider's Log Book]
BILL OF FARE, OCTOBER 12TH

Mulligatawny Soup
Salt Fish and Egg Sauce
Roast Haunch of Mutton
Boiled Shoulder and Onion Sauce
Boiled Beef
Roast Fowls
Pillow ditto
Ham
Haricot Mutton
Curry and Rice

Cabbage
French Beans
Boiled Potatoes
Baked ditto

Damson Tart
Currant ditto
Rice Puddings
Currant Fritters

WE were just at the port's mouth – and could see the towers and buildings of Alexandria rising purple against the sunset, when the report of a gun came booming over the calm golden water; and we heard, with much mortification, that we had no chance of getting *pratique* that night.[1] Already the ungrateful passengers had begun to tire of the ship, – though in our absence in Syria it had been carefully cleansed and purified; though it was cleared of the swarming Jews, who had infected the decks all the way from Constantinople; and though we had been feasting and carousing in the manner described in the last page.

But very early next morning we bore into the harbour, busy with a great quantity of craft. We passed huge black hulks of mouldering men-of-war, from the sterns of which trailed the dirty red flag, with the star and crescent; boats, manned with red-capped seamen, and captains and steersmen in beards and tarbooshes, passed continually among these old hulks, the rowers bending to their oars, so that at each stroke, they disappeared bodily in the boat. Besides these, there was a large fleet of country ships, and stars and stripes, and tricolors, and union jacks; and many active steamers, of the French and English companies, shooting in and out of the harbour, or moored in the briny waters. The ship of our company, the *Oriental*,[2] lay there – a palace upon the brine, and some of the Pasha's steam vessels likewise, looking very like Christian boats; but it was queer to look at some un- intelligible Turkish flourish painted on the stern, and the long-tailed Arabian hieroglyphics gilt on the paddle-boxes. Our dear friend and comrade of Beyrout (if we may be permitted to call her so), HMS *Trump*, was in the harbour; and the captain of that gallant ship, coming to greet us, drove some of us on shore in his gig.

I had been preparing myself overnight, by the help of a cigar and a moonlight contemplation on deck, for sensations on landing in Egypt. I was ready to yield myself up with solemnity to the mystic grandeur of the scene of initiation. Pompey's pillar must stand like a mountain,[3] in a yellow plain, surrounded by a grove of obelisks, as tall as palm trees. Placid sphinxes, brooding o'er the Nile – mighty Memnonian countenances calm – had revealed Egypt to me in a sonnet of Tennyson's,[4] and I was ready to gaze on it with pyramidal wonder and hieroglyphic awe.

The landing quay at Alexandria is like the dockyard quay at Portsmouth: with a few score of brown faces scattered among the population. There are slop-sellers, dealers in marine stores, bottled porter shops, seamen lolling about; flies and cabs are plying for hire; and a yelling chorus of donkey

boys, shrieking, 'Ride, sir! – donkey, sir! – I say, sir!' in excellent English, dispel all romantic notions. The placid sphinxes, brooding o'er the Nile, disappeared with that shriek of the donkey boys. You might be as well impressed with Wapping, as with your first step on Egyptian soil.

The riding of a donkey is, after all, not a dignified occupation. A man resists the offer first, somehow as an indignity. How is that poor little, red-saddled, long-eared creature to carry you? Is there to be one for you and another for your legs? Natives and Europeans, of all sizes, pass by it is true, mounted upon the same contrivance. I waited until I got into a very private spot, where nobody could see me,

The Author's Entry into Alexandria, hand-coloured wood engraving from Samuel Bevan's *Sand and Canvas*, published in 1849. The experience of a donkey ride on arrival in Alexandria was apparently as undignified for Bevan as it had been for his friend, Thackeray.
Victoria and Albert Museum (Searight Collection).

[123]

broad street (like a street of Marseilles) where the principal hotels and merchants' houses are to be found, and where the consuls have their houses, and hoist their flags. The palace of the French Consul General makes the grandest show in the street,[5] and presents a great contrast to the humble abode of the English representative, who protects his fellow country-men from a second floor.

But that Alexandrian two-pair-front of a Consulate, was more welcome and cheering than a palace to most of us. For there lay certain letters, with postmarks of *Home* upon them; and kindly tidings, the first heard for two months: – though we had seen so many men and cities since, that Cornhill seemed to be a year off, at least, with certain persons dwelling (more or less) in that vicinity. I saw a young Oxford man seize his dispatches, and slink off with several letters, written in a tight, neat hand, and sedulously crossed; which any man could see, without looking farther, were the handywork of Mary Ann, to whom he is attached. The lawyer received a bundle from his chambers, in which his clerk eased his soul regarding the state of Snooks v. Rodgers, Smith *ats* Tomkins, etc. The statesman had a packet of thick enve-lopes, decorated with that profusion of sealing wax, in which official recklessness lavishes the resources of the country: and your humble servant got just one little, modest letter, containing another, written in pencil characters, varying in size between one and two inches; but how much pleasanter to read than my lord's dispatch, or the clerk's account of Smith *ats* Tomkins, -yes, even than the Mary Ann corres-pondence!... Yes, my dear madam, you will understand me, when I say, that it was from little Polly at home, with some confidential news about a cat, and the last report of her new doll.[6]

It is worth while to have made the journey for this pleas-ure: to have walked the deck on long nights, and have thought of home. You have no leisure to do so in the city. You don't see the heavens shine above you so purely there, or the stars so clearly. – How, after the perusal of the above documents, we enjoyed a file of the admirable *Galignani*;[7] and what O'Connell was doing;[8] and the twelve last new victories of the French in Algeria; and, above all, six or seven numbers of *Punch*! There might have been an avenue of Pompey's pillars within reach, and a live sphinx sporting on the banks of the Mahmoodieh canal, and we would not have

and then ascended – why not say descended, at once – on the poor little animal. Instead of being crushed at once, as per-haps the rider expected, it darted forward, quite briskly and cheerfully, at six or seven miles an hour; requiring no spur or admonitive to haste, except the shrieking of the little Egyp-tian Jamin, who ran along by asinus' side.

The character of the houses, by which you pass, is scarcely Eastern at all. The streets are busy with a motley population of Jews and Armenians, slave-driving looking Europeans, large-breeched Greeks, and well-shaven buxom merchants, looking as trim and fat as those on the Bourse or on 'Change; only, among the natives, the stranger can't fail to remark (as the Caliph did of the Calendars, in the *Arabian Nights*), that so many of them *have only one eye*. It is the horrid ophthalmia which has played such frightful ravages with them. You see children sitting in the doorways, their eyes completely closed up with the green sickening sore, and the flies feeding on them. Five or six minutes of the donkey ride brings you to the Frank quarter, and the handsome stirred to see them, until *Punch* had had his interview, and *Galignani* was dismissed.

The curiosities of Alexandria are few, and easily seen. We went into the bazaars, which have a much more Eastern look than the European quarter, with its Anglo-Gallic-Italian inhabitants, and Babel-like civilisation. Here and there a large hotel, clumsy and white-washed, with Oriental trellised windows, and a couple of slouching sentinels at the doors, in the ugliest composite uniform that ever was seen, was pointed out as the residence of some great officer of the Pasha's court, or of one of the numerous children of the Egyptian Solomon. His Highness was in his own palace, which was consequently not visible. He was in deep grief, and strict retirement. It was at this time that the European newspapers announced that he was about to resign his empire; but the quidnuncs of Alexandria hinted that a love affair, in which the old potentate had engaged with senile extravagance, and the effects of a potion of hashish, or some deleterious drug, with which he was in the habit of intoxicating himself, had brought on that langour and desperate weariness of life and governing, into which the venerable Prince was plunged. Before three days were over, however, the fit had left him, and he determined to live and reign a little longer. A very few days afterwards several of our party were presented to him at Cairo, and found the great Egyptian ruler perfectly convalescent.

This, and the Opera, and the quarrels of the two *prime donne*, and the beauty of one of them, formed the chief subject of conversation; and I had this important news in the shop of a certain barber in the town, who conveyed it in a language composed of French, Spanish, and Italian, and with a volubility quite worthy of a barber of *Gil Blas*.

Then we went to see the famous obelisk presented by Mehemet Ali to the British Government, who have not shown a particular alacrity to accept this ponderous present.[9] The huge shaft lies on the ground prostrate, and desecrated by all sorts of abominations. Children were sprawling about, attracted by the dirt there. Arabs, negroes, and donkey boys, were passing, quite indifferent, by the fallen monster of a stone, – as indifferent as the British Government, who don't care for recording the glorious termination of their Egyptian campaign of 1801. If our country takes the compliment so coolly, surely it would be disloyal upon our

Interview with the Viceroy of Egypt at his palace at Alexandria, lithograph after David Roberts. When Roberts met Muhammad Ali in Alexandria in May 1839 he had just completed his long tour of Egypt and the Holy Land, and was awaiting the arrival of a P&O steamship for the passage home. On this occasion he was accompanying the British Consul-General, Colonel Patrick Campbell, and Thomas Waghorn, promoter of the Overland Route, who were explaining to the Viceroy the advantages of the transit through Egypt of India-bound mail and passengers. This lithograph is one of the magnificent series of 124 by Louis Haghe after David Roberts, published in three volumes as *Egypt and Nubia*, 1846-49.
Victoria and Albert Museum.

parts to be more enthusiastic. I wish they would offer the Trafalgar Square Pillar to the Egyptians; and that both of the huge, ugly monsters, were lying in the dirt there, side by side.

Pompey's Pillar is by no means so big as the Charing Cross trophy. This venerable column has not escaped ill-treatment either. Numberless ship's companies, travelling cockneys, etc., have affixed their rude marks upon it. Some daring ruffian even painted the name of 'Warren's blacking' upon it, effacing other inscriptions, – one, Wilkinson says, of 'the second Psammetichus'. I regret deeply, my dear friend, that I cannot give you this document respecting a lamented monarch, in whose history I know you take such an interest.

The best sight I saw in Alexandria, was a negro holiday; which was celebrated outside of the town by a sort of negro village of huts, swarming with old, lean, fat, ugly, infantine, happy faces, that nature has smeared with a preparation even more black and durable than that with which

Psammetichus's base has been polished. Every one of these jolly faces was on the broad grin, from the dusky mother to the India-rubber child sprawling upon her back, and the venerable jetty senior, whose wool was as white as that of a sheep in Florian's pastorals.

To these dancers a couple of fellows were playing on a drum and a little banjo. They were singing a chorus, which was not only singular, and perfectly marked in the rhythm, but exceedingly sweet in the tune. They danced in a circle; and performers came trooping from all quarters, who fell into the round, and began waggling their heads, and waving their left hands, and tossing up and down the little thin rods which they each carried, and all singing to the very best of their power.

I saw the chief eunuch of the Grand Turk at Constantinople pass by —

(the above is an accurate likeness of his beautiful features) – but with what a different expression! Though he is one of the greatest of the great in the Turkish Empire (ranking with a Cabinet minister or Lord Chamberlain here), his fine countenance was clouded with care, and savage with *ennui*.

Here his black brethren were ragged, starving, and happy; and I need not tell such a fine moralist as you are, how it is the case, in the white as well as the black world, that happiness (republican leveller, who does not care a fig for the fashion) often disdains the turrets of kings, to pay a visit to the '*tabernas pauperum.*'

We went the round of the coffee-houses in the evening, both the polite European places of resort, where you get ices and the French papers, and those in the town, where Greeks, Turks, and general company resort, to sit upon uncomfortable chairs, and drink wretched muddy coffee, and to listen to two or three miserable musicians, who keep up a variation of howling for hours together. But the pretty song of the negroes had spoiled me for that abominable music.

Left. *The Chief Black Eunuch of the Ottoman Sultan,* wood engraving by William Thackeray.

Right. *Negroes celebrating a holiday in Alexandria,* wood engraving by William Thackeray.

[126]

Chapter XV: TO CAIRO

Mahmoudie Canal, watercolour attributed to Henry Fitzcook, for *The Route of The Overland Mail to India,* 1850-52. At Atfah, where the Mahmudiyyah Canal from Alexandria joined the Nile, passengers had to disembark from their barges (or fly boats, as Thackeray called them) and transfer on to steamers for the journey up river to Cairo.
The Peninsular and Oriental Steam Navigation Company.

WE had no need of hiring the country boats which ply on the Mahmoodieh canal to Atfeh,[1] where it joins the Nile, but were accommodated in one of the Peninsular and Oriental Company's fly boats; pretty similar to those narrow Irish canal boats, in which the enterprising traveller has been carried from Dublin to Ballinasloe. The present boat was, to be sure, tugged by a little steamer, so that the Egyptian canal is ahead of the Irish in so far: in natural scenery, the one prospect is fully equal to the other; it must be confessed that there is nothing to see. In truth, there was nothing but this: you saw a muddy bank on each side of you, and a blue sky overhead. A few round mud huts and palm trees were

[127]

planted along the line here and there. Sometimes we would see, on the water side, a woman in a blue robe, with her son

Fallahin beside the Nile, wood engraving by William Thackeray.

Facing Page, Top. *Approach to the Pyramids of Gizah,* watercolour by William Prinsep, 1842. In Thackeray's day the road to the Pyramids of Gizah from Cairo ran through fields and villages, where the *fallahin* went about their daily activities.
Photograph: Martyn Gregory Gallery.

Facing Page, Bottom. *Shepheard's Hotel, Cairo,* c.1849. At least two hotels for European visitors to Cairo were established on al-Azbakiyyah Square in the 1840s, the Hôtel d'Orient where Thackeray stayed, and, a few years later, Shepheard's. This lithograph, after a drawing by Machereau, a little-known French artist, bears out Thackeray's description of the busy square.
Victoria and Albert Museum (Searight Collection).

by her, in that tight brown costume with which Nature had supplied him. Now, it was a hat dropped by one of the party into the water; a brown Arab plunged and disappeared incontinently after the hat, re-issued from the muddy water, prize in hand, and ran naked after the little steamer (which was by this time far ahead of him), his brawny limbs shining in the sun: then, we had half-cold fowls and bitter ale: then, we had dinner – bitter ale and cold fowls; with which incidents the day on the canal passed away, as harmlessly as if we had been in a Dutch *track-schuyt.*

Towards evening we arrived at the town of Atfeh – half land, half houses, half palm trees, with swarms of half-naked people crowding the rustic shady bazaars, and bartering their produce of fruit or many-coloured grain. Here the canal came to a check, ending abruptly with a large lock. Some little fleet of masts and country ships were beyond the lock, and it led into THE NILE.

After all, it is something to have seen these red waters. It is only low green banks, mud-huts, and palm clumps, with the sun setting red behind them, and the great, dull, sinuous river, flashing here and there in the light. But it is the Nile,

the old Saturn of a stream – a divinity yet, though younger river-Gods have deposed him. Hail! O venerable father of crocodiles! We were all lost in sentiments of the profoundest awe and respect; which we proved, by tumbling down into the cabin of the Nile steamer that was waiting to receive us, and fighting and cheating for sleeping berths.

At dawn in the morning we were on deck; the character had not altered of the scenery about the river. Vast flat stretches of land were on either side, recovering from the subsiding inundations: near the mud villages, a country ship or two was roosting under the date trees; the landscape everywhere stretching away level and lonely. In the sky in the east was a long streak of greenish light, which widened and rose until it grew to be of an opal colour, then orange; then, behold, the round red disk of the sun rose flaming up above the horizon. All the water blushed as he got up; the deck was all red; the steersman gave his helm to another, and prostrated himself on the deck, and bowed his head eastward, and praised the Maker of the sun: it shone on his white turban as he was kneeling, and gilt up his bronzed face, and sent his blue shadow over the glowing deck. The distances, which had been grey, were now clothed in purple; and the broad stream was illuminated. As the sun rose higher, the morning blush faded away; the sky was cloudless and pale, and the river and the surrounding landscape were dazzlingly clear.

Looking ahead in an hour or two, we saw the Pyramids. Fancy my sensations, dear M. —— ; – two big ones and a little one:

! ! !

There they lay, rosy and solemn in the distance – those old, majestical, mystical, familiar edifices. Several of us tried to be impressed; but breakfast supervening, a rush was made at the coffee and cold pies, and the sentiment of awe was lost in the scramble for victuals.

Are we so *blasé* of the world that the greatest marvels in it do not succeed in moving us? Have society, Pall Mall clubs, and a habit of sneering, so withered up our organs of veneration that we can admire no more? My sensation with regard to the pyramids was, that I had seen them before: then came a feeling of shame that the view of them should awaken no respect. Then I wanted (naturally) to see whether my neighbours were any more enthusiastic than myself – Trinity College, Oxford, was busy with the cold ham: Downing Street was particularly attentive to a bunch of grapes: Fig Tree Court behaved with decent propriety; he is in good practice, and of a conservative turn of mind, which leads him to respect from principle *les faits accomplis;* perhaps he remembered that one of them was as big as Lincoln's Inn Fields.[2] But, the truth is, nobody was seriously moved . . And why should they, because of an exaggeration of bricks ever so enormous? I confess, for my part, that the pyramids are very big.

After a voyage, of about thirty hours, the steamer brought up at the quay of Boulak, amidst a small fleet of dirty comfortless *cangias*, in which cottons and merchandise were loading and unloading, and a huge noise and bustle on the shore.[3] Numerous villas, parks and country houses, had begun to decorate the Cairo bank of the stream ere this: residences of the Pasha's nobles, who have had orders to take their pleasure here and beautify the precincts of the capital; tall factory chimneys also rise here; there are founderies and steam-engine manufactories.[4] These, and the pleasure-houses, stand as trim as soldiers on parade; contrasting with the swarming, slovenly, close, tumble-down, eastern old town, that forms the out-port of Cairo, and was built before the importation of European taste and discipline.

Here we alighted upon donkeys, to the full as brisk as those of Alexandria, invaluable to timid riders, and equal to any weight. We had a Jerusalem pony race into Cairo; my animal beating all the rest by many lengths. The entrance to the capital, from Boulak, is very pleasant and picturesque – over a fair road, and the wide planted plain of the Ezbekieh; where are gardens, canals, fields, and avenues of trees, and where the great ones of the town come and take their pleasure. We saw many barouches driving about with fat Pashas, lolling on the cushions; stately looking colonels and doctors taking their ride, followed by their orderlies or footmen; lines of people taking pipes and sherbet in the coffee-houses; and one of the pleasantest sights of all, – a fine new white building with HÔTEL D'ORIENT written up in huge French characters, and which, indeed, is an establishment as large and comfortable as most of the best inns of the South of France.[5] As a hundred Christian people, or more, come

Boulac, the port of Cairo, where Thackeray disembarked and was conveyed by express donkey to his hotel in the city. The watercolour, attributed to Henry Fitzcook, is another lively scene from the series for *The Route of The Overland Mail to India*, 1850-52.
The Peninsular and Oriental Steam Navigation Company.

Lieutenant Waghorn's Travelling Carriage. Although it appeared in a feature on Waghorn in the *Illustrated London News* (8 November 1845), this caricature of the energetic entrepreneur's speedy vehicle could as well have been intended to illustrate Thackeray's hilarious description.

Facing page. *Ghawazi, or Dancing Girls, Rosetta*, after Emile Prisse d'Avennes. One of the exotic eastern customs that fascinated western visitors was the stylised but alluring dancing performed by *ghawazi* or *almahs*. The lithograph is from Prisse's *Oriental Album. Characters, Costumes, and Modes of Life, in the Valley of the Nile,* published in 1848.
Victoria and Albert Museum (Searight Collection).

from England and from India every fortnight, this inn has been built to accommodate a large proportion of them; and twice a month, at least its sixty rooms are full.

The gardens from the windows give a very pleasant and animated view: the hotel gate is besieged by crews of donkey-drivers; the noble stately Arab women, with tawny skins (of which a simple robe of floating blue cotton enables you liberally to see the colour) and large black eyes, come to the well hard by for water: camels are perpetually arriving and setting down their loads: the court is full of bustling dragomans, ayahs, and children from India; and poor old venerable he-nurses, with grey beards and crimson turbans, tending little white-faced babies that have seen the light at Dumdum or Futtyghur: a copper-coloured barber, seated on his hams, is shaving a camel driver at the great inn gate. The bells are ringing prodigiously; and Lieutenant Waghorn is bouncing in and out of the courtyard full of business.[6] He only left Bombay yesterday morning, was seen in the Red Sea on Tuesday, is engaged to dinner this afternoon in Regent's Park, and (as it is about two minutes since

I saw him in the courtyard) I make no doubt he is by this time at Alexandria or at Malta, say, perhaps, at both. *Il en est*

capable. If any man can be at two places at once (which I don't believe or deny) Waghorn is he.

Six o'clock bell rings. Sixty people sit down to a *quasi* French banquet: thirty Indian officers in mustachoes and jackets; ten civilians in ditto and spectacles; ten pale-faced ladies with ringlets, to whom all pay prodigious attention. All the pale ladies drink pale ale, which, perhaps, accounts for it; in fact the Bombay and Suez passengers have just arrived, and hence this crowding and bustling, and display of military jackets and mustachoes, and ringlets and beauty. The windows are open, and a rush of mosquitoes from the Ezbekieh waters, attracted by the wax candles, adds greatly to the excitement of the scene.[7] There was a little tough old Major, who persisted in flinging open the windows, to admit these volatile creatures, with a noble disregard to their sting – and the pale ringlets did not seem to heed them either, though the delicate shoulders of some of them were bare.

All the meat, *ragoûts, fricandeaux,* and roasts, which are served round at dinner, seem to me to be of the same meat: a black uncertain sort of viand do these 'flesh pots of Egypt' contain. But what the meat is no one knew: is it the donkey? The animal is more plentiful than any other in Cairo.

After dinner, the ladies retiring, some of us take a mixture of hot water, sugar and pale French brandy, which is said to be deleterious, but is by no means unpalatable. One of the Indians offer a bundle of Bengal cheroots; and we make acquaintance with those honest bearded white-jacketed Majors and military Commanders, finding England here in a French hotel kept by an Italian, at the city of Grand Cairo, in Africa.

On retiring to bed you take a towel with you into the sacred interior, behind the mosquito curtains. Then your duty is, having tucked the curtains closely around, to flap and bang violently with this towel, right and left, and backwards and forwards, until every mosquito shall have been massacred that may have taken refuge within your muslin canopy.

Do what you will, however, one of them always escapes the murder: and as soon as the candle is out the miscreant begins his infernal droning and trumpeting; descends playfully upon your nose and face, and so lightly that you don't know that he touches you. But that for a week afterwards you bear about marks of his ferocity, you might take the invisible little being to be a creature of fancy – a mere singing in your ears.

This, as an account of Cairo, dear M.——, you will probably be disposed to consider as incomplete: the fact is, I have seen nothing else as yet. I have peered into no harems. The magicians, proved to be humbugs, have been bastinadoed out of town. The dancing girls, those lovely Alme, of whom

I had hoped to be able to give a glowing and elegant, though strictly moral, description, have been whipped into Upper Egypt, and as you are saying in your mind * * Well it *isn't* a good description of Cairo; you are perfectly right. It is England in Egypt? I like to see her there with her pluck, enterprise, manliness, bitter ale and Harvey sauce. Wherever they come they stay and prosper. From the summit of yonder pyramids forty centuries may look down on them if they are minded; and I say, those venerable daughters of time ought to be better pleased by the examination, than by regarding the French bayonets and General Bonaparte, Member of the Institute, fifty years ago, running about with sabre and pigtail.[8] Wonders he did to be sure, and then ran away, leaving Klèber, to be murdered, in the lurch – a few hundred yards from the spot where these disquisitions are written. But what are his wonders compared to Waghorn? Nap. massacred the Mamelukes at the pyramids: Wag. has conquered the pyramids themselves; dragged the unwieldly structures a month nearer England than they were, and brought the country along with them. All the trophies and captives, that ever were brought to Roman triumph, were not so enormous and wonderful as this. All the heads that Napoleon ever caused to be struck off (as George Cruikshank says) would not elevate him a monument as big. Be ours the trophies of peace! O my country! O Waghorn! *Hae tibi erunt artes.* When I go to the pyramids I will sacrifice in your name, and pour out libations of bitter ale and Harvey sauce in your honour.

One of the noblest views in the world is to be seen from the citadel, which we ascended today. You see the city stretching beneath it, with a thousand minarets and mosques, – the great river curling through the green plains, studded with innumerable villages. The pyramids are beyond, brilliantly distinct; and the lines and fortifications of the height, and the arsenal lying below. Gazing down, the guide does not fail to point out the famous Mameluke leap, by which one of the corps escaped death, at the time that his Highness the Pasha arranged the general massacre.[9]

The venerable Patriarch's harem is close by, where he received, with much distinction, some of the members of our party. We were allowed to pass very close to the sacred precincts, and saw a comfortable white European building, approached by flights of steps, and flanked by pretty gardens. Police and law-courts were here also, as I understood;

but it was not the time of the Egyptian assizes. It would have been pleasant, otherwise, to see the chief Cadi in his hall of justice; and painful though instructive, to behold the immediate application of the bastinado.

The great lion of the place is a new mosque which Mehemet Ali is constructing very leisurely. It is built of alabaster of a fair white, with a delicate blushing tinge; but the ornaments are European – the noble, fantastic, beautiful Oriental art is forgotten. The old mosques of the city, of which I entered two, and looked at many, are a thousand times more beautiful.[10] Their variety of ornament is astonishing, – the difference in the shapes of the domes, the beautiful fancies and caprices in the forms of the minarets, which violate the rules of proportion with the most happy, daring grace, must have struck every architect who has seen them. As you go through the streets, these architectural beauties keep the eye continually charmed: now it is a marble fountain, with its arabesque and carved overhanging roof, which you can look at with as much pleasure as an antique gem, so neat and brilliant is the execution of it; then, you come to the arched entrance to a mosque, which shoots up like – like what? – like the most beautiful pirouette by Taglioni, let us say.[11] This architecture is not sublimely beautiful, perfect loveliness and calm, like that which was revealed to us at the Parthenon (and in comparison of which the Pantheon and Colosseum are vulgar and coarse, mere broad-shouldered Titans before ambrosial Jove); but these fantastic spires, and cupolas, and galleries, excite, amuse, *tickle* the imagination so to speak, and perpetually fascinate the eye. There were very few believers in the famous mosque of Sultan Hassan when we visited it, except the moslem beadle, who was on the look out for *backsheesh*, just like his brother officer in an English cathedral; and who, making us put on straw slippers, so as not to pollute the sacred pavement of the place, conducted us through it.[12]

It is stupendously light and airy; the best specimens of Norman art that I have seen (and surely the Crusaders must have carried home the models of these heathenish temples in their eyes) do not exceed its noble grace and simplicity. The mystics make discoveries at home, that the Gothic architecture is Catholicism carved in stone (in which case, and if architectural beauty is a criterion or expression of religion, what a dismal barbarous creed must that, expressed by the

Street in Cairo, watercolour by Max Schmidt, 1844 *(detail).*
Photograph: Mathaf Gallery.

Facing Page, Left. *Cairo and the Valley of the Nile from the Citadel,* watercolour by William Bartlett, 1845-49. In *The Nile Boat,* Bartlett's account of his visit to Egypt in 1845, he describes this view with its multitude of domes and minarets as 'one of the grandest prospects in the world'. It extends from the great 14th-century mosque of Sultan Hasan across the city to the distant Pyramids on the far side of the Nile.
Photograph: The Fine Art Society.

Facing Page, Right. *Portrait of Muhammad Ali Pasha,* watercolour by John Frederick Lewis, 1844. Painted in the year that Thackeray visited Cairo, this imposing portrait shows the elderly Viceroy of Egypt in a room in his palace in the Citadel. Independent of the Ottoman Sultan in all but name, he is presented as ruler of all he surveys, from ancient Egypt, symbolised by the Pyramids, on the one hand, to modern Egypt, indicated by a corner of the mosque of Sultan Hasan, on the other.
Victoria and Albert Museum.
Photograph: The Peninsular and Oriental Steam Navigation Company.

Bethesda meeting-house and Independent chapels, be?); if, as they would gravely hint, because Gothic architecture is beautiful, Catholicism is therefore lovely and right, – why, Mahommedanism must have been right and lovely too once. Never did a creed possess temples more elegant; as elegant as the Cathedral at Rouen, or the Baptistery at Pisa.

But it is changed now. There was nobody at prayers; only the official beadles, and the supernumerary guides, who came for *backsheesh*. Faith has degenerated. Accordingly they can't build these mosques, or invent these perfect forms, any more. Witness the tawdry incompleteness and vulgarity of the Pasha's new temple, and the woeful failures among the very late edifices in Constantinople!

However, they still make pilgrimages to Mecca in great force. The mosque of Hassan is hard by the green plain on which the *Hajj* encamps before it sets forth annually on its pious perigrination.[13] It was not yet its time, but I saw in the bazaars that redoubted Dervish, who is the Master of the *Hajj* – the leader of every procession, accompanying the sacred camel; and a personage almost as much respected as Mr O'Connell in Ireland.

This fellow lives by alms (I mean the head of the *Hajj*). Winter and summer he wears no clothes but a thin and scanty white shirt. He wields a staff, and stalks along scowling and barefoot. His immense shock of black hair streams behind him, and his brown, brawny body is curled over with black hair, like a savage man. This saint has the largest harem in the town; he is said to be enormously rich by the contributions he has levied; and is so adored for his holiness by the infatuated folk, that when he returns from the *Hajj* (which he does on horseback, the chief Mollahs going out to meet him and escort him home in state along the Ezbekieh road), the people fling themselves down under the horse's feet, eager to be trampled upon and killed, and confident of Heaven if the great Hajji's horse will but kick them into it.

a clown and a knowing one, like Widdicombe and the clown with us, – the buffoon answering with blundering responses, which made all the audience shout with laughter; but the only joke which was translated to me would make you do anything but laugh, and shall therefore never be revealed by these lips. All their humour, my dragoman tells me, is of this questionable sort; and a young Egyptian gentleman, son of a Pasha, whom I subsequently met at Malta, confirmed the statement, and gave a detail of the practices of private life, which was anything but edifying. The great aim of the women, he said, in the much maligned Orient, is to administer to the brutality of her lord; her merit is in knowing how to vary the beast's pleasures. He could give us no idea, he said, of the *wit* of the Egyptian women, and their skill in *double entendre*; nor, I presume, did we lose much by our ignorance. What I would urge, humbly, however, is this – Do not let us be led away by German writers and aesthetics, Semilassoisms, Hahnhahnisms, and the like. The life of the East is a life of brutes. The much-maligned Orient, I am confident, has not been maligned near enough; for the good reason that none of us can tell the amount of horrible sensuality practised there.

Beyond the jack pudding rascal and his audience, there was on the green a spot, on which was pointed out to me, a mark, as of blood. That morning the blood had spouted from the neck of an Arnaoot soldier, who had been executed for murder.[14] The Arnaoots are the curse and terror of the citizens. Their camps are without the city; but they are always brawling, or drunken, or murdering within, in spite of the rigid law which is applied to them, and which brings one or more of the scoundrels to death almost every week.

Some of our party had seen this fellow borne by the hotel the day before, in the midst of a crowd of soldiers who had apprehended him. The man was still formidable to his score of captors; his clothes had been torn off; his limbs were bound with cords; but he was struggling frantically to get free; and my informant described the figure and appearance of the naked, bound, writhing savage, as quite a model of beauty.

Walking in the street, this fellow had just before been struck by the looks of a woman who was passing, and laid hands on her. She ran away, and he pursued her. She ran into the police barrack, which was luckily hard by; but the

Was it my fault if I thought of Hajji Daniel, and the believers in him.

There was no Dervish of repute on the plain when I passed; only one poor, wild fellow, who was dancing, with glaring eyes and grizzled beard, rather to the contempt of the by-standers, as I thought, who by no means put coppers into his extended bowl. On this poor devil's head there was a poorer devil still – a live cock, entirely plucked, but ornamented with some bits of ragged tape and scarlet and tinsel, the most horribly grotesque and miserable object I ever saw.

A little way from him, there was a sort of play going on –

Arnaoot was nothing daunted, and followed into the midst of the police. One of them tried to stop him. The Arnaoot pulled out a pistol, and shot the policeman dead. He cut down three or four more before he was secured. He knew his inevitable end must be death: that he could not seize upon the woman: that he could not hope to resist half a regiment of armed soldiers: yet his instinct of lust and murder was too strong; and so he had his head taken off quite calmly this morning, many of his comrades attending their brother's last moments. He cared not the least about dying; and knelt down and had his head off as coolly as if he were looking on at the same ceremony performed on another.

When the head was off, and the blood was spouting on the ground, a married woman, who had no children, came forward very eagerly out of the crowd, to smear herself with it, – the application of criminals' blood being considered a very favourable medicine for women afflicted with barrenness, – so she indulged in this remedy.

But one of the Arnaoots, standing near, said 'What, you like blood, do you? (or words to that effect) – Let's see how yours mixes with my comrades' and thereupon, taking out a pistol, he shot the woman in the midst of the crowd and the guards who were attending the execution; was seized of course by the latter; and no doubt tomorrow morning will have his head off too. It would be a good chapter to write – the *Death of the Arnaoot* – but I shan't go. Seeing one man hanged is quite enough in the course of a life. *J'y ai été*, as the Frenchman said of hunting.

These Arnaoots are the terror of the town. They seized hold of an Englishman the other day, and were very nearly pistolling him. Last week one of them murdered a shopkeeper at Boulak, who refused to sell him a watermelon at a price which he, the soldier, fixed upon it. So, for the matter of three half-pence, he killed the shopkeeper; and had his own rascally head chopped off, universally regretted by his friends. Why, I wonder, does not his Highness the Pasha invite the Arnaoots to a *déjeuner* at the Citadel, as he did the *Mamluks*, and serve them up the same sort of breakfast? The walls are considerably heightened since Emin Bey and his horse leapt them, and it is probable that not one of them would escape.

This sort of pistol practice is common enough here it would appear; and not among the Arnaoots merely, but the

higher orders. Thus, a short time since, one of his Highness's grandsons, whom I shall call Bluebeard Pasha[15] (lest a revelation of the name of the said Pasha might interrupt our good relations with his country) – one of the young Pashas being backward rather in his education, and anxious to learn mathematics, and the elegant deportment of civilized life – sent to England for a tutor. I have heard he was a Cambridge man, and had learned both algebra and politeness under the Reverend Doctor Whizzle, of —— College.

One day when Mr MacWhirter, B.A., was walking in Shoubra gardens, with His Highness the young Bluebeard Pasha, inducting him into the usages of polished society, and favouring him with reminiscences of Trumpington,[16] there came up a poor fellah, who flung himself at the feet of young Blubeard, and calling for justice in a loud and pathetic voice, and holding out a petition, besought his Highness to cast a gracious eye upon the same, and see that his slave had justice done him.

Bluebeard Pasha was so deeply engaged and interested by his respected tutor's conversation, that he told the poor *fellah* to go to the deuce, and resumed the discourse which his ill-timed outcry for justice had interrupted. But the unlucky wight of a *fellah* was pushed by his evil destiny, and thought he would make yet another application. So he took a short cut down one of the garden lanes, and as the Prince and the Reverend Mr MacWhirter, his tutor, came along once more engaged in pleasant disquisition, behold the *fellah* was once more in their way, kneeling at the august Bluebeard's feet, yelling out for justice as before, and thrusting his petition into the royal face.

When the Prince's conversation was thus interrupted a second time, his royal patience and clemency were at an end: 'Man,' said he, 'once before I bade thee not to pester me with thy clamour, and lo! you have disobeyed me, – Take the consequences of disobedience to a Prince, and thy blood be upon thine own head.' So saying, he drew out a pistol and blew out the brains of that *fellah*, so that he never bawled out for justice any more.

The Reverend Mr MacWhirter was astonished at this sudden mode of proceeding: 'Gracious Prince,' said he, 'we do not shoot an undergraduate at Cambridge even for walking over a college grass-plot. – Let me suggest to your Royal Highness that this method of ridding yourself of a poor

Darb al-Ahmar, drawing by Prosper Marilhat, 1831-32 *(detail)*. The principal mosque is that of Amir Khayrbak. The precise rendering of architectural detail in pencil and red chalk is characteristic of this French artist.
Victoria and Albert Museum (Searight Collection).

devil's importunities, is such as we should consider abrupt and almost cruel in Europe. Let me beg you to moderate your royal impetuosity for the future; and, as your Highness's tutor, entreat you to be a little less prodigal of your powder and shot.'

'O Mollah!' said his Highness, here interrupting his governor's affectionate appeal, – 'You are good to talk about Trumpington and the Pons Asinorum, but if you interfere with the course of justice in any way, or prevent me from shooting any dog of an Arab who snarls at my heels, I have another pistol; and, by the beard of the Prophet! a bullet for you too.' So saying he pulled out the weapon, with such a terrific and significant glance at the Reverend Mr MacWhirter, that that gentleman wished himself back in his Combination Room again; and is by this time, let us hope, safely housed there.

Another facetious anecdote, the last of those I had from a well-informed gentleman residing at Cairo, whose name (as many copies of this book that is to be, will be in the circulating libraries there) I cannot, for obvious reasons, mention.[17] The revenues of the country come into the august treasury through the means of farmers, to whom the districts are let out, and who are personally answerable for their quota of the taxation. This practice involves an intolerable deal of tyranny and extortion on the part of those engaged to levy the taxes, and creates a corresponding duplicity among the fellahs, who are not only wretchedly poor among themselves, but whose object is to appear still more poor, and guard their money from their rapacious overseers. Thus the Orient is much maligned: but everybody cheats there: that is a melancholy fact. The Pasha robs and cheats the merchants; knows that the overseer robs him, and bides his time, until he makes him disgorge by the application of the tremendous bastinado;[18] the overseer robs and squeezes the labourer; and the poverty-stricken devil cheats and robs in return; and so the government moves in a happy cycle of roguery.

Deputations from the *fellahs* and peasants come perpetually before the august presence, to complain of the cruelty and exactions of the chiefs set over them: but, as it is known that the Arab never will pay without the bastinado, their complaints, for the most part, meet with but little attention. His Highness's treasury must be filled, and his officers supported in their authority.

However, there was one village, of which the complaints were so pathetic, and the inhabitants so supremely wretched, that the royal indignation was moved at their story, and the chief of the village, Skinflint Beg, was called to give an account of himself at Cairo.

When he came before the presence, Mehemet Ali reproached him with his horrible cruelty and exactions; asked him how he dared to treat his faithful and beloved subjects in this way, and threatened him with disgrace, and the utter confiscation of his property, for thus having reduced a district to ruin.

'Your Highness says I have reduced these *fellahs* to ruin', said Skinflint Beg; 'what is the best way to confound my enemies, and to show you the falsehood of their accusations that I have ruined them? – To bring more money from them. If I bring you five hundred purses from my village, will you acknowledge that my people are not ruined yet?'.

The heart of the Pasha was touched: 'I will have no more bastinadoing, O Skinflint Beg; you have tortured these poor people so much, and have got so little from them, that my royal heart relents for the present, and I will have them suffer no farther.'

'Give me free leave – give me your Highness's gracious pardon, and I will bring the five hundred purses as surely as my name is Skinflint Beg. I demand only the time to go home, the time to return, and a few days to stay, and I will come back as honestly as Regulus Pasha did to the Carthaginians, – I will come back and make my face white before your Highness.'

Skinflint Beg's prayer for a reprieve was granted, and he returned to his village, where he forthwith called the elders together: 'O friends,' he said, 'complaints of our poverty and misery have reached the royal throne, and the benevolent heart of the sovereign has been melted by the words that have been poured into his ears. 'My heart yearns towards my people of El Muddee,' he says; "I have thought how to relieve their miseries. Near them lies the fruitful land of El Guanee. It is rich in maize, and cotton, in sesame, and barley: it is worth a thousand purses; but I will let it to my children for seven hundred, and I will give over the rest of the profit to them, as an alleviation for their affliction."'

The elders of El Muddee knew the great value and fertil-

Minaret of the Mosque El Rhamree, watercolour by David Roberts, c.1839 *(detail)*. An example of the architectural variety found in the streets of Cairo that so delighted Thackeray. *Photograph:* Sotheby's.

ity of the lands of Guanee, but they doubted the sincerity of their governor, who, however, dispelled their fears, and adroitly quickened their eagerness to close with the proffered bargain: 'I will myself advance two hundred and fifty purses', he said; 'do you take counsel among yourselves, and subscribe the other five hundred; and when the sum is ready, a deputation of you shall carry it to Cairo, and I will come with my share; and we will lay the whole at the feet of His Highness.' So the grey-bearded ones of the village advised with one another; and those who had been inaccessible to bastinadoes, somehow found money at the calling of interest; and the sheikh, and they, and the five hundred purses, set of on the road to the capital.

When they arrived, Skinflint Beg and the elders of El Muddee sought admission to the royal throne, and there laid down their purses. 'Here is your humble servant's contribution,' said Skinflint, producing his share; 'and here is the offering of your loyal village of El Muddee. Did I not before say that enemies and deceivers had maligned me before the august presence, pretending that not a piastre was left in my village, and that my extortion had entirely denuded the peasantry? See! here is proof that there is plenty of money still in El Muddee: in twelve hours the elders have subscribed five hundred purses, and lay them at the feet of their lord.'

Instead of the bastinado, Skinflint Beg was instantly rewarded with the royal favour, and the former mark of attention was bestowed upon the *fellahs* who had maligned him: Skinflint Beg was promoted to the rank of Skinflint Bey; and his manner of extracting money from his people, may be studied with admiration in a part of the United Kingdom.*

At the time of the Syrian quarrel,[19] and when, apprehending some general rupture with England, the Pasha wished to raise the spirit of the *fellahs*, and *relever la morale nationale*, he actually made one of the astonished Arabs a colonel. He degraded him three days after peace was concluded. The young Egyptian colonel, who told me this, laughed and enjoyed the joke with the utmost gusto. 'Is it not a shame,' he said, 'to make me a colonel at three-and-twenty; I, who have no particular merit, and have never seen

* At Derrynane Beg, for instance

The Street and Mosque of the Ghooreyah, watercolour and gouache painting by John Fredrick Lewis, ?1876. Lewis was one of many artists who took up Thackeray's challenge to paint the streets and bazaars of Cairo. Many of his highly acclaimed watercolours and oils were, like this one, based on the numerous sketches that Lewis had made while living in Cairo between 1841 and 1851. The Forbes Magazine Collection, New York. *Photograph:* The Fine Art Society.

Facing Page. *Bab Zooayleh,* watercolour by William Bartlett, 1845-49. The Bab Zuwaylah marked the southern boundary to the old Fatimid city. Above the gate rise the elegant twin minarets of the 15th-century Mosque of Sultan Muayyad Shaykh. Victoria and Albert Museum (Searight Collection).

A JOURNEY TO CAIRO

Female Costume, Cairo, watercolour by William Prinsep, 1842 *(detail)*. The women are enveloped in a *khabara* or outer robe covering the head and arms, and a *burqa*, the white muslin veil extending to below the knees. Women of the wealthier classes usually rode on donkeys through the Cairo streets.
Photograph: Martyn Gregory Gallery.

Facing Page, Left. *In the Bezestein, El Khan Khalil, Cairo,* oil painting by John Frederick Lewis, 1860. Thackeray's vivid description of the picturesque streets and bazaars of Cairo is brilliantly matched in Lewis's paintings, with their rich colours, closely observed detail and almost magical rendering of light and shade. Here, a dignified, elderly merchant, in sumptuous Ottoman dress, sits in a section of the Khan al Khalili that specialised in the sale of rugs, embroideries and other luxury textiles.
Photograph: The Fine Art Society.

any service?'. Death has since stopped the modest and good-natured young fellow's further promotion. The death of —— Bey was announced in the French papers, a few weeks back.

My above kind-hearted and agreeable young informant used to discourse, in our evenings in the Lazaretto at Malta, very eloquently about the beauty of his wife, whom he had left behind him at Cairo – her brown hair, her brilliant complexion, and her blue eyes. It is this Circassian blood, I suppose, to which the Turkish aristocracy that governs Egypt, must be indebted for the fairness of their skin. Ibrahhim Pasha, riding by in his barouche, looked like a bluff, jolly-faced English dragoon officer, with a grey mustache and red cheeks, such as you might see on a field day at Maidstone. All the numerous officials riding through the town, were quite as fair as Europeans. We made acquaintance with one dignitary, a very jovial and fat pasha, the proprietor of the inn, I believe, who was continually lounging about the Ezbekieh garden, and who, but for a slight Jewish cast of countenance, might have passed any day for a Frenchman. The ladies whom we saw were equally fair; that is, the very slight particles of the persons of ladies which our

lucky eyes were permitted to gaze on. These lovely creatures go through the town by parties of three or four, mounted on donkeys, and attended by slaves holding on at the crupper, to receive the lovely riders lest they should fall, and shouting out shrill cries of *Schmaalek, Ameenek* (or however else these words may be pronounced), and flogging off the people right and left with the buffalo thong. But the dear creatures are even more closely disguised than at Constantinople: their bodies are enveloped with a large black silk hood, like a cab-head; the fashion seemed to be to spread their arms out, and give this covering all the amplitude of which it was capable, as they leered and ogled you from under their black masks with their big rolling eyes.

Everybody has big rolling eyes here (unless to be sure they lose one of ophthalmia). The Arab women are some of the noblest figures I have ever seen. The habit of carrying jars on the head always gives the figure grace and motion; and the dress the women wear certainly displays it to full advantage. I have brought a complete one home with me, at the service of any lady for a masqued ball. It consists of a coarse blue dress of calico, opened in front, and fastened with a horn button. Three yards of blue stuff for a veil; on the top of the veil a jar to be balanced on the head; and a little black strip of silk to fall over the nose, and leave the beautiful eyes full liberty to roll and roam. But such a costume, not aided by any stays or any other article of dress whatever, can be worn only by a very good figure. I suspect it won't be borrowed for many balls next season.

The men, a tall handsome noble race, are treated like dogs. I shall never forget riding through the crowded bazaars, my interpreter, or *laquais de place*, ahead of me to clear the way – when he took his whip, and struck it over the shoulders of a man who could not or would not make way!

The man turned round – an old, venerable, handsome face, with awfully sad eyes, and a beard long and quite grey. He did not make the least complaint, but slunk out of the way, piteously shaking his shoulder. The sight of that indignity gave me a sickening feeling of disgust. I shouted out to the cursed lackey to hold his hand, and forbade him ever in my presence to strike old or young more; but everybody is doing it. The whip is in everybody's hands: the pasha's running footman, as he goes bustling through the bazaar; the doctor's attendant, as he soberly threads the crowd on his

follow him; and should any artist (by some rare occurrence) read this, who has leisure, and wants to break new ground, let him take heart, and try a winter in Cairo, where there is the finest climate and the best subjects for his pencil.

A series of studies of negroes alone, would form a picture-book delightfully grotesque. Mounting my donkey today, I took a ride to the desolate, noble old buildings outside the city, known as the Tombs of the Caliphs. Every one of these edifices, with their domes, and courts, and minarets is strange and beautiful. In one of them there was an encampment of negro slaves newly arrived: some scores of them were huddled against the sunny wall; two or three of their masters lounged about the court, or lay smoking upon carpets. There was one of these fellows, a straight-nosed

mare; the negro slave, who is riding by himself, the most insolent of all, strikes and slashes about without mercy, and you never hear a single complaint.

How to describe the beauty of the streets to you! – the fantastic splendour; the variety of the houses, and archways, and hanging roofs, and balconies, and porches; the delightful accidents of light and shade which chequer them; the noise, the bustle, the brilliancy of the crowd; the interminable vast bazaars with their barbaric splendour! There is a fortune to be made for painters in Cairo, and materials for a whole Academy of them. I never saw such a variety of architecture, of life, of picturesqueness, of brilliant colour, and light and shade. There is a picture in every street, and at every bazaar stall. Some of these, our celebrated water-colour painter, Mr Lewis,[20] has produced with admirable truth and exceeding minuteness and beauty; but there is room for a hundred to

ebony-faced Abyssinian, with an expression of such sinister, good humour in his handsome face, as would form a perfect type of villainy. He sat leering at me, over his carpet, as I endeavoured to get a sketch of that incarnate rascality. 'Give me some money,' said the fellow. 'I know what you are about. You will sell my picture for money when you get back to Europe; let me have some of it now!' But the very rude and humble designer was quite unequal to depict such a consummation and perfection of roguery; so flung him a cigar, which he began to smoke, grinning at the giver. I requested the interpreter to inform him, by way of assurance of my disinterestedness, that his face was a great deal too ugly to be popular in Europe, and that was the particular reason why I had selected it.

Then one of his companions got up and showed us his black cattle. The male slaves were chiefly lads, and the

Cairo from the Valley of Petrifications, watercolour by William Prinsep, 1842 *(detail)*. Like Thackeray, and apparently also on a donkey, Prinsep visited the so-called Tombs of the Caliphs in the Eastern Cemetery and the desert immediately beyond. *Photograph:* Martyn Gregory Gallery.

women young, well formed, and abominably hideous; the dealer pulled her blanket off one of them and bade her stand up, which she did with a great deal of shuddering modesty. She was coal black, her lips were the size of sausages, her eyes large and good-humoured; the hair or wool on this young person's head was curled and greased into a thousand filthy little ringlets. She was evidently the beauty of the flock.

They are not unhappy; they look to being bought, as many a spinster looks to an establishment in England; once in a family they are kindly treated and well clothed, and fatten, and are the merriest people of the whole community. These were of a much more savage sort than the slaves I had seen in the horrible market at Constantinople where I recollect the following young creature —

Negro slave girl,
wood engraving by William Thackeray.

(indeed it is a very fair likeness of her) whilst I was looking at her and forming pathetic conjectures regarding her fate – smiling very good humouredly, and bidding the interpreter ask me to buy her for twenty pounds.

From these Tombs of the Caliphs the Desert is before you. It comes up to the walls of the city, and stops at some gardens which spring up all of a sudden at its edge. You can see the first station house on the Suez Road; and so from distance point, to point, could ride thither alone without a guide.[21]

Asinus trotted gallantly into this desert for the space of a quarter of an hour. There we were (taking care to keep our backs to the city walls), in the real actual desert: mounds upon mounds of sand, stretching away as far as the eye can see, until the dreary prospect fades away in the yellow horizon! I had formed a finer idea of it out of *Eothen*. Perhaps in a *simoom* it may look more awful.[22] The only adventure that befell in this romantic place was that asinus' legs went deep into a hole: whereupon his rider went over his head, and bit the sand, and measured his length there; and upon this hint rose up, and rode home again. No doubt one should have gone out for a couple of days' march – as it was, the desert did not seem to me sublime, only *uncomfortable*.

Very soon after this perilous adventure the sun likewise dipped into the sand (but not to rise therefrom so quickly as I had done); and I saw this daily phenomenon of sunset with pleasure, for I was engaged at that hour to dine with our old

friend J. ——, who has established himself here in the most complete Oriental fashion.

You remember J. ——, and what a dandy he was, the faultlessness of his boots and cravats, the brilliancy of his waistcoats and kid gloves; we have seen his splendour in Regent Street, in the Tuilleries, or on the Toledo. My first object on arriving here was to find out his house, which he has taken far away from the haunts of European civilization, in the Arab quarter. It is situated in a cool, shady, narrow alley; so narrow, that it was with great difficulty – His Highness Ibrahim Pasha happening to pass at the same moment – that my little procession of two donkeys mounted by self and *valet de place*, with the two donkey-boys, our attend-

The Hôsh (Courtyard) of the House of the Coptic Patriarch, Cairo, oil painting by John Frederick Lewis, 1864. Despite the title this in fact depicts the house in which Lewis lived during his decade in Cairo, and which Thackeray describes in such vivid detail, even down to the pigeons 'flapping, and hopping, and fluttering, and cooing about . . . fed with crumbs from the henna-tipped fingers of Zuleikah!'. Private Collection.

Facing Page, Far Left. *Caged Doves, Cairo*, oil painting by John Frederick Lewis, 1864 *(detail)*. Lewis's model, sumptuously dressed in Turkish attire, was his wife, Marian, whom he married in Alexandria in 1847, and presumably took back to Cairo to the splendid house that provided the setting of many of his paintings. *Photograph*: Agnew's.

Facing Page, Right. *Hotel near Cairo*, lithograph by William Delamotte, from *Views of the Overland Journey to India*, 1847. This shows the first of several station houses on the road to Suez, where travellers could refresh themselves. Victoria and Albert Museum (Searight Collection).

ants, could range ourselves along the wall, and leave room for the august cavalcade. His Highness having rushed on (with an affable and good-humoured salute to our imposing party), we made J.'s quarters; and, in the first place, entered a broad covered court or porch, where a swarthy tawny attendant, dressed in blue, with white turban, keeps a perpetual watch. Servants in the east lie about all the doors, it appears; and you clap your hands, as they do in the dear old *Arabian Nights*, to summon them.

This servant disappeared through a narrow wicket, which he closed after him; and went into the inner chambers to ask if his lord would receive us. He came back presently, and rising up from my donkey, I confided him to his attendant

(lads more sharp, arch, and wicked, than these donkey-boys don't walk the *pavé* of Paris or London), and passed the mysterious outer door.

First we came into a broad open court, with a covered gallery running along one side of it. A camel was reclining on the grass there; near him was a gazelle to glad J. with his dark blue eye; and a numerous brood of hens and chickens, who furnish his liberal table. On the opposite side of the covered gallery rose up the walls of his long, queer, many-windowed, many-galleried house. There were wooden lattices to those arched windows, through the diamonds of one of which I saw two of the most beautiful, enormous, ogling, black eyes in the world, looking down upon the interesting stranger. Pigeons were flapping, and hopping, and fluttering, and cooing about. Happy pigeons you are, no doubt, fed with crumbs from the henna-tipped fingers of Zuleikah! All this court, cheerful in the sunshine, cheerful with the astonishing brilliancy of the eyes peering out from

Zuleikah peeping through the wooden lattice of Lewis's house, wood engraving by William Thackeray.

the lattice bars, was as mouldy, ancient, and ruinous, as any gentleman's house in Ireland, let us say. The paint was peeling off the rickety, old, carved, galleries; the arabesques over the windows were chipped and worn; – the ancientness of the place rendered it doubly picturesque. I have detained you a long time in the outer court. Why the deuce was Zuleikah there, with the beautiful black eyes!

Hence we passed into a large apartment, where there was a fountain; and another domestic made his appearance, taking me in charge, and relieving the tawny porter of the gate. This fellow was clad in blue too, with a red sash and a grey beard. He conducted me into a great hall, where there was a great, large Saracen oriel window. He seated me on a divan; and stalking off, for a moment, returned with a long pipe and a brass chafing dish: he blew the coal for the pipe, which he motioned me to smoke, and left me there with a respectful bow. This delay, this mystery of servants, that outer court with the camels, gazelles, and other beautiful-eyed things, affected me prodigiously all the time he was staying away; and while I was examining the strange apart-

ment and its contents, my respect and awe for the owner increased vastly.

As you will be glad to know how an Oriental nobleman (such as J. undoubtedly is) is lodged and garnished, let me describe the contents of this hall of audience. It is about forty feet long, and eighteen or twenty high. All the ceiling is carved, gilt, painted and embroidered with arabesques, and choice sentences of Eastern writing. Some Mameluke Aga, or Bey, whom Mehemet Ali invited to breakfast and massacred, was the proprietor of this mansion once; it has grown dingier, but, perhaps, handsomer, since his time. Opposite the divan is a great bay-window, with a divan likewise round the niche. It looks out upon a garden about the size of Fountain Court, Temple; surrounded by the tall houses of the quarter. The garden is full of green. A great palm tree springs up in the midst, with plentiful shrubberies, and a talking fountain. The room besides the divan is furnished with one deal table, value, five shillings; four wooden chairs, value, six shillings; and a couple of mats and carpets. The tables and chairs are luxuries imported from Europe. The regular Oriental dinner is put upon copper trays, which are laid upon low stools. Hence J. —— Effendi's house may be said to be much more sumptuously furnished than those of the Beys and Agas his neighbours.

When these things had been examined at leisure, J. —— appeared. Could it be the exquisite of the *Europa* and the *Trois Frères?*[23] A man – in a long yellow gown, with a long beard, somewhat tinged with grey, with his head shaved, and wearing on it first a white wadded cotton night-cap, second, a red tarboosh – made his appearance and welcomed me cordially. It was some time, as the Americans say, before I could 'realise' the *semillant* J. of old times.

He shuffled off his outer slippers before he curled up on the divan beside me. He clapped his hands, and languidly called 'Mustapha'. Mustapha came with more lights, pipes, and coffee; and then we fell to talking about London, and I gave him the last news of the comrades in that dear city. As we talked, his oriental coolness and languor gave way to British cordiality; he was the most amusing companion of the —— club once more.

He has adapted himself outwardly, however, to the oriental life. When he goes abroad he rides a grey horse with red housings, and has two servants to walk beside him. He wears a very handsome grave costume of dark blue, consisting of an embroidered jacket and gaiters, and a pair of trousers, which would make a set of dresses for an English family. His beard curls nobly over his chest, his Damascus scimitar on his thigh. His red cap gives him a venerable and Bey-like appearance. There is no gewgaw or parade about him, as in some of your dandified young agas. I should say that he is a Major General of Engineers, or a grave officer of State. We and the Turkified European, who found us at dinner, sat smoking in solemn divan.

His dinners were excellent; they were cooked by a regular Eyptian female cook. We had delicate cucumbers stuffed with forced meats; yellow smoking pilaffs, the pride of the oriental cuisine; kid and fowls *à l'Aboukir* and *à la Pyramide*; a number of little savoury plates of *légumes* of the vegetable-marrow sort; kibobs with an excellent sauce of plums and piquant herbs. We ended the repast with ruby pomegranates, pulled to pieces, deliciously cool and pleasant. For the meats, we certainly ate them with the Infidel knife and fork; but for the fruit, we put our hands into the dish and flicked them into our mouths in what cannot but be the true oriental manner. I asked for lamb and pistachio nuts, and cream tarts *au poivre*; but J.'s cook did not furnish us with either of those historic dishes. And for drink, we had water freshened in the porous little pots of grey clay, at whose spout every traveller in the East has sucked delighted. Also it must be

confessed, we drank certain sherbets, prepared by the two great rivals, Hadji Hodson and Bass Bey – the bitterest and most delicious of draughts![24] O divine Hodson! a camel's load of thy beer came from Beyrout to Jerusalem while we were there. How shall I ever forget the joy inspired by one of those foaming cool flasks?

We don't know the luxury of thirst in English climes. Sedentary men in cities at least have seldom ascertained it; but when they travel, our countrymen guard against it well. The road between Cairo and Suez is *jonché* with soda-water

corks. Tom Thumb and his brothers might track their way across the desert by those land marks.

Cairo is magnificently picturesque: it is fine to have palm trees in your gardens, and ride about on a camel; but, after all, I was anxious to know what were the particular excitements of Eastern life, which detained J., who is a town-bred man, from his natural pleasures and occupations in London; where his family don't hear from him, where his room is still kept ready at home, and his name is on the list of his Club; and where his neglected sisters tremble to think that their Frederick is going about with a great beard and a crooked sword, dressed up like an odious Turk. In a 'lark' such a costume may be very well; but home, London, a razor, your sister to make tea, a pair of moderate Christian breeches in lieu of those enormous Turkish *shulwars*, are vastly more convenient in the long run. What was it that kept him away

The Mid-day Meal, oil painting by John Frederick Lewis, 1875 *(detail).* The men on the balcony – overlooking the courtyard of Lewis's house – are participating in a meal similar to the dinner prepared for Thackeray by Lewis's Egyptian cook.
Photograph: Sotheby's.

Left. *Self-portrait smoking a çubuk,* wood engraving by William Thackeray.

The Hhareem, watercolour by John Frederick Lewis, 1850. A new slave-girl is brought into the harem for the master of the house to inspect. As the pasha leans forward, his three wives regard the new inmate with suspicion, while an Abyssinian girl – perhaps Thackeray's Zuleikah with the beautiful black eyes – watches with amusement. The exotic subject matter and elaborate treatment of it caused a sensation when the painting was exhibited at the Old Water-Colour Society in London, shortly before Lewis's return.
Nippon Life Insurance Company, Osaka.

Egyptian boy on top of a Pyramid, wood engraving by William Thackeray.

from these decent and accustomed delights?

It couldn't be the black eyes in the balcony – upon his honour she was only the black cook, who has done the pilaff, and stuffed the cucumbers. No, it was an indulgence of laziness such as Europeans, Englishmen at least, don't know how to enjoy. Here he lives like a languid Lotus-eater – a dreamy, hazy, lazy, tobaccofied life. He was away from evening parties, he said: he needn't wear white-kid gloves, or starched neckcloths, or read a newspaper. And even this life at Cairo was too civilized for him; Englishmen passed through; old acquaintances would call: the great pleasure of pleasures was life in the desert, – under the tents, with still *more* nothing to do than in Cairo; now smoking, now cantering on Arabs, and no crowd to jostle you; solemn contemplations of the stars at night, as the camels were picketed, and the fires and the pipes were lighted.

The night scene in the city is very striking for its vastness and loneliness. Everybody has gone to rest long before ten o'clock. There are no lights in the enormous buildings; only the stars blazing above, with their astonishing brilliancy, in the blue, peaceful sky. Your guides carry a couple of little lanterns, which redouble the darkness in the solitary, echoing street. Mysterious people are curled up and sleeping in the porches. A patrol of soldiers passes, and hails you. There is a light yet in one mosque, where some devotees are at prayers all night; and you hear the queerest nasal music proceeding from those pious believers. As you pass the mad-house, there is one poor fellow still talking to the moon – no sleep for him. He howls and sings there all the night – quite cheerfully, however. He has not lost his vanity with his reason; he is a Prince in spite of the bars and the straw.

What to say about those famous edifices, which has not been better said elsewhere? – but you will not believe that we visited them, unless I bring some token from them. Here is one: —

That white-capped lad skipped up the stones with a jug of water in his hand, to refresh weary climbers; and, squatting himself down on the summit, was designed as you see. The vast, flat landscape stretches behind him; the great winding river; the purple city, with forts, and domes, and spires; the green fields, and palm groves, and speckled villages; the plains still covered with shining inundations – the landscape stretches far, far away, until it is lost and mingled in the golden horizon. It is poor work this landscape painting in print. Shelley's two sonnets are the best views that I know of the Pyramids – better than the reality;[25] for a man may lay down the book, and in quiet fancy conjure up a picture out

of these magnificent words, which shan't be disturbed by any pettiness or mean realities, – such as the swarms of howling beggars, who jostle you about the actual place, and scream in your ears incessantly, and hang on your skirts, and bawl for money.

The ride to the Pyramids is one of the pleasantest possible. In the fall of the year, though the sky is almost cloudless above you, the sun is not too hot to bear; and the landscape, refreshed by the subsiding inundations, delightfully green and cheerful. We made up a party of some half dozen from the hotel, a lady (the kind soda-water provider, for whose hospitality the most grateful compliments are hereby offered) being of the company, bent like the rest upon going to the summit of Cheops. Those who were cautious and wise, took a brace of donkeys. At least five times during the route did my animals fall with me, causing me to repeat the desert experiment over again, but with more success. The space between a moderate pair of legs and the ground, is not many inches. By eschewing stirrups, the donkey could fall, and the rider alight on the ground, with the greatest ease and

grace. Almost everybody was down and up again in the course of the day.

We passed through the Ezbekieh and by the suburbs of the town, where the garden-houses of the Egyptian *noblesse* are situated, to old Cairo, where a ferry boat took the whole party across the Nile, with that noise and bawling volubility in which the Arab people seem to be so unlike the grave and silent Turks; and so took our course for some eight or ten miles over the devious tract which the still outlying waters obliged us to pursue. The Pyramids were in sight the whole way. One or two thin, silvery clouds were hovering over them, and casting delicate, rosy shadows, upon the grand, simple, old piles. Along the track, we saw a score of pleasant pictures of Eastern life: – The Pasha's horses and slaves stood caparisoned at his door; at the gate of one country house, I am sorry to say, the Bey's gig was in waiting, – a most unromantic chariot: the husbandmen were coming into the city, with their strings of donkeys, and their loads; as they arrived, they stopped and sucked at the fountain: a column of red-capped troops passed to drill, with slouched gait,

The Sphinx and Pyramids of Gizah, watercolour by William Prinsep, 1842. 'There they rose up enormous under our eyes, and the most absurd, trivial things were going on under their shadow.' In contrast to the effusions of most contemporary visitors to the Pyramids, Thackeray's attitude was characteristically derisive. *Photograph:* Martyn Gregory Gallery.

Left. *Female of the Middle Class drawing Water from the Nile*, after Emile Prisse d'Avennes, lithograph from *Oriental Album*, 1848. The *fallahah*, with her long blue robe and water-jar, is portrayed just as Thackeray describes. Victoria and Albert Museum (Searight Collection).

who every moment expected to be pitched into one of the many holes with which the treacherous lake abounded.

It was nothing but joking and laughter, bullying of guides, shouting for interpreters, quarrelling about six-pences. We were acting a farce, with the Pyramids for the scene. There they rose up enormous under our eyes, and the most absurd, trivial things were going on under their shadow. The sublime had disappeared, vast as they were. Do you remember how Gulliver lost his awe of the tremen-dous Brobdingnag ladies? Every traveller must go through all sorts of chaffering and bargaining, and paltry experiences, at this spot. You look up the tremendous steps, with a score of savage ruffians bellowing round you; you hear faint cheers

View on the Nile. Isle of Rhoda, and Ferry to Gizah, watercolour by David Roberts, 1840s. 'The busy and bustling scene near the great ferry is full of animation; picturesque boats lie near, and everywhere groups of Turks, Arabs, and Nubians, present subjects for the pencil of the artist.' The text accompanying Roberts's lithographs of Cairo and the Pyramids in *Egypt and Nubia* (vol. III, 1849) was as reverential in tone as Thackeray's was supercilious. *Photograph:* Mathaf Gallery.

white uniforms, and glittering bayonets.

Then we had the pictures at the quay: the ferry boat, and the red-sailed river boat, getting underway, and bound up the stream. There was the grain market, and the huts on the opposite side; and that beautiful woman, with silver armlets, and a face the colour of gold, which (the nose-bag having been luckily removed) beamed solemnly on us Europeans, like a great, yellow harvest moon. The bunches of purpling dates were pending from the branches; grey cranes or herons were flying over the cool, shining lakes, that the river's over-flow had left behind; water was gurgling through the courses by the rude locks and barriers formed there, and overflowing this patch of ground; whilst the neighbouring field was fast budding into the more brilliant fresh green. Single dromedaries were stepping along, their riders lolling on their haunches; low sail boats were lying in the canals; now, we crossed an old marble bridge; now, we went, one by one, over a ridge of slippery earth; now, we floundered through a small lake of mud. At last, at about half-a-mile off the Pyramid, we came to a piece of water some two score yards broad, where a regiment of half-naked Arabs, seizing upon each individual of the party, bore us off on their shoul-ders, to the laughter of all, and the great perplexity of several,

and cries high up, and catch sight of little reptiles crawling upwards; or, having achieved the summit, they come hop-ping and bouncing down again from degree to degree, – the cheers and cries swell louder and more disagreeable; pres-ently the little jumping thing, no bigger than an insect a moment ago, bounces down upon you expanded into a panting major of Bengal cavalry. He drives off the Arabs with an oath, – wipes his red, shining face, with his yellow handkerchief, drops puffing on the sand in a shady corner, where cold fowl and hard eggs are awaiting him, and the next minute you see his nose plunged in a foaming beaker of brandy and soda-water. He can say now and for ever, he has

been up the Pyramid. There is nothing sublime in it. You cast your eye once more up that staggering perspective of a zigzag line, which ends at the summit, and wish you were up there – and down again. Forwards! – Up with you! It must be done. Six Arabs are behind you, who won't let you escape if you would.

The importunity of these ruffians is a ludicrous annoyance to which a traveller must submit. For two miles before you reach the Pyramids, they seize on you, and never cease howling. Five or six of them pounce upon one victim, and never leave him until they have carried him up and down. Sometimes they conspire to run a man up the huge stair, and bring him, half-killed and fainting, to the top. Always a couple of brutes insist upon impelling you sternwards; from whom the only means to release yourself is to kick out vigorously and unmercifully, when the Arabs will possibly retreat. The ascent is not the least romantic, or difficult, or sublime: you walk up a great broken staircase, of which some of the steps are four feet high. It's not hard, only a little high. You see no better view from the top than you beheld from the bottom; only a little more river, and sand, and rice field. You jump down the big steps at your leisure; but your meditations you must keep for after times, – the cursed shrieking of the Arabs prevents all thought or leisure.

—— And this is all you have to tell about the Pyramids? O! for shame! Not a compliment to their age and size? Not a big phrase, – not a rapture? Do you mean to say that you had no feeling of respect and awe? Try, man, and build up a monument of words as lofty as they are – they, whom

imber edax, and *aquilo impotens*,[26] and the flight of ages, have not been able to destroy!

— No: be that work for great geniuses, great painters, great poets! This quill was never made to take such flights; it comes of the wing of an humble domestic bird, who walks a common; who talks a great deal (and hisses sometimes); who can't fly far or high, and drops always very quickly; and whose unromantic end is, to be laid on a Michaelmas or Christmas table, and there to be discussed for half-an-hour – let us hope, with some relish.

——

Another week saw us in the Quarantine Harbour at Malta,[27] where seventeen days of prison and quiet were almost agreeable after the incessant sight-seeing of the last two months. In the interval, between the 23rd of July and the 27th of October, we may boast of having seen more men and cities than most travellers have seen in such a time: – Lisbon, Cadiz, Gibraltar, Malta, Athens, Smyrna, Constantinople, Jerusalem, Cairo. I shall have the carpet-bag, which has visited these places in company with its owner, embroidered with their names; as military flags are emblazoned, and laid up in ordinary, to be looked at in old age. With what a number of sights and pictures, – of novel sensations, and lasting and delightful remembrances, does a man furnish his mind after such a tour! You forget all the annoyances of travel; but the pleasure remains with you, after that kind provision of nature by which a man forgets being ill, but thinks with joy of getting well, and can remember all the minute circumstances of his convalescence. I forget what sea-sickness is now; though it occupies a woeful portion of my Journal. There was a time on board, when the bitter ale was decidedly muddy; and the cook of the ship deserting at Constantinople, it must be confessed his successor was some time before he got his hand in. These sorrows have passed away with the soothing influence of time: the pleasures of the voyage remain, let us hope, as long as life will endure. It was but for a couple of days that those shining columns of the Parthenon glowed under the blue sky there; but the experience of a life could scarcely impress them more vividly. We saw Cadiz only for an hour; but the white buildings, and the glorious blue sea, how clear they are to the memory! – with the tang of that gipsy's guitar dancing in the market-

Left: *From the Top of the Great Pyramid*, watercolour by William Prinsep, 1842. 'The vast flat landscape stretches behind him; the great winding river; the purple city, with forts, and domes, and spires; the green fields, and palm groves, and speckled villages . . .'. *Photograph:* Martyn Gregory Gallery.

Facing Page, Right. *The Ascent of the Pyramids*, wood engraving from *The Overland Guide-Book; a complete vademecum for the Overland Traveller*, by Captain James Barber, published in 1845. Like it or not, no visitor to the Great Pyramid (Pyramid of Khufu), could escape the indignity of being hauled to the top.
The Peninsular and Oriental Steam Navigation Company.

place, in the midst of the fruit, and the beggars, and the sunshine. Who can forget the Bosphorus, the brightest and fairest scene in all the world; or the towering lines of Gibraltar; or the great piles of Mafra, as we rode into the Tagus? As I write this, and think, back comes Rhodes, with its old towers and artillery, and that wonderful atmosphere, and that astonishing blue sea which environs the island. The Arab riders go pacing over the plains of Sharon, in the rosy twilight, just before sunrise; and I can see the ghastly Moab mountains, with the Dead Sea gleaming before them; from the mosque on the way towards Bethany. The black, gnarled trees of Gethsemane lie at the foot of Olivet, and the yellow ramparts of the city rise up on the stony hills beyond.

But the happiest and best of all the recollections, perhaps, are those of the hours passed at night on the deck, when the stars were shining overhead, and the hours were tolled at their time, and your thoughts were fixed upon home far away. As the sun rose I once heard the priest, from the minaret of Constantinople, crying out, 'Come to prayer,' with his shrill voice ringing through the clear air; and saw, at the same hour, the Arab prostrate himself and pray, and the Jew rabbi, bending over his book, and worshipping the Maker of Turk and Jew. Sitting at home in London, and writing this last line of farewell, those figures come back the clearest of all to the memory, with the picture, too, of our ship sailing over the peaceful Sabbath sea, and our own prayers and services celebrated there. So each, in his fashion, and after his kind, is bowing down, and adoring the Father, who is equally above all. Cavil not, you brother or sister, if your neighbour's voice is not like yours; only hope, that his words are honest (as far as they may be), and his heart humble and thankful.

Entrance to Valletta Harbour, watercolour by Andrew Nicholl, 1837.
The Peninsular and Oriental Steam Navigation Company.

DEDICATION AND PREFACE TO THE 1865 EDITION

NOTES AND INDEX

DEDICATION

Dedicated To
CAPTAIN SAMUEL LEWIS,
Of the Peninsular and Oriental
Steam Navigation Company's Service[1]

MY DEAR LEWIS,

After a voyage, during which the captain of the ship has displayed uncommon courage, seamanship, affability, or other good qualities, grateful passengers often present him with a token of their esteem, in the shape of teapots, tankards, trays, etc., of precious metal. Among authors, however, bullion is a much rarer commodity than paper, whereof I beg you to accept a little in the shape of this small volume. It contains a few notes of a voyage which your skill and kindness rendered doubly pleasant; and of which I don't think there is any recollection more agreeable, than that it was the occasion of making your friendship.

If the noble Company in whose service you command (and whose fleet alone makes them a third-rate maritime power in Europe) should appoint a few admirals in their navy, I hope to hear that your flag is hoisted on board one of the grandest of their steamers. But, I trust, even there you will not forget the *Iberia*,[1] and the delightful Mediterranean cruise we had in her in the Autumn of 1844.

Most faithfully yours,

My dear Lewis,

W. M. THACKERAY
London, Dec. 24th, 1845.

PREFACE

On the 24th of July, 1844, the writer of this little book went to dine at the —— Club,[2] quite unconscious of the wonderful events which Fate had in store for him.

Mr William was there,[3] giving a farewell dinner to his friend, Mr James (now Sir James).[4] These two asked Mr Titmarsh to join company with them, and the conversation naturally fell upon the tour Mr James was about to take. The Peninsular and Oriental Company had arranged an excursion in the Mediterranean, by which, in the space of a couple of months, as many men and cities were to be seen as Ulysses surveyed and noted in ten years. Malta, Athens, Smyrna, Constantinople, Jerusalem, Cairo were to be visited, and everybody was to be back in London by Lord Mayor's day.

The idea of beholding these famous places inflamed Mr Titmarsh's mind; and the charms of such a journey were eloquently impressed upon him by Mr James. 'Come,' said that kind and hospitable gentleman, 'and make one of my family party; in all your life you will never probably have a chance again to see so much in so short a time. Consider – it is as easy as a journey to Paris or to Baden.' Mr Titmarsh considered all these things; but also the difficulties of the situation: he had but six-and-thirty hours to get ready for so portentous a journey – he had engagements at home – finally, could he afford it? In spite of these objections, however, with every glass of claret the enthusiasm somehow rose, and the difficulties vanished.

But when Mr James, to crown all, said he had no doubt that his friends, the Directors of the Peninsular and Oriental Company, would make Mr Titmarsh the present of a berth for the voyage, all objections ceased on his part: to break his outstanding engagements – to write letters to his amazed family, stating that they were not to expect him at dinner on Saturday fortnight, as he would be at Jerusalem on that day – to purchase eighteen shirts and lay in a sea stock of Russia ducks, – was the work of four-and-twenty hours; and on the 26th of July, the *Lady Mary Wood* was sailing from Southampton with the 'subject of the present memoir,' quite astonished to find himself one of the passengers on board.[5]

These important statements are made partly to convince some incredulous friends – who insist still that the writer never went abroad at all, and wrote the following pages, out of pure fancy, in retirement at Putney; but mainly, to give him an opportunity of thanking the Directors of the Company in question for a delightful excursion.

It was one so easy, so charming, and I think profitable – it leaves such a store of pleasant recollections for after days – and creates so many new sources of interest (a newspaper letter from Beyrout, or Malta, or Algiers has twice the interest now that it had formerly), – that I can't but recommend all persons who have time and means to make a similar journey – vacation idlers to extend their travels and pursue it: above all, young well-educated men entering life, to take this course, we will say, after that at college; and, having their book-learning fresh in their minds, see the living people and their cities, and the actual aspect of Nature, along the famous shores of the Mediterranean.

NOTES

Chapter I

1. P&O's vessels all left England from Southampton docks, passing the Isle of Wight with passengers often bidding tearful farewells to the Needles.
2. Early voyages aboard P&O vessels were celebrated for their luxuries which always included champagne on Sunday. Voyages to India were also famous for the gargantuan meals which were served on board; Thackeray describes a 'bill of fare' later.
3. The contract for carrying mails to Egypt or India was essential to the profitability of early steam routes and far more crucial in that respect than carrying passengers.
4. Among the 'tallest and fattest' was Thackeray himself, already styling himself 'The Fat Contributor' to *Punch*, over six foot tall and weighing between fifteen and eighteen stone (210-252 lb).
5. Pump Court is in Middle Temple, London where Thackeray studied law.
6. Astley's amphitheatre in London was famous for its equestrian performers and the staging of set pieces of military achievement, such as Nelson's victory at Trafalgar.
7. *Gil Blas*, an eighteenth century picaresque romance by Le Sage, translated into English by Smollett.

Chapter II

1. The church of St Roch in Lisbon was famous for an inner chapel decorated with mosaics and marbles.
2. Lisbon was devastated by an earthquake in 1755, in which 80,000 people are believed to have died.
3. By Louis XV fashions Thackeray is referring to the flamboyant style which characterises much Portuguese architecture, including the Belem

convent church and that of St Roch.
4. The exuberant Belem convent church adjoins the palace of the Kings of Portugal in Lisbon.
5. The Necessidades Palace used to be the royal residence but already by Thackeray's day was used mainly for ceremonial purposes.
6. Napoleon's commanders Marshal Soult and Androche Junot led Napoleon's armies into Spain and subsequently Portugal in 1808. As a small boy sailing to England from India via the Cape of Good Hope, Thackeray had stopped at St Helena and been taken to see the exiled Napoleon walking in his garden.
7. Corks were stuck on bull's horns in Portuguese bullfights because it was illegal for either bull or man to kill the opponent.
8. François d'Orléans, Prince de Joinville, was the third son of Louis Philippe and Admiral of a fleet sent to bombard the Moroccan port of Mogador in 1844. French forces under Marshal Bugeaud fighting the Algerian leader Abd al-Kader had pursued him in 1842 to the border of Morocco (defeating him at Isly) where he was then able to take refuge. In 1844, with the Amir of Morocco having refused to expel Abd al-Kader, the French government decided to teach him a lesson, sending Joinville in August to bombard first Tangier and then Mogador (now Essaoira). In September the Amir sued for peace, Abd al-Kader was banned from using Morocco as a base and Bugeaud was made Duc d'Isly.
9. Figaro was the mischievous barber of Seville invented by Beaumarchais and subsequently made into an operatic hero by Mozart and Rossini. Luigi Lablache (1794-1858), an Italian, was the most famous bass of his generation

who made his London début in 1830 and sang there every season until 1852. He taught singing to Queen Victoria.
10. The British Admiral Sir George Rooke (1650-1709) seized Gibraltar from Spain in 1704.

Chapter III

1. The combination of a lateen mizzen sail and square rigging had enabled the Portuguese caravelles to make their astonishing voyages of discovery in the fifteenth century.

Chapter IV

1. Edward Bulwer-Lytton (1803-73), first Lord Lytton, would have been known to Thackeray as a literary figure in London; his prodigious literary output had brought on ill health and he was advised in the early 1840s to travel to regain his health, hence his visit to Gibraltar.
2. Sir Robert Wilson (1777-1849) had a distinguished military career during the Napoleonic Wars and was appointed Governor of Gibraltar in 1842.
3. The name Gibraltar comes from the Arabic Jabal al-Tarik, after the Arab conqueror Tarik who landed there in 711; the Moorish or Arab castle was built in 725.
4. Harry Lorrequer was a swashbuckling character in the *Dublin Magazine* which Thackeray would have come across during his travels in Ireland in the early 1840s.
5. Thackeray was a qualified admirer of Sir Walter Scott, writing in *Fraser's Magazine* in 1844: 'How astonishingly Sir Walter Scott has influenced the world; how he changed the character of novelists, then of historians, whom he brought from their philosophy to the

study of pageantry and costume.'
6. George Augustus Eliott (1717-90), later Viscount Heathfield, defended Gibraltar from 1779-82 when the Spanish took advantage of British involvement in the American War of Independence to challenge British possession of Gibraltar. The 'magnificent portrait' of Heathfield by Reynolds hangs in the National Gallery.
7. Thackeray moved to P&O's ss *Tagus* in Gibraltar, leaving *Lady Mary Wood* to continue her voyage round the Cape to Calcutta, P&O's headquarters in India. In Constantinople he was to join P&O's *Iberia*.
8. T.P. Cooke (1786-1864) was a celebrated actor whom Thackeray would have seen at Covent Garden and Drury Lane.
9. 'anerithmon gelasma', endless bout of laughter. In fact, Thackeray spares his reader further Greek quotations.
10. '*Que diable allais je faire dans un galère d'un Turc?*' was first exclaimed in 1654 by Cyrano de Bergerac in his *Le Pedant Joué*. Thackeray's version comes from Molière's *Les Fourberies de Scapin* (1671), Act II, sc.9. The expression obviously had great appeal for it was then misquoted by Dickens in *Tale of Two Cities* ('what the devil do you do in that gallery there?' – vol I, Ch.5).
11. Valletta was named after the Grand Master of the Order of Knights of St John of Jerusalem, Jean Parisot de la Valette, who directed the defenders of Malta during its siege by the Turks in 1565. The Order of the Knights of St John was founded in 1099 to look after pilgrims and sick Christians in Jerusalem. They became a military order in 1113, to ward off Muslim attacks. Gradually driven out of Palestine they withdrew first to Rhodes

and later, when driven from there in 1530, to Malta.

12. Don Basilio was Rosina's singing teacher in Rossini's Il *Barbiere de Siviglia*.

13. Alof de Vignacourt (1547-1622) was Grand Master of the Order of the Knights of Malta (1601-22) and was responsible for rebuilding its fortunes in the seventeenth century. Among his achievements was the construction of the aqueduct mentioned by Thackeray bringing water (always a problem in Malta) to Valletta. The portrait of Alof de Vignacourt in full armour (now Louvre, Paris) is one of four known pictures painted by Michelangelo Merisi da Caravaggio (1573-1610) during his stay in Malta in 1607-08.

14. Napoleon invaded Malta in 1798 on his way to Egypt; the British obtained possession of Malta in 1803; and it subsequently became an essential link in the steam route to India, providing coaling facilities as well as acting as a quarantine station for those emerging from the east. The Knights put up virtually no resistance to Napoleon's invasion of the island in 1798, although they were far from 'extinguished': the order was established in Rome and still owns a number of hospitals throughout the world.

15. Malta was the principal of several quarantine stations in the Mediterranean, the name quarantine derived from the forty days it was originally considered necessary to free travellers from the east of their infections – plague and cholera being the main fears. The number of days spent in quarantine depended on the length of time spent since leaving the place of infection. Three of Thackeray's party died during his trip, two of them while in quarantine on the return stretch and the third in Egypt.

Chapter V

1. '*Tooke's Pantheon*', a collection of classical (Greek) stories about the gods.

2. Thackeray uses his visit to Greece for a diatribe against the classical education he had so detested at Charterhouse. He had particularly harsh memories of being thrashed by a 'brute of a schoolmaster' for not mastering Greek grammar.

3. Xantippe was the wife of Socrates, proverbial as a scolding and quarrelsome woman.

4. Aristides, an Athenian general of the 6th century BC who helped defeat the Persians at Marathon (pelting them with holy oyster shells).

5. Cape Sunium, a promontory north of Piræus and the site of a temple dedicated to Poseidon.

6. Aristophanes satirised Socrates lying in a hammock in the '*Clouds*'.

7. By all accounts King Otho of Greece disliked his role as much as Thackeray estimated. Son of King Leopold of Bavaria, he was installed as king by the allied powers – France, Britain, Russia and Austria – after the Greek War of Independence in 1831. His reign was marked by turbulence and he was eventually deposed, as much to his relief, it seems, as to that of his subjects.

8. '*gobemouche*', one who credulously accepts all news.

9. The eulogy of Byron in relation to Missolonghi, in John Murray's handbook to Greece, first published in 1840, is as excessive as Thackeray maintains.

10. Sir Robert Peel (1750-1850), British industrialist, reformer and politician who became Prime Minister in 1834 and again in 1842 was responsible for the repeal of the Corn Laws, the subject of political uproar in the year of Thackeray's voyage.

11. John Cam Hobhouse, Lord Broughton (1786-1869), was Byron's close friend and travelling companion in the eastern Mediterranean, describing his travels in *Journey through Albania, and other provinces of Turkey in Europe and Asia, to Constantinople*, published in 1813.

Chapter VI

1. Smyrna, now Izmir.

2. The *Arabian Nights, Alf laila wa lailah*, was first translated directly into English in 1830 but was already well known as a popular medium for gothic romances and sentimental tales. Thackeray would have been familiar with the 1841 translation, still heavily expurgated, by Edward Lane. Burton's version was published between 1885 and 1888; the third volume was dedicated to Thackeray's friend Richard Monkton Milnes (see Ch.10).

3. Shackabac/Shaccabac, the name of the Barber's sixth brother, in the *Arabian Nights* story of that name. Shaccabac is treated by a rich noble of the Barmaki family to an imaginary feast, hence (according to a later translator Richard Burton) the term 'Barmecide feast' meaning an illusion.

4. The great Afreet (a *jinn*) occurs in *The Tale of the Trader and the Afreet*.

5. Morgiana was the female slave of Ali Baba whose life she preserved by pouring boiling oil into the vats containing the forty thieves; she was rewarded not only with her freedom but also with the honour of marrying Ali Baba's son.

6. King Schahriar, usually known as Shahryar, to amuse whom the beautiful Princess Shahrazad in the *Arabian Nights* spun her tales of kings, barbers and cooks.

7. *Ramazan*, the Muslim lunar month during which nothing may pass between the lips of a devout Muslim between sunrise and sunset. It is not an ideal time to be a tourist in the Muslim world, as Thackeray found.

8. 'narghiles' or *narghilah*, the water pipe popularly smoked in Arab homes and coffee houses.

9. Harun Alraschid – Harun al-Rashid, Abbasid Caliph on whom King Shahryar of *Arabian Nights* was based.

10. An Ovid reference.

11. 'Giaour', a term of reproach applied by Turks to non-Muslims, particularly Christians.

12. Robert Fulton was an American pioneer in the development of steam transport on water. He was aboard the *Charlotte Dundas* in 1801 and returned to the United States to test his own paddle steamer Clermont in 1807, later the same year initiating a service between New York and Albany.

13. Marshal Bugeaud led the French forces to the defeat of the Algerian leader, Abd al-Kader, at Isley (Isly) in 1842.

14. The so-called tomb of Achilles is to the north-west of the main site of Troy.

Chapter VII

1. Clarkson Stanfield (1793-1867) was a marine and landscape painter but most notably in this context – given Thackeray's enthusiasm for the theatre – a painter of theatrical scenes. He painted the popular diorama, *Spithead to Gibraltar*, displayed at Drury Lane in 1828. Baker and Diddear appeared in other slightly later productions – spectacles and melodramas – for which Stanfield painted the scenery.

2. Hollar's print of London: Wenceslaus Hollar (1607-77) was an engraver from Prague who spent much of his working life in London. The reference is probably to a celebrated engraving of the city before and after the Great Fire of 1666.

3. Misseri, now married to an English woman and running the best hotel in Pera, was the faithful servant and companion of Alexander Kinglake during his travels through the Ottoman Empire in 1834-35.

4. Kinglake had just published his anonymous account of these travels, *Eothen*, when Thackeray set out, though Thackeray seems to have known the authorship and was reading it between Malta and Athens.

5. '*Aut diabolus aut*', literally 'either the devil, or someone else' with '*aut diabolus aut amicus*' meaning 'either the devil or a friend'.

6. Lady Mary Wortley Montagu(e) was the intellectual wife of Edward Montagu, sent in 1716 as British ambassador to Constantinople. Lady Mary was introduced to the Turkish bath there and was struck by the beauty of the women bathing therein.

7. The word dragoman is derived from the Arabic *tarjama* meaning to translate. It came to mean the Mr Fix-it so essential to operations in the Middle East, and later little more than a guide for tourists.

8. Tophana was originally a cannon foundry just outside the walls of Galata in Constantinople; the name was later applied to the district.

9. Mahound is the archaic name for the Prophet Muhammad.

10. Miss MacWhirter's flaxen wig: Thackeray is probably referring to the *loofah* with which one is traditionally scrubbed clean in a Turkish bath.

11. Victor Hugo travelled on the Rhine in 1839 and subsequently published two volumes of travels, entitled *Le Rhin*, in 1842; a third volume appeared in 1845.

12. 'Sweet Waters' exist on either side of the Bosphorous where inland springs descended through hills and meadows to the sea; they were popular picnic spots for the inhabitants of Constantinople and were frequently painted by European artists.

13. 'His Highness the Sultan' was Sultan Abdul Mecid (1839-61).

14. David Urquhart's russophobia and turcophilia were well demonstrated in the pages of his periodical *The Portfolio* and a number of other publications.

15. The obscure *Palm Leaves* typifies to Thackeray the romanticised and melodramatic vision of the Orient which he goes to some pains to refute in his own account.

16. Ibrahim Pasha (1789-1848) was the eldest son of Muhammad Ali who led the Egyptian invasion of Syria.

17. A Muslim is obliged to wash before praying. 'Approach not prayers with a mind befogged ... nor in a state of ceremonial impurity ... until after washing your whole body,' orders the Quran.

18. Potential successors were usually viewed with great suspicion by ruling sultans, and Abdul Mecid's predecessor, Sultan Mahmud, was no exception, and certainly responsible for the death of his brother Mustafa. He himself spent much of his youth imprisoned in a cage-like kiosk in the Saray. Thackeray comments that the violence would make a good subject for a poem and indeed various melodramatic episodes in Turkish history furnished themes for European writers.

19. The Atmeidan is the ancient hippodrome of Constantinople.

20. The mosque of Sultan Ahmed Camii, also known as the Blue Mosque, was built between 1609 and 1616 by the architect Mehmet Aga.

21. 'Henné' or *hennah* is a leaf related to privet that is ground, made into a paste and used to decorate by staining the face, hands and hair of women throughout the Near and Middle East.

22. John Leech (1817-64), a humorous artist most celebrated for his association with *Punch*, was a friend of Thackeray from Charterhouse schooldays.

23. Topkapi Saray is the complex of buildings, kiosks and gardens occupied by the Sultan and his household.

24. 'ichoglan', a page-in-waiting at the Sultan's palace.

25. Thackeray is referring to the old Vauxhall pleasure gardens on the south bank of the Thames in London.

26. The Sublime Porte was the gate leading to the palaces and offices of the Grand Vizier, where most Imperial business was conducted.

27. The church nearby is Haghia Eirene, built mostly in the sixth century and later used by the Sultan's Janissaries as an arsenal.

Chapter VIII

1. Broussa or Bursa was famous for its silk industry.

2. Rhodes became the headquarters of the Knights of St John in 1308; they remained there until 1522 when they were forced by the Turks to leave.

3. Thackeray is here voicing an opinion – on the brutality of the Crusaders – more accepted today than in the nineteenth century when, as he points out, most people followed Walter Scott's glamorisation of the Crusaders, notably in *The Talisman* and *Tales of the Crusades*.

4. By Bajazet Ilderim, Thackeray is probably referring to Sultan Beyazit I. He ruled the Ottoman Turks from 1389 to 1402 and was celebrated in English literature by his inclusion in Marlowe's *Tamburlaine the Great*.

5. By 'Calmucs' Thackeray is referring loosely to Russians, although the Kalmuks themselves come from the north-west Caspian shore. They became subject to the Russians in 1646.

6. Ali and Umar were early rivals in claiming the caliphate, or succession, to the Prophet Muhammad, 'the awful camel driver' (Muhammad was a merchant of Mecca, hence his connection with camel caravans); Kadisheh, more correctly Khadijah, was a rich Meccan widow who became his wife.

Chapter X

1. The Bay of Glaucus is now known as the Bay of Fethiye.

2. Richard Monckton Milnes (1809-65), politician, writer and champion of Keats, was a Cambridge friend of Thackeray whom he later knew in Paris and Yorkshire.

3. Henry Vizetelly (1820-94) was the editor of *Pictorial Times* and a friend of Thackeray.

4. Sir Francis Beaufort, author of *Memoir of a Survey of the Coast of Caramania*, published in 1820, was Hydrographer to the Admiralty and creator of the Beaufort Scale for measuring wind speeds. His book drew the attention of Charles Fellowes to antiquities in south-west Turkey and in 1841 Beaufort transported Fellowes to Turkey on board his vessel *Beacon* and brought back the Lycian marble sculptures now in the British Museum.

5. Sir Charles (not John, as Thackeray calls him) Fellowes brought the antiquities to the Museum, including the exquisite Xanthian marbles, after excavations in Asia Minor, 1838-44.

6. Telmessus, the ancient name for Fethiye.

7. Makri, the Greek name for Fethiye, still in use in the nineteenth century.

8. Antiphilos, now Kaş has a small Hellenistic theatre.

9. By St George's Bay Thackeray may be referring to the Gulf of Antalya.

10. The *Trump* had been lying off Beirut to help guarantee the peace achieved by British and Austrian governments after ending the Egyptian occupation of Syria in 1840.

11. C.R. Leslie (1754-1859), painter of historical scenes and also portrait painter.

12. The blue-veiled women from the Lebanon were the Druze women, famous for their strange headdresses, known as tantour, 'sticking out two feet from the upper forehead, never taken off even at night', according to Thackeray's contemporary, Eliot Warburton.

Chapter XI

1. Consuls and consuls-general in Constantinople, Smyrna and Beirut were empowered to appoint lesser consuls and consular agents in towns within their jurisdiction. Generally unpaid and usually Jewish, Italian, Armenian or Greek, their main responsibility was the administration of British justice for British subjects in consular courts. The Jaffa consul also found himself offering hospitality to British pilgrims to the Holy Land. The honorary nature of their services left plenty of scope for malpractice, hence Thackeray's later comment on 'the mean consular flag'.

2. A 'cadi' or *qadi* is the Arabic for a judge of Islamic or Shari'a law.

3. 'casino' or cassino, a card game.

4. 'thimblerig' is a gambling (and swindling) game.

5. Antar was a legendary pre-Islamic hero; in his diary Thackeray notes that he is reading *Antar, a Bedooeen Romance*, published in 1820.

6. *haick*, an oblong piece of cloth which Arabs wrap around the head and body as a garment.

Chapter XII

1. 'Sardanapaluse', one who indulges in effeminate luxury, after Sardanapalus, the last King of Nineveh.

2. *'yataghan'*, a sword in the Islamic world which has a handle without a guard and often a double curved blade.

3. Both the Honourable Hoggin Armer and Lord Oldgent are admirable caricatures of the 'typical' well-to-do tourist who liked to extend his Grand Tour of Europe to slightly more exotic spots such as the Levant.

4. The plain of Sharon extends from Jaffa to Mount Carmel and inland. It was celebrated for its fertility but Jewish commentators reckon that the roses praised in the Song of Solomon (ii,1) and mentioned by Thackeray were in fact narcissi.

5. Richard and Saladin, refers to Richard Coeur de Lion who led the English forces in the Third Crusade in 1191 and his principal opponent the Kurdish general Salah al-Din.

6. 'diachylon', an ointment or dye made from vegetable juices.

7. A US consul in Beirut, Jacques Chasseaud, appointed a US consular agent in Jerusalem in 1840 under pressure from American missionaries working in Beirut and Jerusalem.

8. *'jereed'*, a wooden javelin, about five feet long, used by Arab, Persian and Turkish horsemen in a game.

9. *'fellah'* is Egyptian Arabic for farmer of peasant.

Chapter XIII

1. Russian claims to support the Greek Orthodox Church and protect the holy places in Jerusalem was the immediate pretext for the Crimean War in 1854.
2. The mosque of Umar is more correctly known as the Dome of the Rock or Haram al-Sharif. The city of Jerusalem surrendered to the Caliph Umar in 637, who built an earlier mosque on this site of the Jewish temple.
3. British missionary activity in Jerusalem was mainly directed, since 1820, at the conversion of the Jews since proselytisation among Muslims was expressly forbidden and among oriental Christians politically dangerous. By 1844 the mission was under the auspices of a joint Anglo-Prussian Protestant see, which became purely Anglican in 1866.
4. Bishop Michael Alexander, a converted Jew originally from Germany, was the first bishop appointed to the joint see. He was not a tactful man, referring to the Ottoman administration as 'the usurped government' and starting to build a cathedral before having permission to do so. Edward Lear in Jerusalem in the later 1840s wrote that 'the idea of converting [the Jews] to Christianity in Jerusalem is to the sober observer fully as absurd as that you should constitute a society to convert all the cabbages and strawberries in Covent Garden into pigeon pies and Turkey carpets.'
5. The Zion gate is sometimes known as the Gate of David. One of several tombs claimed to be of David was south of the mosque of Nabi (Prophet) Daoud.
6. Mar Elyas, Monastery of Elijah or Convent of St George as it was also known.
7. George Cattermole (1800-68), a watercolour painter and book illustrator, particularly popular for his historical scenes showing gallant knights and fair ladies in romantic, medieval interiors.

8. The party going to the Dead Sea were to some extent displaying the over-caution typical of many tourists: arming with pistols adds to the exoticism of the tour. But Ottoman control of such outlying territories had a poor reputation and for this reason archaeologists, for instance, found it virtually impossible to investigate the antiquity of the Holy Land outside the main cities.
9. The French had assumed the protection of the Maronites in Syria and Mount Lebanon since the sixteenth century, developing religious and economic links through Catholic missionaries as well as French traders living in Sidon. The relationship continues to the present day, with the French government offering protection to the Lebanese Christians in their war-torn country.
10. Alphonse de Lamartine's *Souvenirs, impressions, pensées et paysages pendant un voyage en Orient 1832-33* was published in Paris in 1835. Vicomte Francois René de Chateaubriand's *Itinéraire de Paris à Jerusalem* was published in Paris in 1812 and a translated version, *Travels in Greece, Palestine, Egypt and Barbary 1806-7,* published in 1811.
11. Charles X ruled France 1824-30, and was known for his public piety.
12. American missionary activity was initiated from Beirut where American missionaries had first settled in the 1820s. It was extended to Jerusalem in 1834 but the activities of the Anglo-Prussian see caused the American mission to withdraw and restrict its own work to Syria. The American mission was responsible for founding the American University of Beirut in 1867.
13. The fatal Syrian fever was probably malaria.
14. Charles Fellowes wrote two books, *An excursion in Asia Minor* (published in 1839) and *Discoveries in Lycia* (published in 1841), in both of which he complains about the mosquitoes – as would anyone who has camped in those parts – and suggests the remedy of a mosquito net in the latter.

Chapter XIV

1. *'pratique'* is the formal permission given to a vessel to enter a foreign port after satisfying local health regulations.
2. P&O's *Oriental* was one of the largest wooden paddle steamers of its day refurbished from the transatlantic run and launched by the company on its Mediterranean service. It was described as 'hermaphrodite', using sail as well as steam power. A passage cost £150 for gentlemen, £153 for ladies; champagne was served on Thursdays as well as Sundays.
3. There is no evidence that Pompey's Pillar had anything to do with the Pompeys; it may have been erected for the Emperor Diocletian in about AD 297.
4. Thackeray may be referring to Tennyson's sonnet to Alexander.
5. The French were pre-eminent among Europeans in Egypt even before Napoleon's invasion in 1798 and curiously enough the invasion and its accompanying teams of savants and technicians sustained that position despite Napoleon's defeat: 'everything in Egypt is growing French,' Waghorn complained in 1838.
6. Thackeray had two daughters, Anne or Anny born in 1837 and Harriet born in 1840. They were both living with Thackeray's mother and stepfather in Paris at the time of his trip.
7. Thackeray worked for *Galignani's Messenger* in Paris in 1835. A. & W. Galignani published a *New Paris Guide* in 1844.
8. Daniel O'Connell (1775-1847), Irish lawyer and political leader.
9. The Viceroy of Egypt Muhammad Ali offered obelisks to both British and French governments, the French accepting theirs in 1833. A special barge was despatched with a removable stern to collect it, towing it by steamer to Rouen with the obelisk eventually erected in Place de la Concorde. The British, disdainful when Muhammad Ali offered it to commemorate the coronation of George IV, only collected theirs in 1877, in a special cylindrical vessel, erecting it on the Adelphi steps on London's Embankment over a cache of contemporary treasures.

Chapter XV

1. The Mahmudiyyah Canal was re-excavated by Muhammad Ali in the 1820s, at the alleged cost of 20,000 lives; the 'country boats' to which Thackeray refers were barges pulled by horses that were inclined to fall into the water; barges also ran the risk of crashing against the water buffalo that regarded the canal as theirs by right. P&O's little steamers were among the several improvements made by the company when it took over the Overland Route through Egypt in the 1840s.
2. Fig Tree Court was in the Middle Temple and denotes a lawyer in this context.
3. Bulaq, the port of Cairo. *'Cangias'* were the magnificent Nile sailing boats which visitors to Egypt hired for their sightseeing voyages up the Nile.
4. The 'steam-engine manufactories' were established by foreign engineers at Muhammad Ali's behest in the 1820s and included a printing press, an arsenal, a silk weaving factory and a boatyard for his steam yacht.
5. The Hôtel d'Orient was one of several hotels that opened on Cairo's al-Azbakiyyah Square in the 1840s on the strength of the Overland Route; another, a later generation of which still survives today, was Shepheard's Hotel.
6. Communications with India had been vastly improved by the development of steam vessels, able to move to a timetable rather than rely on erratic winds. Once P&O took over both ends of the voyage as well as the organisation of the stretch through Egypt, the whole journey from Southampton to Calcutta could be achieved in around six weeks. Thomas Waghorn, so warmly praised here by Thackeray, was the original organiser of the Egyptian stretch.
7. Al-Azbakiyyah Square was developed in the centre of 'European' Cairo. Inclined to swamp, it flooded during the annual inundation of the Nile so that boats could sail on it. It was drained by Muhammad Ali and later, under the Khedive Ismail, became a formal garden with fountains, trees and cafés.
8. Napoleon invaded Egypt in 1798, moving into Syria a year later. Forced by

the British to retreat to Cairo, Napoleon returned to France in October 1799, leaving General Klèber in command. Klèber himself was assassinated early in 1800 and the French finally driven out of Egypt by a joint Turkish-British force in the spring of 1801. The invasion highlighted the paucity of British communications with India, leading eventually to the campaign to develop steamboats on the route.

9. The French invasion seriously undermined the ruling Mamluks in Egypt, enabling Muhammad Ali to seize power in 1805. This he consolidated in 1811 when, at a notorious banquet in the citadel of Cairo (built by Salah al-Din in the twelfth century), he had all invited Mamluks assassinated except for one who leapt on horseback over the castle's precipitous walls.

10. Cairo's old mosques are, as Thackeray says, much more impressive than Muhammad Ali's new mosque, finished only after his death in 1849. They include some of the oldest mosques in the world: including that of Ibn Tulun (finished 879) and the Sultan Hasan mosque, also visited by Thackeray and one of the grandest in Cairo, built between 1356 and 1358. These were, indeed, a far cry from the Nonconformist 'Bethesda meeting-house and Independent chapels' which spurned architectural splendour for places of worship.

11. Marie Taglioni was a famous ballet dancer whom Thackeray saw on his first visit to Paris in 1829.

12. No one may enter a mosque wearing (unclean) outdoor shoes and in some cases slippers are provided as an alternative to bare feet.

13. To make the pilgrimage or *hajj* to re-enact Muhammad's migration from Mecca to Madina is one of the five pillars of Islam whose observance is required of every Muslim. The annual departure of the pilgrims from Cairo was an occasion of great ceremony; Egypt provided each year a new canopy, or *mahmil*, for the Kaaba, the revered stone in the middle of the Great Mosque in Mecca which pilgrims parade around.

14. The Arnauts or Arnaoot soldiers came from Albania, as did Muhammad Ali

himself, recruited into the Ottoman armies and renowned for their ferocity in battle.

15. The story of Bluebeard Pasha recounted by Thackeray belongs to the mixture of fact and fiction which often surrounded tales from Egypt, notably in that curious medieval collection, *Travels of Sir John Mandeville.*

16. Trumpington, Cambridge: Thackeray was an undergraduate at Cambridge for a year.

17. The well-informed gentleman could have been one of a number of people, among them Edward Lane, author *of Manners and Customs of the Modern Egyptians*, or Henry Abbott, founder in Cairo of the Literary Association.

18. 'Bastinado' was a particularly nasty form of punishment or torture that involved beating the soles of the feet.

19. The 'Syrian quarrel' was Muhammad Ali's invasion of Syria in 1833 which by 1839 had led to a general confrontation with several European powers, including Britain, afraid of its destabilising effect on the Ottoman Empire.

20. British painters were indeed making their way to Cairo and one of them, J.F. Lewis, Thackeray clearly knew well. John Frederick Lewis set out for Cairo in 1839, arriving in 1841, and for ten years followed the life of a well-to-do Turk in a suitably elegant Cairo house. His sketches provided him with the basis, on his return to London, for a successful career as a painter of oriental street scenes, markets and harems. He was also a skilled animal painter and, for example, one of the few artists to draw a respectable camel.

It is surprising, given his interest in the theatre, that Thackeray does not mention David Roberts, a celebrated theatrical painter who had returned from a most successful visit to the East in 1839, and whose paintings made a dramatic impact when displayed in the Royal Academy and published as lithographs between 1842 and 1849. Another artist of whom Thackeray would most probably have been aware was Sir David Wilkie who died on his way home from the east in 1841.

21. This first station house on the road to the port of Suez on the Red Sea was one of about a dozen at which travellers

could refresh themselves on the overland stretch of their journey to or from India. Originally haphazardly organised by Waghorn, they were soon taken over by Messrs Hill & Raven and later still by P&O.

22. The *'simoom'* or *khamsin* is a notoriously hot southerly wind that can blow for as many as fifty days between March and May (the name derives from the Arabic for 'fifty').

23. By *Europa* and the *Trois Frères* Thackeray may have been referring to contemporary paintings.

24. Hadji Hodson and Bass Bey were brand names of different beers of the period.

25. Shelley's two sonnets were *Ozymandias* and *Month after month the gathered rains descend*, the latter composed as a competition with Keats and Leigh Hunt to see who could compose the best poem on the Nile.

26. *'imber edax'*, literally 'the rain that washes away'; *'aquilo impotens'* is 'the harmless northerly wind.'

27. Quarantine in Malta was no fun; the regulations were strict, everything going in and out of the station had to be fumigated and in Thackeray's day there was a fair chance of dying while thus incarcerated. Two of his companions died in quarantine. He spent the time finishing off *Barry Lyndon* and writing articles for *Punch*, ultimately published as *Punch in the East*. Thackeray spent seventeen days in quarantine, 'very weary of an imprisonment which I had hoped to put to much greater profit,' according to his diary for November 12th, 1844.

1865 Edition – Dedication and Preface

1. The Dedication is written to Captain Samuel Lewis of the steamer *Iberia*, built by Peninsular & Oriental, the 'noble Company' of the dedication, for its Mediterranean service. The Peninsular Steam Navigation Company, later Peninsular & Oriental, was founded in 1837 from offices off Cornhill, in the City of London. Thackeray joined the *Iberia* in Constantinople.

2. The Reform Club in Pall Mall, London. Thackeray became a member in 1840.

3. William, brother of Samuel Bevan,

author of an account of the Overland Route through Egypt, *Sand and Canvas*, published in 1849, and Thackeray's host in Rome after he had completed his journey to the east.

4. James Emerson Tennent (1804-1869), politician and writer who in 1844 was MP for Belfast and Secretary to the India Board.

5. *Lady Mary Wood*, a paddle steamer built for P&O for their Calcutta-Suez run; Thackeray left her at Gibraltar as she was continuing her maiden voyage to Calcutta via the Cape of Good Hope.

INDEX